Enhancing Productivity with Notion

Save time on projects by supercharging your productivity with Notion's powerful features and templates

Danny Hatcher

BIRMINGHAM—MUMBAI

Enhancing Productivity with Notion

Copyright © 2022 Packt Publishing

Group Product Manager: Alok Dhuri

Publishing Product Manager: Shweta Bairoliya

Senior Editor: Ruvika Rao

Content Development Editor: Urvi Shah

Technical Editor: Maran Fernandes

Copy Editor: Safis Editing

Language Support Editor: Safis Editing

Project Coordinator: Deeksha Thakkar

Proofreader: Safis Editing

Indexer: Subalakshmi Govindhan

Production Designer: Vijay Kamble

Marketing Coordinator: Deepak Kumar

First published: February 2022

Production reference: 2140322

Published by Packt Publishing Ltd.

Livery Place

35 Livery Street

Birmingham

B3 2PB, UK.

ISBN 978-1-80323-208-9

www.packt.com

To my family, who let me follow this opportunity, supplying technology, food, and shelter while giving me the freedom to write this book.

To all of the individuals in the Notion communities across the internet that engage, ask, and answer questions about this great tool.

– Danny Hatcher

Contributors

About the author

Danny Hatcher is a researcher in educational science and a digital tool enthusiast. He has made over 100 video tutorials about Notion on YouTube, as well as speaking on other YouTube channels and podcasts about this tool. He is also a Notion ambassador, frequently looking out for new features, use cases, and ideas. Having used the tool himself personally over the years, he has also helped countless others use it for personal and team applications and use cases ranging from trading, accounting, and content creation to sport, teaching, music, and life organization.

I want to thank my subscribers and followers on the various social media platforms, first for listening to me, second for believing in me, and third for your continued support throughout the writing of this book.

About the reviewer

Jonathan Stewart is the guy you call when you've had it with working hard and not getting ahead. He's a systems specialist and Notion Certified Consultant who has spent years talking to business owners who are smart, busy, and frustrated. Jonathan understands the need for productivity hacks and systems but often finds that these same hacks and systems can hamper business owners' ability to keep up with their own brains.

Through his work, Jonathan strives to help frustrated fast-thinkers design the systems they need in order to build a business that's a joy to run.

Table of Contents

3

Templates, Imports, Account Settings, and Workspace Settings

4

All the Building Blocks

Section 2: Database Options, Features, and Functions

5

All the Basic Database Properties

6

Database Views

7

Database Features and Functions

8

Basic Formula Functions

9
Advanced Formula Combinations

Section 3: Creating Advanced Workflows

10
Creating an Action Management Contextual Dashboard and Workflow

11
Using API Integration and Add-on Options

12

Note Taking, Knowledge Management, and a Wiki Example

13

Other Example Use Cases

Index

Other Books You May Enjoy

Preface

Through this book you will learn about Notion 2.0.21 and the the initial struggles of setting up an account and workspace and learning the blocks, database views, and database properties to create dashboards, workflows, and systems. It allows you to create tasks, wiki, and project management systems for any productivity use case. By the end of this book, you'll be able to create a task management system, project management system, or any other system while combining it with other tools that speed up your work for better efficiency.

Who this book is for

This book is for business users, power users, IT professionals, or anyone from a non-technical background looking to use Notion to increase their productivity.

What this book covers

Chapter 1, *Setting up the Application*, teaches you how to set up your account through the Notion online onboarding process.

Chapter 2, *Workspace Navigation, Sharing, and Appearance*, shows you how to set up your account and manage the workspaces.

Chapter 3, *Templates, Imports, Account Settings, and Workspace Settings*, outlines how to alter settings, import data, and use the default templates provided.

Chapter 4, *All the Building Blocks*, shows you all the different building blocks available in the Notion application.

Chapter 5, *All the Basic Database Properties*, teaches you the core functions of the database.

Chapter 6, *Database Views*, demonstrates how to use the table view, list view, board view, calendar view, gallery view, and timeline view.

Chapter 7, Database Features and Functions, shows you how to use the relation and rollup properties to link databases together, along with the database sorting, filtering, and grouping features.

Chapter 8, Basic Formula Functions, teaches you how to create basic formulas using the formula database property.

Chapter 9, Advanced Formula Combinations, shows you how to use the formula property in databases to use variable inputs to create different outputs.

Chapter 10, Creating an Action Management Contextual Dashboard and Workflow, explains why and how to leverage a master database for a specific purpose.

Chapter 11, Using API Integration and Add-on Options, helps you learn how to use the API integration inside a workspace, along with a discussion of the advantages and concerns of using an API.

Chapter 12, Note Taking, Knowledge Management, and Wiki Example, shows you how to capture, organize, and share information through Notion.

Chapter 13, Other Example Use Cases, has a look at how other users have built templates and systems to help them in their daily lives.

To get the most out of this book

You will only require a browser for running Notion.

While reading through the book, we suggest trying out each block feature or setting option mentioned to give yourself some practice time. Then, after completing the book, have a look around the communities and creators mentioned in *Chapter 13, Other Example Use Cases*, to further understand how all the features mentioned can be put together.

Download the color images

We also provide a PDF file that has color images of the screenshots and diagrams used in this book. You can download it here: `https://static.packt-cdn.com/downloads/9781803232089_ColorImages.pdf`

Conventions used

There are a number of text conventions used throughout this book.

`Code in text`: Indicates code words in text, database table names, folder names, filenames, file extensions, pathnames, dummy URLs, user input, and Twitter handles. Here is an example: "A task is completed by using the `if` statement `prop("Done")` ? `"☑"` : `((now() < prop("Due Date")) ? "● OVERDUE" : "● ON TIME")`."

Bold: Indicates a new term, an important word, or words that you see onscreen. For instance, words in menus or dialog boxes appear in **bold**. Here is an example: "The **Projects** database view uses the timeline view to see when a project will finish, showing the **Name** property, **Department** select property, **Percentage** rollup property, and **Project Manager** person property."

> **Tips or important notes**
> Appear like this.

Get in touch

Feedback from our readers is always welcome.

General feedback: If you have questions about any aspect of this book, email us at `customercare@packtpub.com` and mention the book title in the subject of your message.

Errata: Although we have taken every care to ensure the accuracy of our content, mistakes do happen. If you have found a mistake in this book, we would be grateful if you would report this to us. Please visit `www.packtpub.com/support/errata` and fill in the form.

Piracy: If you come across any illegal copies of our works in any form on the internet, we would be grateful if you would provide us with the location address or website name. Please contact us at `copyright@packt.com` with a link to the material.

If you are interested in becoming an author: If there is a topic that you have expertise in and you are interested in either writing or contributing to a book, please visit `authors.packtpub.com`.

Share Your Thoughts

Once you've read *Enhancing Productivity with Notion*, we'd love to hear your thoughts!
Scan the QR code below to go straight to the Amazon review page for this book and share
your feedback.

https://packt.link/r/1-803-23208-0

Your review is important to us and the tech community and will help us make sure
we're delivering excellent quality content.

Section 1: Settings and Structure

By the end of this section, you will be able to navigate the **heads-up display** (**HUD**) and change the settings to your preference. This section contains the following chapters:

- *Chapter 1, Setting up the Application*
- *Chapter 2, Workspace Navigation, Sharing, and Appearance*
- *Chapter 3, Templates, Imports, Account Settings, and Workspace Settings*
- *Chapter 4, All the Building Blocks*

1

Setting Up the Application

Notion is a software application that can help individuals and teams get things done. It offers many of the benefits of paper, writing down notes, ideas, and thoughts. However, it also has the benefits of digital tools such as searching, database structures, and remote collaboration.

In this chapter, we're going to cover the following main topics:

- Creating an account
- Downloading the application
- Using Notion on multiple devices

You will learn how to create an account in the Notion application for yourself or a team of people, resulting in at least one created account. Note that you cannot use the Notion app without at least one account, so this step cannot be avoided.

Additionally, you will learn how to download the application onto multiple devices if you use them, such as a PC, Mac, laptop, tablet, and mobile. Following this, you will learn how to access an account that you have created on any of those devices. This will give you synced access to your information across each device while remaining safe with your data.

Technical requirements

In this chapter, you will need a device that has access to the internet. The device you use will impact the navigation and guidance given in this chapter, so a PC or laptop is advised but not necessary. Additionally, a phone or tablet can be used, but they might have limited functionality when setting up. Having multiple devices around you will allow for all the setup to be done in one sitting.

Creating an account

Now you will learn how to create an account in Notion. This is so that you can access the application to keep your information and data private while also storing the information linked to the account you create:

1. When you first go looking for Notion, you can find it by searching in your browser (such as Google, Bing, or Yahoo). In the results section, you should see the Notion website, which is titled **Notion – The all-in-one workspace for your notes, tasks, wikis**.

2. When you click through to the main page, you will be able to view their website. However, if you have made an account previously, it will take you into the workspace you are currently logged into; in this case, you can move on to the next section of this chapter.

3. At the top of the main page, there is a section for you to add your email address and sign up, as shown in *Figure 1.1*. The email address that you enter in that box is the email address you will use for your account. This email will receive all the emails and notifications that the Notion app sends out:

All-in-one workspace

One tool for your whole team. Write, plan, and get organized.

Enter your email...   Sign up

For teams & individuals — web, mobile, Mac, Windows.

Figure 1.1 – The Notion website – enter your email account to sign up

Alternatively, you can navigate to the upper-right corner of the main page and click on **Log in**, if you have an account, or **Sign up** to create a new account. Going through this option will take you to a different page where you can use your Google or Apple sign-in details to create a new account. This will use the email address from that account as your Notion account email.

4. Once you have entered an email address for the Notion account, a confirmation code will be sent to that email address. The main page you are on will change and ask for a confirmation code. Go to your email inbox to find the Notion sign-up code. If the email is not in your inbox, you might need to check your spam folder due to your email settings.

5. Once you have found the sign-up email, there will be two options to choose from:

  - A link that will take you to a Notion page

  - A code that you need to put into the main page you just left, asking for the confirmation code

6. Having entered the code or gone through the magic link in the email, you will be taken to a **Privacy & Data** collection page. This page shares how Notion uses cookies to securely identify your account along with how Intercom, Amplitude, Segment, Snowflake, Crashlytics, and Loggly are used to collect analytics for improving the product and troubleshooting customer issues.

7. You can withdraw your consent to analytics at any time by emailing
    `team@makenotion.com`, which is linked on the page. Additionally, they mention
    the product updates and marketing emails that will be sent out with an unsubscribe
    link, if you don't want to receive them, along with their terms of service and privacy
    policy information.

8. When you are happy to proceed, you will be taken to a profile page. This will give
    you the option to add a name, image, and password to your profile. Notion asks for
    a password that is longer than 15 letters or longer than 10 characters with letters
    and numbers.

    There is no need to add a profile picture at this point, as the account can be created
    with just a username and password. Once you have entered a username and
    password, click to continue. You will be given two options:

    - A team options

    - An individual option

9. If you select the team option, it will ask you for a workspace name, company size,
    and your starting team. You can add a logo, but it is not mandatory. As you continue
    through this process, it will ask you to invite your teammates into the workspace.
    You can invite them via their email address, and if they do not already have
    a Notion account, they will go through the account creation process. Again, this is
    not mandatory at this point, and you can move forward without inviting anyone
    into the space.

10. When you pick a team plan, you will be put on the trial package, so you will be
    limited in terms of some of the features that you have access to. To check which
    features are limited, navigate to your workspace settings and look at the **plan**
    section. This will be covered, in more detail in *Chapter 3, Template Import Options,
    Account Settings, and Workspace Settings*.

11. If you select the individual option, you will be directed to your Notion workspace.
    At this point, if you decide that you want to test out the team plan as a trial, you can;
    however, again, you would need to go through the workspace settings.

12. When you enter the Notion workspace, you will go through an onboarding process
    that shows you some templates that you can choose to import into your workspace.

Templates will be covered in more detail in *Chapter 3, Template Import Options, Account
Settings, and Workspace Settings*, but you will also be given a **Getting Started** page in your
private section. The **Getting Started** page goes over some of the basics that will be fully
covered throughout this book.

Downloading the application

In this section, we will download Notion onto our PC, Mac, or laptop device. The process of downloading Notion to our mobile or tablet devices will also be explained. While downloading Notion to your computer has little storage or speed benefits, it does provide some added functionality alongside the ability to add Notion to your taskbar for easy startup access. However, downloading Notion to multiple devices does give you many more options, in terms of its use cases and applications, to create a more productive system overall.

> **Note**
> Before I continue, I want to mention that Notion, like most software applications, uses words and terms that might cross over with other words that you are familiar with. This can get confusing at times, but I will explain each term as we come across them.

Having created an account, you will have access to a workspace. A **workspace** in Notion is at the core of collaboration. It is the digital space that stores the pages and databases that house all your information. A workspace can have multiple members, guests, and admins, which will be covered further in *Chapter 3, Template Import Options, Account Settings, and Workspace Settings*, but a person who is logged into an account can also have access to multiple workspaces.

If you look at the upper-left corner of the sidebar on your screen, it will show you what workspace you are in. Note that at this point, you will be logged into one account, which will have access to one workspace.

When you are looking to download Notion, you can either search for the Notion website to download the app, or you can go through the workspace you are logged into.

When going through the Notion website, there is an option in the menu bar at the top of the screen that says **Download**, as shown in *Figure 1.2*:

Figure 1.2 – Hover over the options menu for local app download

When hovering over it with the mouse, you are presented with different download options. Once you have clicked on the appropriate option, you can download the app using the App Store or Play Store for mobiles and tablets. You can also download it to the device using the Mac or Windows download options.

Alternatively, if you have Notion open on your PC, Mac, or laptop device and are logged into a workspace, you can navigate to the upper-left corner and open the **workspace** menu. At the bottom of the menu, you will see three options: **Add another account**, **Log out all**, and **Get Mac/Windows app**. When you click on the **Get Windows app** button, it will take you to the same page on the website, giving you the relevant download button.

Once you have started the download, your system will start downloading Notion to your local device. The application will be stored on the device you are downloading it to, which can take up the system's memory. If the device memory is low, the download might fail, or your device might decrease in speed, so checking the system memory before downloading would be wise.

If you are on a mobile or tablet device, the first option to go through the Notion website is still available, but if you were to log into your account through a browser, it would give you another option to download Notion from the App Store or Play Store, depending on the device you are using.

Alternatively, if you are on your mobile, you could navigate directly to the App Store if you are on iOS or Play Store if you are on Android. Then, you can search for Notion, which should show a result with the same icon as the PC/Mac app, and an app saying made by **Notion Labs, inc** should appear. Click **Install** and then open the app on your device.

Irrespective of the device or system you have downloaded the app on, you will then come to a sign-in page that is consistent across all devices. You can sign in through Google, using that email account, sign in through Apple, using that email account, or continue with email, giving you the option to type in an email account. To gain access to the same account you created on the PC, Mac, or laptop, the email address needs to be the same when you sign in, as that is the account it will log you in as.

When you are on your PC, Mac, or laptop device, look over to the upper-right corner of the screen. There will be a three-dot menu that you can click on, giving you a drop-down list of options. About halfway down the list, there will be an **Open in Windows app** option on Windows or an **Open in Mac app** option on Mac. After you have downloaded Notion to your system, this will then open your workspace page in the local Notion app.

At this point, you can have your Notion account logged into multiple devices that are all synced together. Personally, I would add a shortcut to Notion on my PC so that I can easily access it from my taskbar and move the Notion app on my devices to a more action-focused location; for example, on mobile, having it on my front page, and the same for the tablet.

Using Notion on multiple devices

In this section, we will go through some of the viewing and functional differences between various devices. There are some actions that you can perform on some devices that are, at the time of writing this, unavailable on other devices. This could impact how you format your pages, build out your workspace, and navigate through the app.

PC, Mac, or laptop

Using a PC, Mac, or laptop will give you the most functionality and flexibility in terms of what you can do with the app. Notion was first built for desktop use, with the mobile and tablet apps being developed later.

When viewing Notion on your screen, you should see the active workspace screen. It includes the active page in the middle, a navigation sidebar on the left-hand side, some options in the upper-right corner for sharing alongside an action menu, and the help button in the lower-right corner of the screen, as shown in *Figure 1.3*:

Figure 1.3 – The workspace home screen for a PC, Mac, or laptop

The sidebar on the left-hand side can be toggled off so that it doesn't show or fill up space. This can be done by clicking the option at the top of the sidebar, as shown in *Figure 1.4*, or using the *Ctrl + * keyboard shortcut:

Figure 1.4 – Closing the left-hand sidebar option on a PC, Mac, or laptop

When you are interacting with the blocks inside the application (note that blocks will be explained further in *Chapter 4, All the Building Blocks*), there are a few options to choose from.

You can either click into the block to add text, interact with the embedded media, or trigger a block action. You could click on the six-dot option at the side of the block, giving you a drop-down menu of actions to apply to the block. Or you could click outside of a block, drag your mouse over the intended blocks you want to interact with, and then use the six-dot option or the *Ctrl + /* shortcut to make any changes.

While on a PC, Mac, or tablet, the only way to move a block is to click and hold the six-dot option, as highlighted in *Figure 1.5*. Then, drag the block to the desired location.

> **Note**
> This could create columns, which will be covered further in *Chapter 4. All the Building Blocks*.

Figure 1.5 – The six-dot option next to a single block

The location of the breadcrumb, which, in Notion, refers to the file tree that shows what page or database the currently active page has gone through, is at the top of the active page just like on all other devices; note that workspace navigation is covered in further detail in *Chapter 2, Workspace Navigation, Sharing, and Appearance*.

Tablet

When viewing Notion on a tablet or iPad screen, the layout will be different. Instead of there being a left-hand sidebar, there is a button to open the sidebar for navigation located in the upper-left corner of the screen, as highlighted in *Figure 1.6*.

The sharing and action options are still in the upper-right corner of the screen, but the share options are in the box and arrow icon menu, and the action options are in the three-dot menu.

At the bottom of the screen, there is the quick search, notification bell, and new page shortcut, which have been taken out of the sidebar from the PC, Mac, or laptop workspace view. In addition to this, there are undo and redo arrows in the lower-right corner of the screen.

On the main working page, there are additional options to add a template to the page, which will be covered further in *Chapter 3, Templates, Imports, Account Settings, and Workspace Settings*:

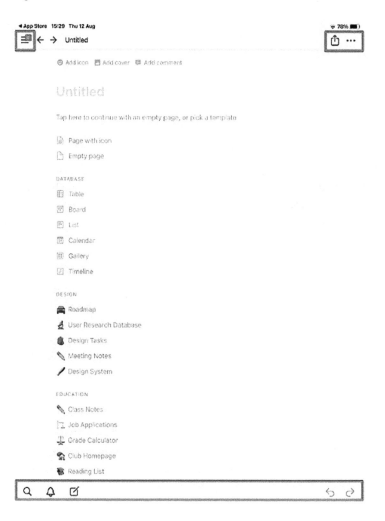

Figure 1.6 – The workspace home screen for the iPad

Unlike the PC, Mac, or laptop view, interacting with blocks doesn't rely on mouse movements or clicks. To add a block, a line of text, or to trigger a block action, you need to click on an active text block on the page to bring up the toolbar or the six-dot menu, as shown in *Figure 1.7*:

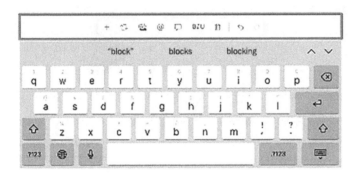

Figure 1.7 – The tablet/iPad toolbar location

To move a block on the tablet or iPad, you need to tap on the block, click on the six-dot option to highlight the block, click off the menu when it appears, then hold the screen on the block with your finger. Finally, you can move it to the desired location.

At the time of writing this book, there is no way to create columns inside a page on the tablet or iPad versions.

Mobile

When viewing Notion on the mobile app, it mimics much of the tablet/iPad workspace view. The sidebar is hidden behind the button in the upper-left corner. The share and action options are still in the upper-right corner, with the share options behind the traditional three-dot and two-line icons and the actions behind the three-dot menu. The search box, notifications bell, and new page shortcut are located at the bottom of the screen. However, unlike the tablet/iPad app, there are no undo or redo buttons, as shown in *Figure 1.8*:

Figure 1.8 – The workspace home screen for mobile

The same can be said for the interaction with blocks on the mobile app. To create a block, go into an active text block on the page by pushing it with your finger to bring up the toolbar. From there, you have access to all the block actions. Similarly, you can move blocks on the mobile app by using the following method:

1. Select a block and then select the drop-down menu for the keyboard.
2. Then, push and hold on to the desired block and move it up and down.

At this point in Notion, there is no way to make columns on a mobile device.

Summary

In summary, before you can access the application, you need to make an account using your preferred email address, which can receive updates and notifications. To access that account on multiple devices, a download of the app needs to be completed per device. Then, you can log in to the account using the same email and password. Despite Notion being available on all of the main devices, such as PC, Mac, laptop, mobile, and tablet/ iPad, the flexibility, usability, and available features are better suited for PC, Mac, and laptop devices.

Now that the account and workspace have been created, we need to gain an understanding of how to navigate around the workspace so that we know where data and information are stored. Additionally, we need to gain an understanding of the main actions that are available when working within the Notion app.

2
Workspace Navigation, Sharing, and Appearance

As an online tool, Notion has many features for collaboration, which means appearance and navigation need to stay consistent across platforms. There are still differences and nuances in how the tool looks and functions for each user, and these differences will be covered in this chapter. In this chapter, we're going to cover the following main topics:

- Quick Find and breadcrumb navigation
- Sidebar navigation
- Sharing and collaboration options
- Page appearance options

You will learn how to navigate Notion through the **Quick Find** search option and **Breadcrumb**, which, in Notion, is similar to a traditional File Explorer path, but instead of showing a folder path leading to a file, it shows page paths going down the hierarchy leading to a page.

Additionally, you will learn how to use the sidebar as a file and folder manager and gain an understanding of how each page will appear in the sidebar for ease of navigation. This can also allow for easier movement from one page to another page, and from pages to databases, making the creation and adaptation process of building out the workspace quicker and more convenient.

One of Notion's strengths is sharing and collaboration—having the option to work with others on the same page at the same time with live updates. This will be covered in more detail, and we will go over all of the sharing privileges that you can set, along with the differences in page appearance.

Technical requirements

In this chapter, you will need a device with internet access. Additionally, you will need access to a Notion account.

Using Quick Find and breadcrumbs

In this section, you will go into your Notion workspace and search for different blocks and pages within the space and learn how the breadcrumb works when navigating through pages. Breadcrumbs are extremely useful when trying to locate specific blocks, pages, or databases when you can't find them, have no quick or easy way to get to them, or you don't remember if you already have a page, block, or database made for a certain purpose.

At this point, you should have an account and a workspace to navigate around, either with some default templates from the onboarding process or just the **Getting Started** page.

Quick Find

The **Quick Find** search option is the most global search option inside Notion. It will go through each block, page, and database in search of the terms that you enter:

1. To access this search option, you can go to the left-hand sidebar, underneath the **workspace** menu, and click on **Quick Find**.

> **Note**
>
> As mentioned in *Chapter 1, Setting up the Application*, the mobile and tablet location of this search feature is at the bottom of the workspace screen. Alternatively, you could use the *Ctrl/cmd + P* keyboard shortcut on a PC or Mac.

2. Once you have opened the **Quick Find** search window, you will be shown the search bar at the top, followed by the recently active pages, the recent past searches, and, finally, the action options at the bottom, as shown in *Figure 2.1*:

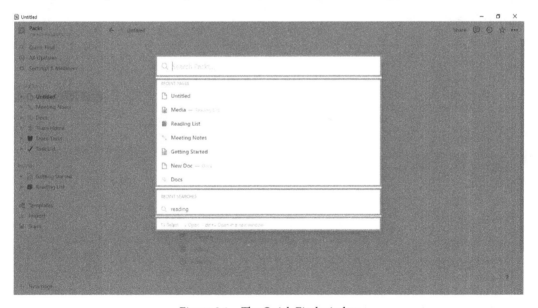

Figure 2.1 – The Quick Find window

3. You can use the arrow keys on your keyboard to navigate up and down the search results. Press *Enter* to open the highlighted result, or press *Ctrl + Enter* to open the result in a different tab.

> **Note**
> When using mobile or tablet devices, the action options are not available at the bottom of the Quick Find window, and you are limited to just opening the page.

4. If you select a recent page, it will take you to that page in your workspace, closing the **Quick Find** window. If you select a recent search, it will input that search term into the Quick Find query, showing the results of that updated search. Additionally, both recent menus can be cleared by selecting the **Clear** option (found on the right-hand side of the Quick Find window when hovering over a result from the desired section, as shown in *Figure 2.2*):

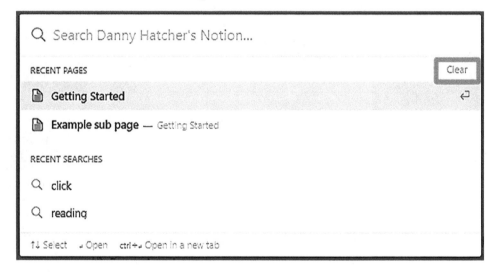

Figure 2.2 – The Quick Find Clear option

5. Once you have started to type in a search query, Notion will start looking for possible results. By default, the results will be sorted by **Best matches,** but they can be changed to **Last edited: Newest first, Last edited: Oldest first, Created: Newest first,** or **Created: Oldest first:**

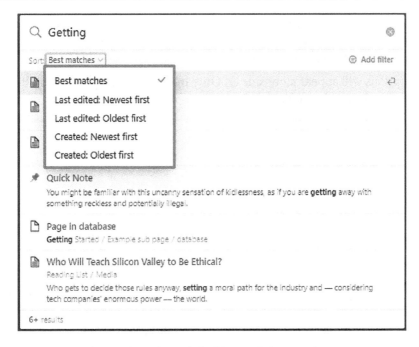

Figure 2.3 – The Quick Find search for "Getting," showing the sorting options

6. The word, term, or sentence you enter will show results with highlighted words that match the requested search, as shown in *Figure 2.4*. The search term could be in a page name, a breadcrumb, or a block page:

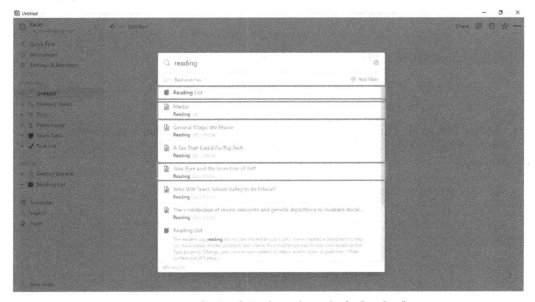

Figure 2.4 – The Quick Find search results for "reading"

7. Once a search has started, an option to filter the search will become available, as shown in blue text, that says **Add filter**. This can be seen just below the search query and above the search results in *Figure 2.4*.

8. Seven options will appear alongside an **Only match titles** toggle, which filters out all of the block-based searches, as shown in *Figure 2.5*:

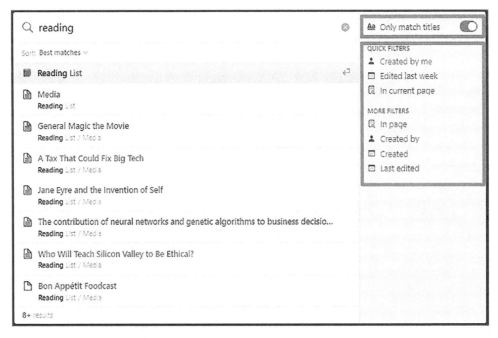

Figure 2.5 – The Quick Find filter options with match titles toggled on

You will find three **QUICK FILTERS**, as follows:

-   **Created by me**: This searches for the query in everything created by you. Once selected, you can add more people to the filter.

-   **Edited last week**: This searches for the query in everything that was edited in the last week. Once selected, you can expand the date range backward in time in the filter.

-   **In current page**: This searches for the query on the current page you are active in. Once selected, you can add multiple pages to the filter.

The **MORE FILTERS** option adds a created time filter alongside some previous filter options:

- The **Created** filter gives you the option to select a start time and an end time in which the block, page, or database was created.

- The **In page** filter gives you the same options as **In Current Page** but goes straight to the search option for pages rather than inputting the current page first.

- The **Created by** filter searches for the account in the workspace that created the block, page, or database. Your account is added by default, but any **guests**, **members**, and **admins** will also become options in this filter.

- The **Last edited** filter also gives you a search range to pick from, instead of inputting the previous week by default.

Breadcrumb

The breadcrumb is located at the top of the screen on all devices. It starts with the **top-level page** going all the way down or from the right-hand side, as you look at it, to the active page you're currently on.

Each page will show up in the breadcrumb. It can be used as a visual understanding of where you are in the workspace but also as a navigation link, as each page in the breadcrumb can be clicked on, taking you to that page. Both a block page and a database page will show up in the breadcrumb. The difference between them will be explained further in *Chapter 4, All the Building Blocks*, but it means you will always have a way to find where you are.

As you can have a long path down to a page, the size of the breadcrumb is impacted. It creates a three-dot menu when it gets too long, which can be clicked on to open a menu of the path, as shown in *Figure 2.6*:

Figure 2.6 – The breadcrumb showing an expanded menu

Combining the **Quick Find** search feature, the breadcrumb, and the sidebar allows for easy navigation when trying to find something or when you are on a page and attempting to access another page quickly.

The sidebar sections, hierarchy, and updates

In this section, you will be going through the left-hand sidebar options, learning the basics of what they are, and how the main page and sidebar hierarchy are organized.

The sidebar hierarchy of pages is similar to **File Explorer** and can be used for navigation and for moving or reorganizing the workspace in a different way. Understanding how the sidebar functions will give you a high-level view of the page privileges, page structure, and workspace foundation.

At the top of the sidebar, there is the workspace menu, which was covered in *Chapter 1, Setting up the Application*. This shows the workspaces and accounts that you are signed in to. You can be signed in to multiple accounts at any one time, with all the workspaces shown underneath the appropriate account.

The **Quick Find** option was covered in the previous section, but finding out what actions are being taken and what notifications you might have in your workspace are located in the **All Updates** menu.

All Updates

The **All Updates** option is where all the notifications for the currently active workspace are. If there are other notifications on a workspace in any logged-in account (which isn't active), the notification number will be shown on the workspace menu. If the notification is from the active workspace, it will be placed in the appropriate sections:

- **Inbox**: This shows any mentions, comments, invites to pages, or reminders, as shown in *Figure 2.7*.

- **Following**: This shows any changes in the upcoming pages.

- **All**: This shows all changes, mentions, comments, and invites made in the workspace.

- **Archived**: This shows all archived notifications from the **Inbox** section:

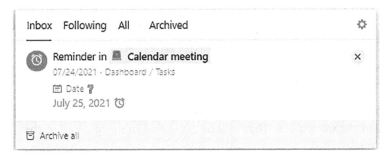

Figure 2.7 – An example reminder notification in the Inbox section

When you are on any page in the workspace, you can go to the upper-right corner of the screen and click on **Updates**. This will show options for you to be updated in Notion or notified in a Slack channel (which will be covered in *Chapter 3, Templates, Account Settings, and Workspace Settings*). Additionally, all the updates that have happened on that page recently are shown in a list, as shown in *Figure 2.8*:

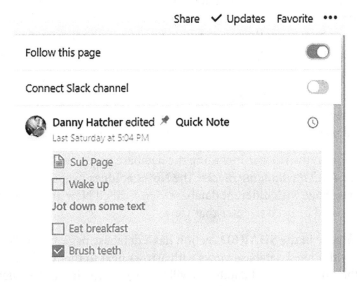

Figure 2.8 – Following a page for updates

Below the **All Updates** option, there is the **Settings & Members** option, which will be covered in full in *Chapter 3, Templates, Account Settings, and Workspace Settings*.

Sidebar hierarchy

The sidebar hierarchy is split into four sections:

- **Favorites**: This is an option you can toggle in the upper-right corner of the page, as illustrated in *Figure 2.7*.

- **Workspace**: These are the pages in the workspace that are shared with other members of the workspace. They will be explained in more detail in the next section.

- **Shared**: These are private pages that you have shared with specific individuals only.

- **Private**: These are pages that can only be accessed by you.

These sections can be viewed in *Figure 2.9*.

The hierarchy works with a **top-level page**, which is a page that is stored and saved in the sidebar. It is visible when all the page toggles have been closed and is the only page in its breadcrumb. The **subpages** option relates to pages with at least one page higher up on the hierarchy, which can be seen on the breadcrumb. By default, the sharing privileges of a top-level page will be put on any subpage, but that can be changed manually afterward.

In *Figure 2.8*, **My Toolkit** is a subpage of **Danny Hatcher**, just like all the other indented pages. This means that **Danny Hatcher** is also in the **Workspace** section. The **My Toolkit** page can be accessed by any member in the workspace unless this option has been manually changed using the sharing status on the **My Toolkit** page.

Every page will show in the sidebar including the database pages, which will be explained further in *Chapter 4, All the Building Blocks*. The **Notes & Ideas** page in the **Workspace** section is a database page with different database views, called **New** and **Table view**. If clicked on, this could be used to enter that view.

The **Notion Book** page in the **SHARED** section has a database page, called **Sections Database**, along with linked database views with arrows next to them, which are displayed underneath, in the sidebar. Linked databases will be covered further in *Chapter 4, All the Building Blocks*.

If you click on any page in the sidebar, it can be dragged up or down to move the page onto another page, move the page to a different order on the top-level page, or drag it onto the active workspace page to create a linked page:

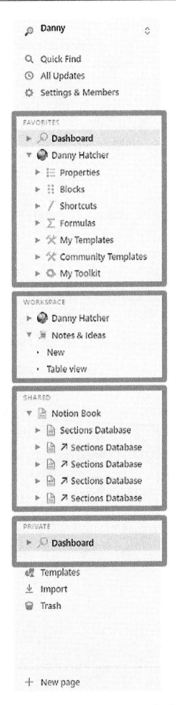

Figure 2.9 – The sidebar hierarchy sections highlighted with
icon differences for pages, databases, and linked databases

Underneath the **Workspace Hierarchy** sections, there is a template option, an import option, and a trash option that shows previously deleted pages that can be restored or permanently deleted. The history of trash is affected by the account plan and will be covered in *Chapter 3*, *Templates, Account Settings, and Workspace Settings*.

Sharing options

In this section, you will learn how to share any page in Notion with anyone publicly on the internet or with specific individuals. This is crucial when looking to collaborate with others using Notion.

We will also cover sharing privileges by going over members, guests, and admin privileges, and their effects in the workspace. The sharing privileges start from the top-level page and work down to the subpages. The privileges can be changed on each subpage individually afterward for more flexibility.

As shown in *Figure 2.9*, there is a share button in the upper-right corner of the screen that allows you to toggle **Share to web**. This opens a menu with four choices:

- **Allow editing**: This allows anyone who accesses the page publicly to edit the page.

- **Allow comments**: This allows anyone who accesses the page publicly to comment on the page.

- **Allow duplicate as template**: This allows anyone who accesses the page publicly to duplicate the top-level page and subpages to their workspace.

- **Search engine indexing**: This is a Personal Pro Plan feature, which will be covered in *Chapter 3*, *Templates, Account Settings, and Workspace Settings*. It allows the page to be found in public search engine results:

Figure 2.10 – The sharing option menu

The section highlighted in red at the bottom of *Figure 2.10* includes the accounts that currently have access to the page, showing the levels of sharing privileges to the right of the accounts. These are in four levels:

- **Full access**: This means they **Can edit and share with others**.
- **Can edit**: This means they **Can edit, but not share with others**.
- **Can comment**: This means they **Can view and comment, but not edit**.
- **Can view**: This means they **Cannot edit or share with others**.

As mentioned in *Chapter 1*, *Setting up the Application*, you can invite people into your workspace using their email account that is linked to an existing Notion account or an email that someone can access your account with.

Members, guests, and admins

The sharing privileges are specific to the pages and can be applied to anyone that has access to the workspace, depending on the plan you and the admin are on:

- **Admins** are the only people in the workspace who can add new members and edit settings. The creator of a workspace is automatically an admin.

- **Members** are the people who can create and edit Notion pages but not edit settings or add members. This is only available on the Team plan or the Enterprise plan.

- **Guests** are people who can work on specific pages that they have been invited to.

> **Note**
>
> The individual accounts that are added into the workspace are the accounts that will appear in the mentioned block. This will be covered in *Chapter 4, All the Basic Blocks*.

When on the Team plan or the Enterprise plan, you can create groups of members, which allows for bulk sharing options. Instead of sharing a page with four members from the same department individually, you could create a department group with the four members in it and just give sharing privileges to the group.

Irrespective of the account status, the privileges on each page can be changed, and the sharing privileges work down from the top-level page. This means that the shared privileges for a top-level page will be the same for every subpage unless it is changed manually.

> **Note**
>
> Linked pages and linked database pages will adopt the privileges from the original page instance. This means that if the account viewing a page doesn't have the sharing privileges of the database page (which it was originally created in), then a linked database view won't show.

Page appearance, actions, and information

In this section, we will go through the native Notion appearance changes we can make to a page that can change the aesthetic. Additionally, we will go through the main actions that are available on a page, which can change its appearance for others viewing the page and yourself when editing the page.

This is useful not just for aesthetics but also when collaborating with others, showing them relevant information or guiding them to specific areas using different features such as **lock page** and **customize page**.

As mentioned in *Chapter 1, Setting up the Application*, the breadcrumb is always located at the top of the screen, irrespective of the device. Additionally, the action menu is located in the same place in the upper-right corner of the screen for each device, which is where the focus of this section will be.

> **Note**
> Multiple community projects work with Notion and that can also provide added functionality and changes to the page appearance. Many of these groups are not associated with Notion, but popular add-ons will be mentioned in *Chapter 11, Using API Integrations and Add-on Options*.

Page appearance options

The **page name** is the title of the page. It is displayed at the top of the page in the breadcrumb and the sidebar for navigation. It is also used as the reference name when linking the page to any other page. Additionally, the name of a database page will be used in advanced database features, as explained in *Chapter 7, Database Features and Functions*.

Every page has the option to **Add icon**, **Add cover**, and **Add comment**. These options can be accessed next to the page name, as shown in *Figure 2.11*:

Figure 2.11 – A page with the name of "Notion Book," an icon (badminton racket),
and the option to add a cover being selected

For the page icon, an emoji could be used, an image link to any address on the web could be used, or you could upload an image (ideally, 280 x 280 pixels). The page icon will also be shown in any place the page is linked to—either on another page or in the databases.

> **Note**
> There are websites and creators from where you can access different icons; some popular examples are Notion Icons and Favicon Icons.

For cover images, you can pick from a preset selection from the Notion gallery using these different sections:

- **COLOR & GRADIENT**
- **NASA ARCHIVE**
- **RIJKSMUSEUM**
- **THE MET MUSEUM – JAPANESE PRINTS**
- **THE MET MUSEUM**

Alternatively, you can upload an image (ideally, 1,500 pixels wide), use a link to an image, or use the free Unsplash library.

When you click on the three-dot menu in the upper-right corner of the page, as you can see in *Figure 2.9*, you will be given a drop-down menu that will show three text style options at the top: **Default**, **Serif**, and **Mono**. These are the only three font styles that will change all the text on the active page. Currently, there is no global setting for text fonts, so each page you create will need a setting change if you want to use **Serif** or **Mono.**

> **Note**
> You can change the font of the text on the page using the inline math block, which will be covered further in *Chapter 4, All the Building Blocks*.

The text size and the page width work in the same way as the text style, having a default size and an option for **small text** with text sizes and **full width** for page size, which would need to be toggled on for each page.

A few differences you will find between devices are that the mobile app doesn't offer the **small text** or **full width** options, and the tablet/iPad app won't show the **small text** option.

The **Customize page** option will differ depending on the type of page you are active on. On every page, there will be the option to adjust **Page comments** and **Backlinks**, but only database pages will have the option to adjust database properties. This will be covered in *Chapter 5*, *All the Basic Database Properties*.

A **Block page** is a page that does not have any properties and can have multiple blocks placed on the page. This is unlike a **database page**, which has properties associated with the page that are from the database it belongs to.

On any page, the backlinks can be **Expanded**. This is so that they appear as a list at the top of the page underneath the page name. **Show in popover** means that they appear as a clickable menu, which can display all of the backlinks, as shown in *Figure 2.12*. Additionally, **Off** means that the backlinks are not shown:

Figure 2.12 – The block page backlink option; the top red box is the location of the clickable backlink menu, and the bottom red bock is the dropdown of backlinks to the block page

On the other hand, **Page comments** are either **Expanded** or **Off**. These are the comments from guests or members on the page who have those privileges.

On a database page, each property will have a drop-down menu for viewing options. **Always show** and **Always hide** are options for every property, but **Hide when empty** is an option for every property except these few: **Last edited by**, **Last edited time**, **Checkbox**, **Created by**, and **Created time**.

This will change how the top of the page looks, as those properties that should be hidden will be put under a clickable menu that can be expanded if they are wanted, as shown in *Figure 2.13*:

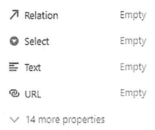

Figure 2.13 – Database properties are shown at the top of a page underneath the page name, with a clickable menu for 14 hidden properties

> **Note**
> When properties are hidden on a page, to reorder them, first, you need to unhide the properties.

Page actions and information

All the page actions are available on each device with no limitations located in the upper-right corner of the workspace screen. In the drop-down menu, the **lock page** feature prevents any editing to be done to the page, including adding, replacing, or moving blocks, and adding filters, sorts, views, or pages in databases. However, it does allow comments to be added.

The **open in app**, **add to favorites**, and **undo** buttons were covered in *Chapter 1, Setting up the Application*. Note that the copy link options allow you to copy the active page link to your clipboard to be used as a link for a block; this will be covered further in *Chapter 4, All the Building Blocks*.

At the bottom of the drop-down menu, **Word count** can be found alongside **Last edited by** and the **Today** time setting.

Summary

In this chapter, we covered how to use the Quick Find option and the breadcrumb of an active page to navigate around the workspace, using the sidebar hierarchy to help us locate where in the workspace we are.

Sharing options for collaborative work can be given to each individual page with different privileges for each account. Additionally, the page appearance can be changed on an individual-page basis with no global formatting, with actions that act directly on the active page.

Now that you understand how to navigate through the workspace, and what options are available when sharing pages, in the next chapter, we will set up the account and workspace so that we can work without issues and import some templates or information to start working.

3
Templates, Imports, Account Settings, and Workspace Settings

Once you have set up your account and are able to navigate around Notion, you can get started. However, when you start building out your workspace, there can be some irritations you come across, which, very often, are in the account settings or the workspace settings. If the solution isn't found in the settings, then it makes us contemplate where to start and which imports and templates to use to help.

In this chapter, we're going to cover the following main topics:

- How to duplicate and import templates
- Other external import options
- The My account settings options
- The Workspace settings setup options

You will learn how to import default templates from the Notion options, what the templates mean and do, and how to duplicate other creators' templates in your workspace. Additionally, we will check what other information you can import into Notion.

Additionally, you will learn how to set up your account so that the account you are on has appropriate notifications, viewing preferences, and privacy preferences enabled. In addition to this, you will learn about all the workspace options in the **settings** menu, covering members, plans, and security.

Often, setting up your account is only done once; however, if things change in the future, knowing where to find these options is useful. However, the workspace settings are a place that you are likely to visit on multiple occasions to check the settings for the other people that have access.

How to duplicate and import templates

In this section, you will learn how to import templates from the native Notion list and duplicate templates from other creators into your workspace. This can help give you a start on a use case for your workspace, or it could give you a solution to a problem you are having.

> **Note**
>
> Templates can be a great place to start from, but understanding how the template works is far more useful, as it allows you to adjust and change the features, functionality, and limitations the template may have.

The term "template" in Notion can mean lots of things, but alone, **template** refers to a set of pages, blocks, and databases that can be duplicated into another workspace. A **template block** is a special type of block that allows you to duplicate pages, blocks, and databases inside a current page, such as a duplication button, which will be covered in *Chapter 4, All the Building Blocks*. A **database template** is a database page that is stored in a database and can be duplicated into any blank database page created in the same database.

In the sidebar, there is a **Templates** option that you can select, which opens a window of duplicatable templates. These are all top-level pages with premade pages, blocks, and databases to serve a specific function and purpose.

The template options window will show the template on the main screen, as illustrated in *Figure 3.1*:

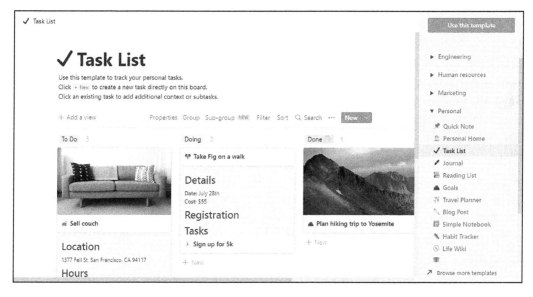

Figure 3.1 – The template options window showing a task list template and the sidebar
option for other template options

On the right-hand side, there will be a drop-down menu of other top-level pages that are
templates you can import into your space. You can access them by using the button in the
upper-right corner of the window, as shown in *Figure 3.2*:

Figure 3.2 – The template import option list

Once the template has been imported into your space, it will have created a top-level page in the workspace and will appear in the sidebar, just like the templates from the onboarding process.

Now that the template is in your workspace, you have full editing privileges and can change it as much as you want, linking it to anything else in your current workspace. More on that will be covered in *Chapter 4*, *All the Building Blocks*, and *Chapter 7*, *Database Features and Functions*. The same process applies to any other creator templates; however, the viewing experience will be different.

If you follow a link to another individual's page that has the **duplicate** setting enabled, you will be taken to a page that doesn't allow for editing but has a **duplicate** option in the upper-right corner of the screen, as shown in *Figure 3.3*:

> **Note**
>
> You can find creator templates through links on YouTube videos, in articles, in blog posts, on websites, and in the Notion gallery located at the bottom of the native Notion template menu list.

Figure 3.3 – An example creator template showing the duplicate template button

Sometimes, you will have information in other applications or pieces of software, and templates won't be able to help you with that. If the data or information is somewhere else and you want to bring it into Notion, you will need to import it.

Other external import options

In this section, you will import data into your Notion workspace and learn how importing data into Notion works. Each import option function goes through the same process, but there are some differences in how the information is shown depending on the type of import.

This is not only useful for starting your Notion workspace with preexisting information but also for importing data when working on other software such as Excel.

> **Note**
> Many online applications will have the option to export the data to a CSV file or Excel. This means that even though there might not be a direct import into Notion, you can still transfer the data.

If you look at the sidebar, underneath **Templates**, and above **Trash**, there is an **Import** option.

There are two main types of data that can be imported into Notion: the first is **Text & Markdown** and the second is a **CSV** file, which imports much like many of the other import options, as shown in *Figure 3.4*:

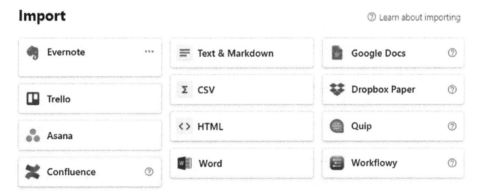

Figure 3.4 – The Import option window

When importing text or markdown files, you will be directed to your local document's **File Explorer** application, where you can select the pages you want to import. Once you have selected a page, it will import that page into Notion as a top-level page. The text will be put into blocks, converting headings and bullet points throughout the page. However, some formatting might still be required.

If you are aware about how all data that is imported from the app, you will be happy to know that imports work in very similar ways:

1. Before Notion can import data, you need to log into the application you are looking to import the data from.

2. Once Notion is connected to the application, you need to grant access to Notion to export the data. This could be by adding your password to the app or, in some cases, ticking a box or selecting a drop-down menu to authorize your access.

3. After the authentication process is successful, Notion will attempt to import the data. In most cases, there will be multiple notebooks, projects, or pages from the app that you can choose from as an import.

4. You can **Select all** or **Deselect all** when navigating the import window. Alternatively, you can use the search option to find exactly what you want to import, as shown in *Figure 3.5*:

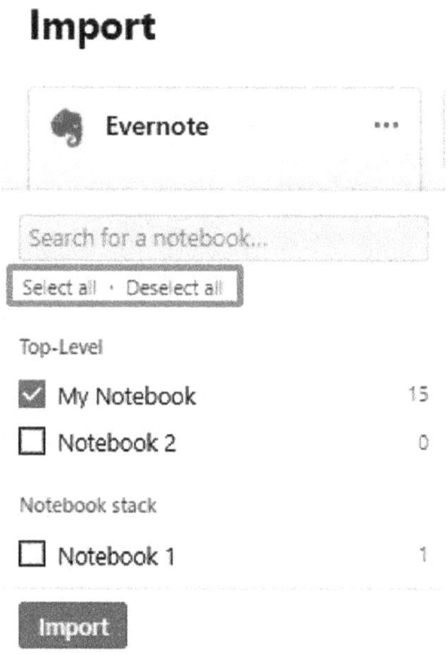

Figure 3.5 – The Evernote Import window with the Select all and Deselect all options highlighted

5. When importing data from an application, if there is any metadata inside the app, the information will be put into a database such as the **CSV** import instead of text on a page. **Metadata** is information that relates specifically to a page entry, which separates it from other pages. *Chapter 5, All the Basic Database Properties*, is full of examples of different types of metadata.

> **Note**
>
> When using spreadsheet software such as Excel, you can copy the cells and paste them into Notion, and this is treated as a CSV import. The information will be imported into Notion and put into a database.

Importing **CSV** files works in the same way as Text & Markdown by taking you to your local **File Explorer** application. The difference is that you can import it as a unique page, or you can import it directly into an existing database. This can be done from the core database page or a linked database view. A **core database page** is a page that only stores information for a database and has no option to add any blocks. A **linked database view** is a copy of the database link, which shows and gives access to the core database page, allowing you to edit from the linked view.

The **Merge with CSV** option can be found in the upper-right section of the core database page and in the three-dot menu found in the upper-right corner of the linked database view.

Once you have information in your workspace through importing templates, importing data from external apps, or inputting information from scratch, you then need to set up your account for collaboration.

The My account settings setup options

In this section, we will go through the account settings, making sure they are safe, connected to the appropriate apps, and show the correct information. Most of the account settings will only be set once and not changed. However, knowing where to look when a change is needed, or to help a co-worker, can really help.

To access the account settings, you need to open the sidebar and click on **Settings & Members**, which will open up the **settings** window. This window will show a sidebar section that is split by a **WORKSPACE** title, as shown in *Figure 3.6*:

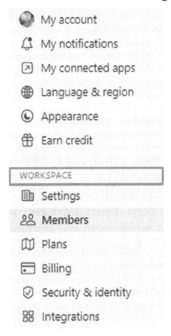

Figure 3.6 – The Settings & Members sidebar section with Members as the currently active window

Every option above the **WORKSPACE** section, as shown in *Figure 3.6*, relates only to the account, whereas the other information is specific to the active workspace (that is, the workspace you are currently in).

> **Note**
> The account settings are accessible irrespective of the workspace you are active in, but the option will appear as **Settings** instead of **Settings & Members**.

The **My account** tab gives you multiple options:

- You can change your photo by uploading one from your local files. This photo is similar to your profile picture and can be viewed in every workspace you are in.

- You can change your email, which is where all of the notifications for this account will be sent.

- You can change the **Preferred name** option, which is what is shown to other users when they hover over your profile picture.

- You can enable **Support access**, which gives the Notion support team access to your account for troubleshooting any issues.

- **Log out of all devices** will log you out of every device except the one you are active on when selecting this option.

- The **Start week on Monday** toggle will change the database views. This is explained further in *Chapter 6, Database Views*.

- The **Danger zone** option is where you can delete your account. This will delete your account, affecting every device and instance of the account.

- The **My notifications** section allows you to toggle on or off the options for Mobile push notifications, Email notifications, and always send email notifications. These notifications apply to the update section in *Chapter 2, Workspace Navigation, Sharing, and Appearance*, that was mentioned earlier, which will trigger when you are following a page.

- The **My connected apps** section shows what apps you are currently connected to that allow for the import options, as explained in the previous section. This section allows you to connect or disconnect from any of those apps.

- The **Language & region** section allows you to select your language and allows you to select the **Start week on Monday** option, just like in the **My account** section.

- The **Appearance** section allows you to move from light mode to dark mode and select **Use system setting**, which will use the settings that are currently on your computer system.

> **Note**
> For those familiar with CSS and Chromium-based applications, Notion does allow you to customize the appearance.

The **Earn credit** section can be very useful to go through when first starting to use Notion. By completing the six tasks that are mentioned next, you can earn credit, which will pay for up to 5 months of the **Personal Pro Plan** subscription:

1. Log in on the web, which can be done by simply creating an account and signing in. Most people will have done this one by signing up. You can also log in on the desktop or the mobile app, as demonstrated in *Chapter 1, Setting Up the Application*.

2. **Import from Evernote**, which was covered earlier in the chapter. For those who don't have an Evernote account, you can create an account, make one note, and import that note into Notion to complete this task.

3. **Use the Web Clipper**, which will be covered in *Chapter 11, Using API Integration and Add-On Options*.

4. **Use the iOS or Android system share menu**, which needs to be done on the mobile app. For this, you need to access an online web page and press the share button option, sharing it to your Notion app. This will create a page in Notion, with the link to the web page in it. This function is very similar to the web clipper.

> **Note**
>
> On the mobile and tablet apps, you will have restricted access to these account options. You will get **Notifications & settings** as an option, giving you access to the **My notifications** section and options to change your password, change the appearance, give support access, and start the week on Monday. When on the Team plan, you will be shown an additional **Members** option, which will be covered in the next section of this chapter.

The Workspace settings setup options

In this section, you will go through the workspace settings, making sure your guests, members, and admins are in order. The plan you are on gives you the features you want and ensures that the billing is correct. Additionally, you will see where the integration and security information is stored; however, this section will mostly focus on the plan and member sections.

This is important because as your team grows or your use case for Notion increases, there might be features you are looking for that require a different plan, as there are limitations to each plan.

> **Note**
>
> The settings you see in each workspace will be dependent on your account privileges in that workspace. If you are accessing a workspace without admin privileges, you won't have access to every settings section.

Settings

The **Settings** section is where you can change the name of the workspace, and this will be seen by any other user. The icon can also be changed—again seen by any other user. The **Icon** setting of the workspace has the same options as the page icon: **Emoji**, **Upload an image**, and **Link**. Please refer to *Figure 3.7*:

Figure 3.7 – The icon pop-up menu with three options, Emoji, Upload an image, and Link

The **Domain** option gives you the option to change the domain that the public pages will be shared under. This changes what will be seen when you share a Notion page publicly.

Then, there is the **Export content** option that allows you to use the **Export all workspace content** option. This will export everything in your Notion workspace into the file format you choose, such as **HTML**, **Markdown & CSV**, or **PDF**, if you have the Enterprise plan. You can remove images and files from this export if you want.

Additionally, you can **Export members** if you are on the Enterprise plan, as a **CSV** document, as shown in *Figure 3.8*:

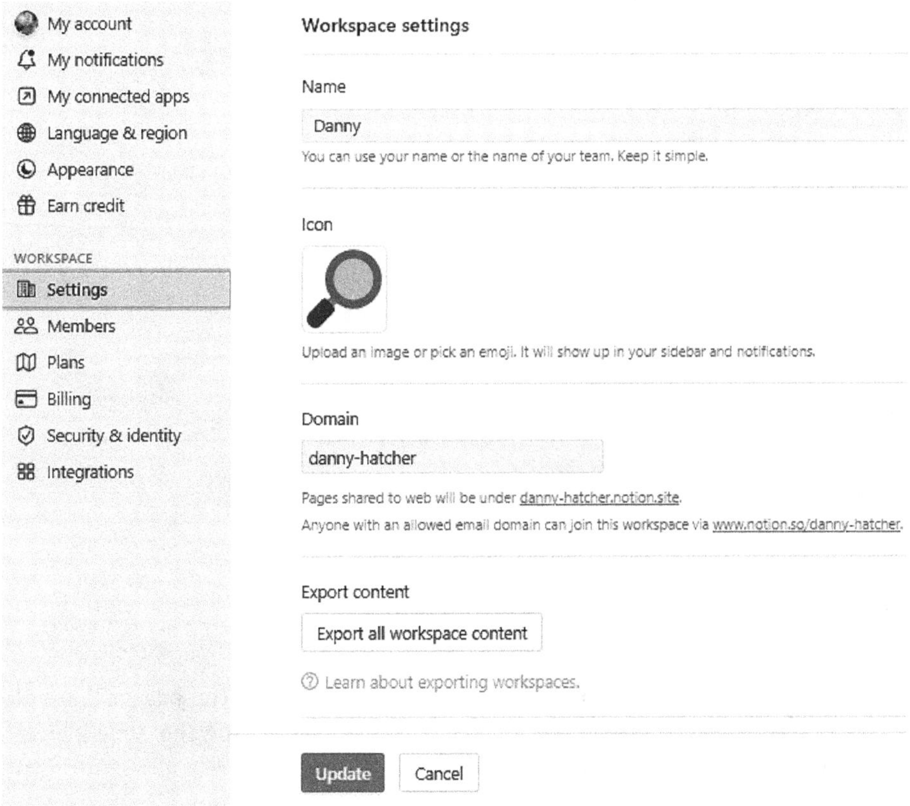

Figure 3.8 – The Settings window tab

> **Note**
> You can export any individual page or database page without the rest of
> the workspace.

If you have admin access to a workspace, you will be shown a **Delete entire workspace**
option, which will delete the workspace you're in, not your account. If you are in another
workspace, this option will say **Leave workspace** if you don't have admin privileges.

> **Note**
> Once you have made any changes, make sure that you click the **Update** button
> at the bottom of the section to save the changes.

Members

In the **Members** section, you will be limited in terms of the functions you have access to,
depending on the plan you're on. Take a look at the three sections shown in *Figure 3.9*:

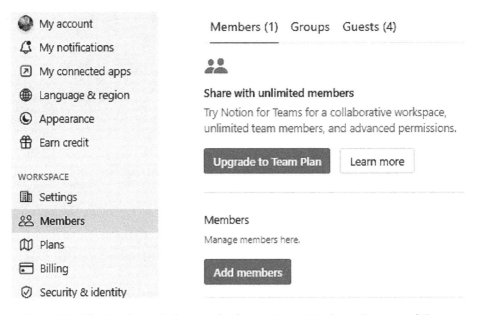

Figure 3.9 – The Members tab showing the three sections, Members, Groups, and Guests

The **Members** area is where you can add members to your space if you have a Team plan
or higher. The members active in the workspace will be shown within the **Access level**
setting they have to the workspace, either **Admin** or **Member**.

Members will have access to all the pages in the workspace, but they cannot change the workspace settings or invite new members to the workspace. Members with admin privileges can change the workspace settings and invite new members to the workspace.

The **Groups** area is where you can group members if you are on the Team plan or higher. This allows you to share pages and databases with groups of members at a time, instead of sharing them with everyone in a group. A department could be an example use case of groups.

Finally, the **Guests** area is where you can see what pages each guest can access, and then remove that access if you want to. When you try to remove access, you will be shown a warning message asking if you are sure, to avoid any mistakes, as they will be removed from every page that they currently have access to.

Plans

The **Plans** area of the workspace settings is where you can look through the features that are available in the app and what plan you might need to move to when the team grows. Alternatively, you can check which plan is appropriate for you if you decide to create a workspace on your own.

> Note
> The rest of this section is subject to Notion updates, and we can change the plans accordingly, so it is worth double-checking before selecting any plan changes.

There are four plans, including the individual user plans:

- **Personal**
- **Personal Pro**
- **Team**
- **Enterprise**

There are many differences between each of these. The main ones to consider are as follows:

- The free **Personal** plan is limited to 5 guests and 5 MB of file upload. That is the individual upload size, not the total upload storage.
- The free **Personal** plan has no version history option, whereas **Personal Pro** and **Team** have 30 days and **Enterprise** is forever.

- The individual user plans don't allow any added members, whereas the multiple user plans are unlimited. This means the multiple user plans can use the **Collaborative workspace** features, allowing others to have sharing privileges.

- The timeline database view is limited to three in the individual user plans, five in the **Team** plan, and is unlimited in the **Enterprise** plan.

- The **Admin & Security** and **Support** sections are where most of the plan differences can be seen, as shown in *Figure 3.9*:

Admin & security	Personal	Personal Pro	Team	Enterprise
Bulk export	✓	✓	✓	✓
Admin tools			✓	✓
Permission groups			✓	✓
Advanced permissions			✓	✓
Advanced security controls				✓
SAML + Single Sign-On (SSO)				✓
User provisioning (SCIM)				✓
Bulk PDF export				✓
Support				
Priority support		✓	✓	✓
Dedicated manager				✓
Custom contract & invoicing				✓
Access new features early				✓

Figure 3.9 – The plan feature differences in the Admin & security section and Support section; from left to right, the columns are Personal, Personal Pro, Team, and Enterprise

> **Note**
> Any student or educator can get the Personal Pro Plan for free by using the school email address. This can be done by creating a new account or by changing the current account email.

Billing

The **Billing** section shows the current plan you are on alongside when the next payment is due. You can change the plan you are on by selecting the **Change plan** button in this section or through any of the other **Upgrade** or **Downgrade** buttons around the Notion workspace, as shown in *Figure 3.10*:

	For individuals		For teams & businesses	
	Personal $0	**Personal Pro** $5 per month	**Team** $10 per member per month	**Enterprise** $25 per member per month
Pay annually ⬤ Monthly	Downgrade	Current plan	Upgrade	Upgrade
				Contact sales
Usage				
Pages and blocks	Unlimited	Unlimited	Unlimited	Unlimited
Members	Just you	Just you	Unlimited	Unlimited
Guests	5	Unlimited	Unlimited	Unlimited
File uploads	5 MB	Unlimited	Unlimited	Unlimited
Version history		30 days	30 days	Forever

Figure 3.10 – The payment plan options for upgrading or downgrading the workspace

You can add specific billing details in this section, such as the following:

- Payment method, whether this is a credit or debit card, Apple Pay, or Google Pay.
- The billing interval shows how frequently you will be charged.
- The billing email is the email associated with the payments and will receive all communication about those payments.
- Your address is just your full name and country.
- The VAT/GST number, making sure to include the country code.
- The workspace balance, which is from the credit earned through the tasks mentioned earlier.
- Apply a coupon.

The **Security & identity** section is accessible by everyone, but only members with the Enterprise plan can change any of the settings, as shown in *Figure 3.9*. The **Integrations** section shows what API integrations have been set up in the workspace, which will be covered in *Chapter 11*, *Using API Integrations and Add-On Options*.

Summary

In this chapter, we learned how to import templates from Notion, the Notion gallery, and creator templates to help you get started. Additionally, we looked at how to import information from other applications by exporting the data into a format that Notion can import, such as into Excel or in a CSV file. We also covered how to set up your account ready for collaboration and how the workspace settings can be changed to alter member privileges alongside the differences between the available plans.

At this point, you now have an account, a workspace, and all the settings ready for you to start building. So, in the next chapter, let's discover what blocks are and what you can do with them.

4

All the Building Blocks

This is where Notion starts to separate itself from other applications that you might already be familiar with. **Notion** is not just an app you use but one that you can build. You are in total control of what information is on each page, what information you see on each page, and how you see it. This is achieved by giving you the power of adding and removing blocks and databases to and from pages.

In this chapter, we're going to cover the following main topics:

- The basic and inline block options

- Creating columns and coloring blocks

- The media and embed block options

- Using advanced blocks, actions, and databases

You will learn how to add a block to a page, move a block around a page, and change existing blocks to a different type. This also includes creating columns on pages and understanding which pages allow for block placement.

Additionally, you will learn about the different blocks that you can put onto a page, from basic blocks to special blocks with added functions, and the database and action block options that require additional knowledge in order to use them effectively.

The basic and inline block options

In this section, you will learn what all the **basic blocks** in Notion are and how they can be used to create various pages for sharing and storing information. Knowledge of each of these blocks not only helps to reduce the page size and page number, but it also creates an aesthetic that is pleasant to work in.

Understanding block uses can also allow other team members, or collaborators, to create pages to their liking, giving some individual personality to their work environment.

> **Note**
>
> You can only add a block to a page or a page to a database, but you cannot do so for a database page. If the page has a database in its full width with no option to add a block underneath, it is a **database page**. You can check this by looking at the upper-right three-dot menu and searching for a database lock. If one is present, then it is a database page.

To insert a block onto a page, you can either click on the + option next to an existing block or push *Enter* while in an existing block, as shown in *Figure 4.1*. Pressing *Enter* will automatically insert a new text block:

Figure 4.1: An empty text block showing the / command option and the + block option

When in an empty text block, you can push / to open a drop-down menu of all the block types. The **basic block** types are as follows:

1. **Text**: This is a basic block for writing words.

2. **Page**: This is used to create a link to a new page. You can use the + shortcut in a text block and type in the name you want the new page to be, and then push *Enter* to create the page.

3. **To-do list**: This is a checkbox that can be checked on or off. You can use the *[]* shortcut followed by a space after each item.

4. **Heading 1**: This is a large size heading. You can use the # shortcut and then push the spacebar.

5. **Heading 2**: This is a medium-size heading. You can use the ## shortcut and then push the spacebar.

6. **Heading 3**: This is a small-size heading. You can use the ### shortcut and then push the spacebar.

7. **Bulleted list**: This is a list with bullets. You can use the – shortcut and then press the spacebar.

8. **Numbered list**: This is a list with numbered bullets. You can use the *1* shortcut followed by the spacebar.

9. **Toggle list**: This is a block that allows you to fold and unfold the list. You can use the > shortcut followed by the spacebar.

10. **Quote**: This is a larger viewing text block. You can use the " shortcut followed by the spacebar.

11. **Divider**: This is a line that goes across the column. You can use the - - - shortcut.

12. **Link to page**: This is similar to a **Page** block, but it links to an existing page. You can use the + shortcut in a text block and type in the name you want to search for by pushing *Enter* to create the link.

13. **Callout**: This is a text block that allows for an icon.

The **Inline** blocks are as follows:

1. **Mention a person**: This sends a notification to the personal account you mention in the block. You can use the @ shortcut and then type in the name of the person you are looking for.

2. **Mention a page**: This is similar to the **Link to page** block but is in line with text instead of being a single block. You can use the @ shortcut and then type in the name of the page you are looking for.

> **Note**
> When you **mention a page,** the drag and drop feature with a linked page is unavailable, so you can't drag blocks onto the mentioned page.

3. **Date or reminder**: This creates a date for viewing or adding a reminder with the date picker for a notification. The difference is shown in *Figure 4.2*. You can use the @ shortcut, and then type in the date you are looking for, or type in **remind** and the date you want to be reminded of:

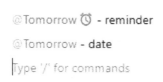

Figure 4.2: A reminder for tomorrow, and a date for tomorrow with an empty text block below

4. **Emoji**: This adds an emoji for the emoji menu inside a text block. You can use the @ shortcut and then type in the name of the person you are looking for.

5. **Inline equation**: This adds a box that allows the *Latex* and *Katex* functions to be added. *Figure 4.3* shows the **Learn more** option in the app:

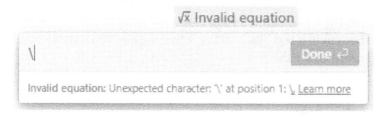

Figure 4.3: The Learn more option in the inline math equation input box,
which is found when entering / into the input bar

All of these blocks can be used straight away without any other knowledge apart from the inline math equation, but that is only for *Latex* or *Katex* use. Once you have added these blocks to a page, you can adjust them by using the formatting tools, which will be explained next.

Creating columns and coloring blocks

In this section, you will learn how to use some of the basic blocks to format a page and create different aesthetics. This is a crucial skill to learn when creating pages in Notion, as some pages suit devices better than others, and some pages can be condensed by using some of the tools available when formatting blocks.

Irrespective of the type of block on the page, there will be two options to the left-hand side of each block—a + option and an ∷ option—as shown in *Figure 4.1*. To move a block, you can use the ∷ icon:

1. First, you need to select the block by clicking on the ∷ icon and dragging your mouse over the desired blocks (or while editing the block, push *Esc* on the keyboard):

New page

A text block

Figure 4.4: A highlighted text block with the words "A text block" written inside

2. Once the desired blocks have been highlighted, you can click and hold the ∷ icon. While holding down on the mouse, drag the block until a blue line appears on the page. At this point, you can release the mouse to place the block, as shown in *Figure 4.5*:

New page

A text block

A text block

Figure 4.5: The text block is being dragged down the page until
a blue line appears underneath an empty text block

Creating columns

To create columns, drag the desired blocks to the side of a current block—on the left or right—until a blue line appears, as shown in *Figure 4.6*:

New page

A text block   A second text block

A second text block   A third text block

A third text block

Figure 4.6: Two blocks are being dragged to the right-hand side of the top block to create two columns

> **Note**
>
> There is no restriction regarding how many columns you can create on a page. However, by making the page full width and hiding the sidebar, you get more room on the page, which allows for easier viewing of multiple columns.

Database blocks work in the same way as regular blocks when moving them up and down the page, but creating columns is not as simple. The same difficulty occurs when creating columns inside a column or a toggle block.

To put inline databases into columns, the columns need to have already been created using another block. Following this, you can drag the inline database into the preexisting columns. This can be done quickly, as follows:

1. Create a text block.

2. Push *Enter* to create a second text block below.

3. Drag the second text block to the left-hand side of the first text block to create columns.

4. Drag the inline databases into each column.

5. The result can be seen in *Figure 4.7*:

Figure 4.7: Two columns made with text blocks with inline databases inside them

Creating columns inside an existing column or a toggle block is more complicated. When dragging a text block to the side of a column or toggle block, Notion will either create a new column next to the existing column or place the block in the neighboring column.

Block actions will be covered in more detail in a future section; however, for this to work correctly, we need to use a block action on a linked page:

1. Create a toggle block or columns on a page.

2. Create a page inside the column or toggle block, as shown in *Figure 4.8*:

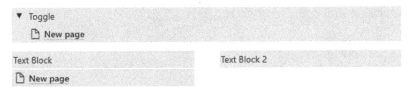

Figure 4.8: Highlighted blocks showing columns with page blocks inside

3. Enter the new page and create the number of columns you want inside the new page.

4. Go back to the original page and click on the ⁝⁝ icon to access the actions menu, as shown in *Figure 4.:9*

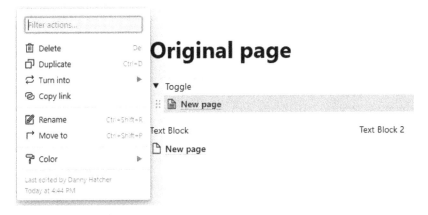

Figure 4.9: The New page block with the columns highlighted with the action menu open

5. Click on **Turn into** and then select **text**.

6. The result will show the name of the page as text, and everything that was on the page is indented underneath, as illustrated in *Figure 4.10*:

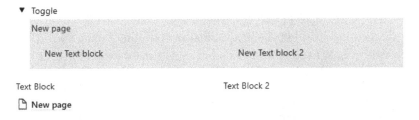

Figure 4.10: Two columns inside a toggle block with the page now as text

7. You can leave the text as it is with the columns indented, or you can delete the text leaving just the columns. The same process can be done inside an existing column. Both results are shown in *Figure 4.11*:

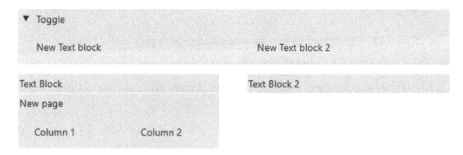

Figure 4.11: The highlighted column block results

Figure 4.9 shows a toggle block with two columns created from a page whose name has been deleted. You can see a text block column with two columns created from a page with the name remaining, leaving indented columns.

Creating columns can be tricky, but this method covers all situations you might want to include. However, block coloring has many more possibilities for customization.

Still using the ⠿ icon, you can click on **color**. This will open a menu for **color** and **background color**, which will be applied to the entire block selection. Additionally, you can highlight text, using the same options as the text toolbar, but note that they only apply to the selected text, as shown in *Figure 4.12*:

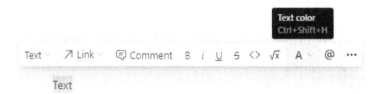

Figure 4.12: The text toolbar is shown after highlighting the text and selecting the Text color option

When inside the menu from either the text toolbar or from the ⠿ icon, you will be shown a list of options with a **Last used** option available using the *Ctrl + Shift + H* keyboard shortcut for Windows and *Cmd + Shift + H* for macOS.

With the 10 color options and 10 background color options, alongside the 2 selection options, there are plenty of combinations of coloring to choose from. An example using orange and the default color is shown in *Figure 4.13*:

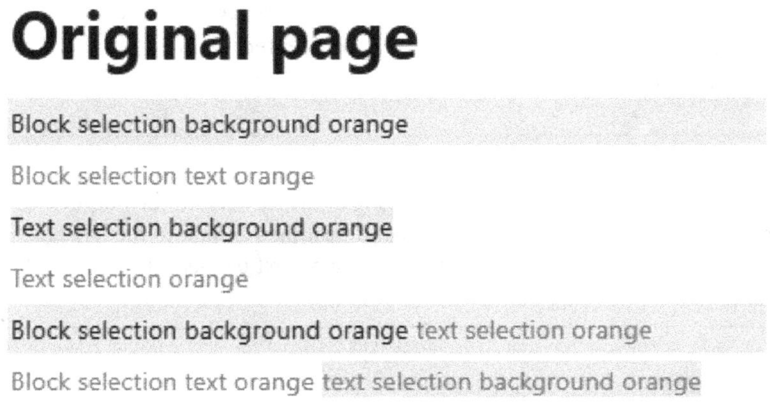

Original page

Block selection background orange

Block selection text orange

Text selection background orange

Text selection orange

Block selection background orange text selection orange

Block selection text orange text selection background orange

Figure 4.13: Colouring options with block and text selections, changing the background
and text color using the default with orange

Changing the background of each block will come out with different aesthetics. Changing
the background and text of a block will also affect anything that is indented underneath
that block. Therefore, a database block will change if indented or inside another block for
that specific instance, as shown in *Figure 4.14*:

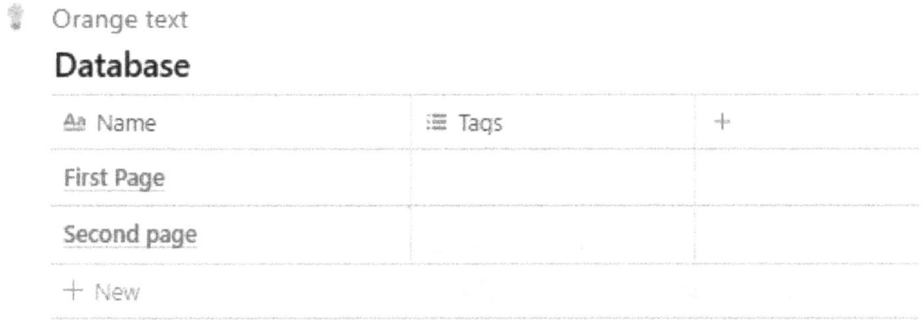

Orange text

Database

Aa Name	≡ Tags	+
First Page		
Second page		
+ New		

Figure 4.14: A database inside a callout block with the block selection of
the callout block being set to orange text

With this massive variety of options to customize the look of the page just with colors,
there is another way to add even more options to the aesthetic, inline, and math equations.

Inline and math equation coloring

The **inline equation block** is in the basic block section, whereas the **block equation** is
in the advanced block section inside the Notion app. They both do the same thing,
except inline equations can be inside a text block, whereas the **math equation block** is
a standalone block.

Latex and **Katex** can be entered into these blocks; therefore, color can be added, fonts can be changed, sizes can be adjusted, and images can be created using symbols, with some examples shown in *Figure 4.15* and *Figure 4.16*:

Note

The block equation can be useful for centering a title by default; the output is centered in the block, whereas text blocks and headings default to the left. An **inline equation block** that is part of the heading or text blocks will also default to the left.

Example text Tiny example

Example text Scriptsize example

Example text Footnotesize example

Example text small example

Example text normalsize example

Example text large example

Example text Large example

Example text LARGE example

Example text huge example

Example text Huge example

In this sentence, there are some words I want to highlight with a yellow box and other words I want an outline for using inline math. This has the two types of highlights applied together

Normal Inline Math – abcdefghijklmnopqrstuvwxyz ABCDEFGHIJKLMNOPQRSTUVWXYZ

text Inline Math - abcdefghijklmnopqrstuvwxyz ABCDEFGHIJKLMNOPQRSTUVWXYZ

sf font – abcdefghijklmnopqrstuvwxyz ABCDEFGHIJKLMNOPQRSTUVWXYZ

bf font – abcdefghijklmnopqrstuvwxyz ABCDEFGHIJKLMNOPQRSTUVWXYZ

tt font – abcdefghijklmnopqrstuvwxyz ABCDEFGHIJKLMNOPQRSTUVWXYZ

Bbb font – abcdefghijklmnopqrstuvwxyz ABCDEFGHIJKLMNOPQRSTUVWXYZ

Figure 4.15: Inline math examples showing different text sizes, font types, and inline text highlighting

Some examples of **inline math equation** blocks and how they can change the aesthetic of pages can be viewed in *Figure 4.16*:

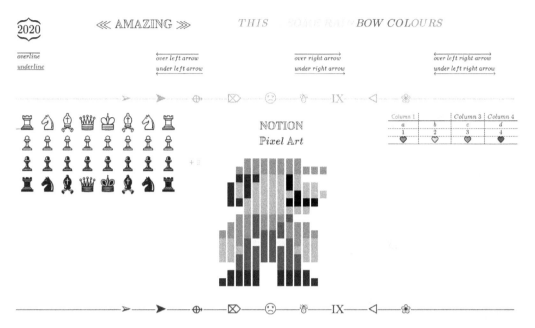

Figure 4.16: Inline and math equation blocks using various Katex,
showing examples of dividers, arrays, images, and alternate heading options

Much of the flexibility in using inline math comes down to the creativity of the user in terms of how they can use the **Learn more** option in Notion for the different functions that are accepted, as shown in *Figure 4.3*. This moves us onto the media and embed blocks.

The media and embed block options

In this section, you will learn how to embed media and other tools in a page. This is often useful for visual users of a tool, for showing images, embedding instructional videos, or including another tool in the space. Another common use is to just have links going to other places on the internet.

Media blocks

The blocks that are underneath the **MEDIA** section are mostly using external links or files to be displayed in Notion:

- The **Image** block allows you to upload an image, embed a linked image from other places on the web, or use **Unsplash** for something such as the page icon.

> **Note**
> The upload size of any file will be limited depending on what payment plan you are on. Some plans limit individual uploads to 5 MB, so it is worth checking this.

- The **Web bookmark** block is a way of showing a web link in a button format instead of seeing the text link, as shown in *Figure 4.15*:

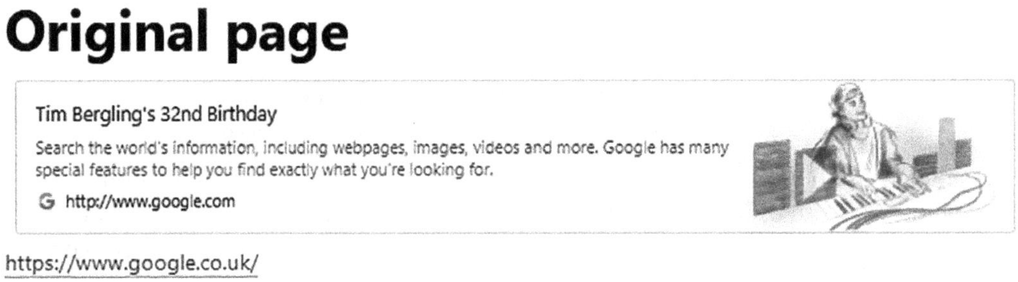

Original page

Tim Bergling's 32nd Birthday

Search the world's information, including webpages, images, videos and more. Google has many special features to help you find exactly what you're looking for.

G http://www.google.com

https://www.google.co.uk/

Figure 4.17: An example of a Web bookmark of Google and the text below for a visual contrast

- The **File**, **Audio**, and **Video** blocks all give the same options: **Upload** or **Embed link**. Each displays the appropriate result; however, when you copy and paste a file or link into Notion, it will come up with an options menu, as shown in *Figure 4.18*:

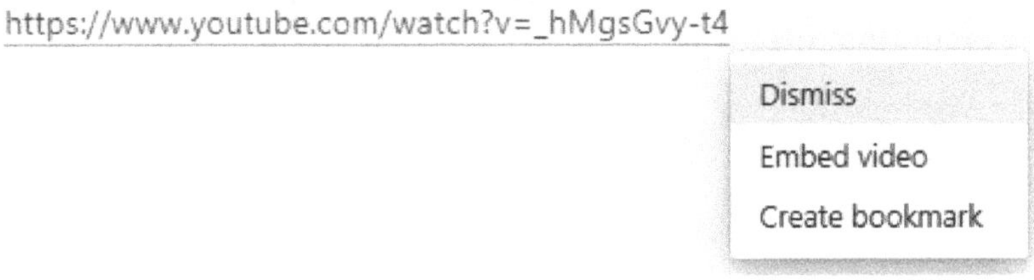

https://www.youtube.com/watch?v=_hMgsGvy-t4

Dismiss

Embed video

Create bookmark

4.18: The copy and paste options menu inside Notion for files and links

> **Note**
>
> This options menu will appear without any interaction with the block selection menu. This means you can print screen an image, copy the URL of a website, or drag a file from File Explorer and put it into Notion, and this menu will appear every time.

- There are also code blocks in this section, and they allow you to write in code, with highlights depending on the language you are using. For example, if you are writing in JavaScript, it will highlight the appropriate code functions. This block also has a copy-to-clipboard button in the upper-right corner of the block.

Before moving on to all of the embed options, it is important to note that the media options and embed options work in very similar ways. The main difference is that the embed list is specific to a tool or app, whereas the media list is generic.

Embeds

The **Embeds** section is available as a list of apps and tools that are typically used by other Notion users, but every copy and paste instance will show the preceding menu:

- **Embed**
- **Google Drive**
- **Tweet**
- **GitHub Gist**
- **Google**
- **Figma**
- **Abstract**
- **Invision**
- **Framer**
- **Whimsical**
- **Miro**
- **Sketch**
- **Excalidraw**
- **PDF**
- **Loom**

- **Typeform**
- **CodePen**
- **Replit**

> **Note**
>
> Some embeds might fail due to sign-in issues, privacy issues, or because the tool or application doesn't allow embeds, which means Notion will default the embed as a web bookmark, acting as a hyperlink. There are plenty of embed options that are not in the list but can be achieved through the same embed process. Once the basic blocks are in place, there are other actions and blocks that might be useful.

Using advanced blocks, actions, and databases

In this section, you will add the advanced blocks onto a page and use the additional functions each block gives you. Navigate through the actions that can be taken on each block, some of which are specific to certain block types. Then, cover the database options when going through the block menu.

The **advanced blocks** are great tools for saving time in a workflow by helping with the creation of blocks, navigating through pages, or ensuring synchronicity across the workspace:

- A **Table of contents** block is a block that is placed on a page, and it will automatically show each heading that is on the page. It will indent **Heading 2** and **Heading 3** under **Heading 1**, and indent **Heading 3** under **Heading 2**, as shown in *Figure 4.17*.

> **Note**
>
> By clicking on the heading in the table of contents block it will take you to that location on the page. To get back to the table of contents you would need to scroll or navigate another way.

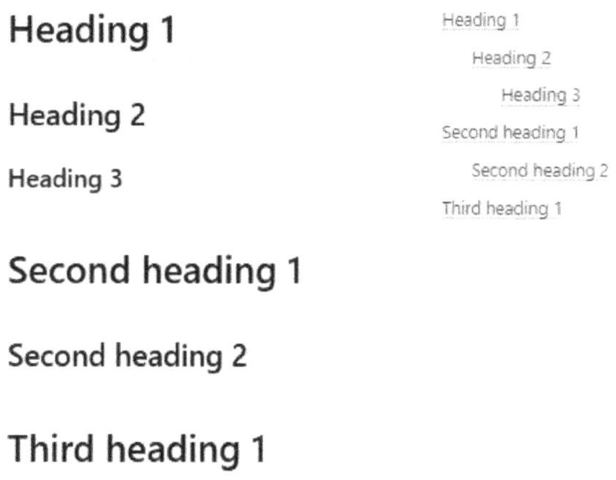

Heading 1

Heading 2

Heading 3

Second heading 1

Second heading 2

Third heading 1

Heading 1
Heading 2
Heading 3
Second heading 1
Second heading 2
Third heading 1

4.19: A table of contents block on the right-hand side of the image mimicking
the different heading blocks shown on the left-hand side

- **Block equation** works in the same way as inline math, as shown in *Figure 4.19* and *Figure 4.20*. But it is a block type rather than a subset of another block type. This means the equation can be moved without text and is centered on the page.

- The **Template button** block is different from the templates you import, as explained in *Chapter 3, Templates, Imports, Account Settings, and Workspace Settings*. This block allows you to put any type of block inside it, and then, when activating the template block, it will duplicate everything inside.

- To configure this block, push the settings cog on the right-hand side of the block, as shown in *Figure 4.20*:

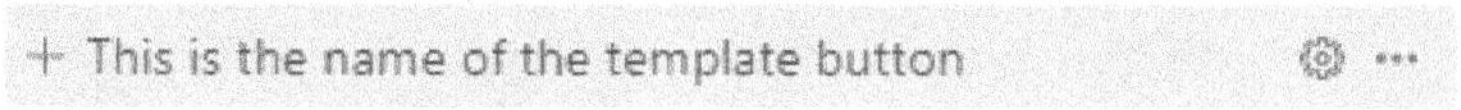

+ This is the name of the template button   ⚙ ⋯

Figure 4.20: The template button block is configured with the settings cog on the far right

- Once pushed, the configure template button window will open, and every block and action you create on a page is available inside the **Template** section, as shown at the bottom of *Figure 4.21*:

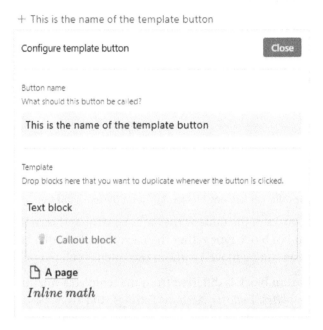

Figure 4.21: The Configure template button window showing the Button name section and the Template section with some blocks included

- The output of this specific template button will look similar to *Figure 2.22* after two clicks of the template block:

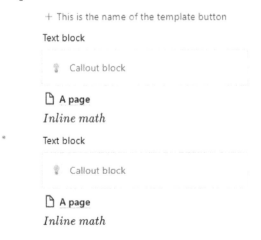

Figure 4.22: The result of two clicks of the template button

Note

When the first block in the template button is a page block, the page will open when the template button is activated, which will put the user on that page. This means that if you don't want to be directed to the page when you activate the template button, there needs to be a block above the page block, just like the callout block shown in *Figure 4.22*.

- The **Breadcrumb** block shows the breadcrumb for the page you are on, just like the breadcrumb at the top of the page, as shown in *Figure 4.23*.

Original page / First page / Second Page

Second Page

Original page / First page / Second Page

Figure 4.23: The breadcrumb block underneath the page heading of Second Page, showing the same result at the top of the page

- The **Synced block** option allows you to create a block and then copy the block to other pages in the workspace with synchronized changes. This means if you have information that needs to be updated in multiple places at once, it can be done in one change. These blocks can be identified with a red outline when clicking on them, alongside additional options such as **Copy and sync** and **Editing in**, and then links to other instances of the synced block, as shown in *Figure 4.24*:

Original page

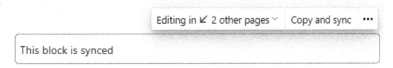

Editing in ↙ 2 other pages ⌄   Copy and sync   •••

This block is synced

Figure 4.24: A synced block with text in it, showing the other pages the block is synced with and the Copy and sync option

---

Note

Each individual synced block can be unsynced at any time. This gives some workflow flexibility when creating documents or when using templates. A sync block can be duplicated in a template, synced to any changes, and then unsynced when appropriate.

Each of these blocks has its use cases from a functional point of view, but the template buttons and synced blocks are the most practical as they can be used to speed up workflows.

- The **Table** block allows you to create a simple table inside a page, which can have columns and rows with a highlighted column or row.

Adding a column or row can be done using the buttons next to the current column or row, or you can add both a column and a row at the same time by dragging diagonally on the + button, as shown in *Figure 4.25*:

Figure 4.25: A table block being enlarged by clicking and dragging the + button

The rows and columns can be moved by clicking and dragging the ⁝⁝ icon at the end of the row or column.

Action options

Each block will have some simple actions that can be taken using the ⁝⁝ icon on the left-hand side of the block or the ⁝ icon on the far right of any block. The actions available will be dependent on the block type, but all basic blocks will have the following:

- **Delete**: This deletes the highlighted block.
- **Duplicate**: This duplicates the highlighted block, inserting the duplication below.
- **Turn into**: This allows for the block type to be changed. This is the action used for creating columns, as mentioned earlier.
- **Turn into page in**: This allows you to turn any block that is not currently a page into a page. That new page can be located in any page or database that is currently in the workspace.
- **Copy link**: This copies the link to the block on the page.

> **Note**
>
> This block link can be pasted on any text or symbol inside a text or heading property. This could be used as a way to jump up and down a page using text or emojis/symbols. Additionally, it could be used to jump between pages if the link of a page has been put into the text. Combining this with the **Table of contents** block can allow for quick page navigation.

- **Move to**: This moves either the block, page, or database to the desired location in the workspace.

- **Comment**: This allows for any comment to be added to any block of text. Mentions can be placed inside comments, sending a notification to that account. Files can be added to the comment for quick navigation. Each comment can be resolved, and the comments show up on the side of the page, as shown in *Figure 4.26* and *Figure 4.27*:

This is a text block with a comment on

Figure 4.26: A text block with a block comment and a text comment

The comment window will open up when clicking on the comment or commented text, as shown in *Figure 4.27*:

Figure 4.27: A text block with both a text comment and a block comment, with the Resolve button visible

Most actions inside Notion are quick to navigate to, but for those who prefer to use shortcuts, there are plenty of them that can speed up how you work.

Shortcuts

There are plenty of keyboard shortcuts within Notion, and they can be shared through the Notion app using the menu in the lower-right corner, as shown in *Figure 4.28*:

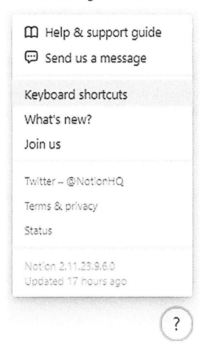

Figure 4.28: The location of the keyboard shortcut menu within the Notion app

Some shortcuts are used more than others. Let's examine them in the following sections:

Most popular

Some of the most popular shortcuts are as follows:

- Press *cmd/ctrl + n* to create a new page (this is for desktop apps only).
- Press *cmd/ctrl + shift + n* or use *cmd/ctrl + click* to open a new Notion window.
- Press *cmd/ctrl + p* to open search or jump to a recently viewed page.
- Press *cmd/ctrl + [* to go back a page.
- Press *cmd/ctrl +]* to go forward a page.
- Press *cmd/ctrl + shift + l* to switch to **Dark Mode** (note that's an "L," not a "1").

> **Note**
>
> You can add any inline emoji to a Notion page by typing in : followed by the name of the emoji, such as :*apple* for 🍎 or :*clapping* for 👏 .

Additionally, you can bring up your computer's emoji picker using the *ctrl + cmd + space* shortcut on a Mac and the Windows key + . or Windows key + ; shortcuts on Windows.

Markdown style

As Notion is based on markdown, you can use its shortcuts to speed up the creation of text and styles. Here is the list:

- Type ** on either side of your text to change to bold.
- Type * on either side of your text to italicize.
- Type ''' on either side of your text to create inline code. (That's the symbol on the left-hand side of your *1* key.)
- Type ~ on either side of your text to add a strikethrough.
- Type in *, -, or +* followed by the spacebar to create a bulleted list.
- Type in *[]* to create a to-do checkbox. (There's no space in between.)
- Type in *1.* followed by the spacebar to create a numbered list.
- Type in # followed by the spacebar to create an H1 heading.
- Type in ## followed by the spacebar to create an H2 sub-heading.
- Type in ### followed by the spacebar to create an H3 sub-heading.
- Type in > followed by the spacebar to create a toggle list.
- Type in " followed by the spacebar to create a quote block.

Creating and styling your content

Some shortcuts can help with styling and changing the contents of blocks. Here is a list:

- Press *enter* to insert a line of text.
- Press *shift + enter* to create a line break within a block of text.
- Press *cmd/ctrl + shift + m* to create a comment.
- Type --- to create a divider. (This is three dashes in a row.)
- With text selected, press *cmd/ctrl + b* to change to bold text.
- With text selected, press *cmd/ctrl + i* to italicize text.

- With text selected, press *cmd/ctrl + u* to underline text.

- With text selected, press *cmd/ctrl + shift + s* to add a strikethrough.

- With text selected, press *cmd/ctrl + k* to add a link. You can also copy and paste a URL over the selected text to turn it into a link using *cmd/ctrl + v*.

- With text selected, press *cmd/ctrl + e* for inline code.

- Press *tab* to indent and nest content.

> **Note**
> Whenever you indent, you're nesting that block inside the block above it. If you select the parent, everything under it will also be selected.

- Press *shift + tab* to un-nest content.

- Type */turn* at the beginning or end of a block to turn it into a different type of block.

- Type */color* at the beginning or end of any text block to change its color or highlight a color. (To remove color or highlight, just type in */default*.)

- Press *cmd/ctrl + option/shift + 0* to create text.

- Press *cmd/ctrl + option/shift + 1* to create an H1 heading.

- Press *cmd/ctrl + option/shift + 2* to create an H2 heading.

- Press *cmd/ctrl + option/shift + 3* to create an H3 heading.

- Press *cmd/ctrl + option/shift + 4* to create a to-do checkbox.

- Press *cmd/ctrl + option/shift + 5* to create a bulleted list.

- Press *cmd/ctrl + option/shift + 6* to create a numbered list.

- Press *cmd/ctrl + option/shift + 7* to create a toggle list.

- Press *cmd/ctrl + option/shift + 8* to create a code block.

- Press *cmd/ctrl + option/shift + 9* to create a new page or turn whatever you have on a line into a page.

- Press *cmd/ctrl + +* to zoom in.

- Press *cmd/ctrl + -* to zoom out.

- Press *cmd/ctrl + shift + u* to go up one level in the page hierarchy.

- Duplicate any content on a Notion page by holding down *option/alt* as you drag and drop.

Editing and moving blocks

Some shortcuts help with editing and moving blocks when creating pages. The following is a list:

- Press *Esc* to select the block you're currently in. Or you can use it to clear selected blocks.

- Press *cmd/ctrl + a* once to select the block your cursor is in.

- Press *space* to open a selected image in full screen. Or you can use it to exit full screen.

- Press *arrow keys* to select a different block.

- Hold down *shift + up/down arrow keys* to expand your selection up or down.

- Use *cmd + shift + click* on Mac and *alt + shift + click* on Windows/Linux to select or de-select an entire block.

- Use *shift + click* to select another block and all blocks in between.

- Press *backspace* or *delete* to delete selected blocks.

- Press *cmd/ctrl + d* to duplicate the blocks you've selected.

- Press *enter* to edit any text inside a selected block (or open a page inside a page). When highlighted pages inside a database.

- Press *cmd/ctrl + /* to edit or change one or more selected blocks.

- Hold down *cmd/ctrl + shift + arrow keys* to move a selected block around.

- Press *cmd/ctrl + option/alt + t* to expand or close all toggles in a toggle list.

- Press *cmd/ctrl + shift + h* to apply the last text or highlight the color you used.

- Press *cmd/ctrl + enter* to modify the current block you're in. Modify refers to the following:

  - Open a page.

  - Check or uncheck a to-do checkbox.

  - Open or close a toggle list item.

  - Make embeds or images fullscreen.

Now, let's understand how using the @ symbol in a block will give you some added options.

The @ commands

Here is a list of @ commands:

- **Mention a person**: Type in @ and another workspace member's name to get their attention on something. They'll be notified. This is useful in comments and discussions.

- **Mention a page**: Type in @ and the name of another page in your workspace to create a link to it. If you change the name of the page, this link will automatically change, too.

- **Mention a date**: Type in @ and a date in any format (such as "yesterday," "today," "tomorrow," or even "next Wednesday"). This helps to give yourself due dates.

- **Add a reminder**: Type in @*remind* followed by a date in any format (including "yesterday," "today," and "tomorrow,"). You can click on the link that appears to adjust the date and exact time you want to be reminded. You'll receive a notification at that time.

- Hit *Esc* to dismiss the @-*command* menu if you simply want to type in @.

In the next section, we will explain how using the *[[* symbols in a block can give you other options to choose from.

The [[commands

Here is a list of *[[* commands:

- **Link a page**: Type in *[[* and the name of another page in your workspace to create a link to it. If you change the name of the page, this link will automatically change, too.

- **Create a subpage**: Type in *[[* and the name of the subpage you want to nest within your current page. Use your cursor or *arrow keys* to **select + Add new sub-page** in the drop-down list that appears.

- **Create a new page somewhere else**: Type in *[[* and the name of the page you want to create. Use your cursor or *arrow keys* to select ↗ **Add new page in**... in the drop-down list that appears, then select the page or database where you'd like that page to be added.

Another option is to use the + symbol in a block for added options.

The + commands

Here is a list of + commands:

- **Create a subpage**: Type in + and the name of the subpage you want to nest within your current page. Use your cursor or arrow keys to **select + Add new sub-page in** the drop-down list that appears.

- **Create a new page somewhere else**: Type in + and the name of the page you want to create. Use your cursor or *arrow keys* to select ↗ **Add new page in** in the drop-down list that appears. Then, select the page or database where you'd like that page to be added.

- **Link a page**: Type in + and the name of another page in your workspace to create a link to it. If you change the name of the page, this link will automatically change, too. With the additional shortcut options completed, there are some databases that can be included in the pages alongside the blocks, which add an entirely new look and function to Notion.

- **Databases**: Databases are classed as blocks in Notion when they are placed on a page. This is the inline block of a database, however when a database block is made, a database page is also made.

The available inline database blocks are as follows:

- Table
- List
- Board
- Gallery
- Calendar
- Timeline

Each of these blocks has its options, features, and functions, which will be covered in *Chapter 5*, *All the Basic Database Properties*.

Summary

In this chapter, you learned about all the basic blocks in Notion, covering media blocks, embed blocks, the formatting of columns, block coloring, math blocks, and the various options you have when building out your pages. You learned that each block has actions that can be taken and shortcuts for actions are available on the keyboard to speed up working inside the application.

The types of databases were also covered briefly. In the next chapter, we will go into more detail about databases—specifically, database properties.

Section 2: Database Options, Features, and Functions

In this section, you will learn how to use databases to store, organize, and resurface information in various ways. This section contains the following chapters:

- *Chapter 5, All the Basic Database Properties*
- *Chapter 6, Database Views*
- *Chapter 7, Database Features and Functions*
- *Chapter 8, Basic Formula Functions*
- *Chapter 9, Advanced Formula Combinations*

5
All the Basic Database Properties

Databases inside Notion are where much of the power and flexibility is introduced. They are more than simply a place to store information, and they can be located, filtered, sorted, and changed to create personalized views. Combining various databases views allows flexible personalized dashboards and individualized workflows.

In this chapter, we're going to cover the following main topics:

- The fundamentals of database properties
- Basic database properties
- Viewing database properties

You will learn how to add a block to a page, move a block around a page, and change existing blocks to a different type. This also includes creating columns in pages and gaining an understanding of what pages allow for block placement.

Additionally, you will learn about all the different options of blocks you can put into a page, from basic blocks to special blocks with added functions, and the database and action block options that require additional knowledge in order to use effectively.

The fundamentals of database properties

In this section, you will create a database and all the basic properties, while also learning about the different types of properties. Learning the various property options allows for better filtering and sorting of information when more data is put into databases. Additionally, it will help you to understand the differences when you are looking to use advanced properties.

This can help with creating personalized views using the metadata on each page. **Page Metadata** refers to the information within the properties that relate to that specific page.

To create a database, you can either make an **inline view** or **create a database**. The full-page **DATABASE** option is shown in *Figure 5.1*:

Figure 5.1 – The drop-down list inside a page after typing /table
into an empty text block, showing the database section

Both will result in a database page being created that you can navigate to. The view type of the database will not affect any future viewing options, just the default properties that are created, as shown in *Figure 5.1*:

- The **Table** view will create a **Multi-select** property called **Tags**.

- The **List** view will create a **Multi-select** property called **Tags** and a **Created time** property called **Created**.

- The **Board** view will create a select property called **Status** and a **Person** property called **Assign**.

- The **Gallery** view will create a **Multi-select** property called **Tags** and **a Created time** property called **Created**.

- The **Calendar** view will create a **Multi-select** property called **Tags** and a **Date** property called **Date**.

- The **Timeline** view will create a **Date** property called **Date**, a **Person** property called **Assign**, and a **Select** property called **Status**.

> **Note**
>
> With the frequent updates made to the application, these defaults could change after the publish date of this book.

Additionally, you will see a **Name** property in every database view. This is not optional, unlike all the other properties. It cannot be removed or changed from a text-style property. This is used for reference when using the relation property, as explained in more detail in *Chapter 7, Database Features and Functions*.

Adding and removing properties

Adding and removing properties can be done in different ways depending on the view, but one method that works in every view is to access the page by clicking on **Open** or clicking on the page and then selecting **Add a property** at the bottom of the menu, as shown in *Figure 5.2*:

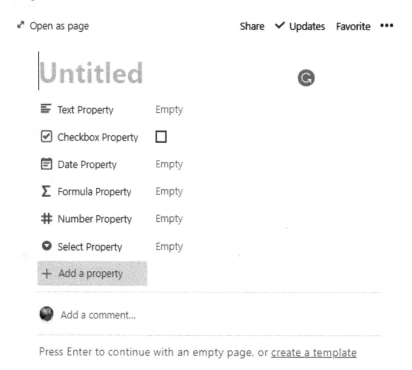

Figure 5.2 – The Open as page window showing the properties list at
the top of a page in a database with the Add a property button highlighted

Removing properties from any view can be done by clicking on the property to bring up the drop-down menu and selecting **Delete**.

Then, you can select the property type from the pop-up list window, as partially shown in *Figure 5.3*:

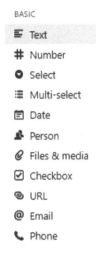

Figure 5.3 – The basic properties pop-up window list

When adding different property types to a database, there are three main styles of properties that you can pick from:

1. A string style includes text properties such as **Name**, **Text**, **Select**, **Multi-select**, **Person**, **URL**, **Email**, **Phone**, **Created by**, **Last edited by**, **Rollup**, and **Formula**.

2. A number style includes properties that only allow numbers, such as **Number**, **Rollup**, and **Formula**.

3. A date style is any property with date information such as **Date**, **Created time**, **Last edited time**, **Rollup**, and **Formula**.

> **Note**
> There is a fourth style, a **Boolean**, which is either true or false and found in either the **Checkbox** or **Formula** properties. This style is mainly used for filtering, sorting, and formulas and will be covered in future chapters.

You might have noticed that the **Rollup** and **Formula** properties are included in all three of the main styles that are unique to those properties. The basic properties only have one viewing style. To check what style the property is, you can use a **Formula** property and look at the icon next to the property, as shown in *Figure 5.4*:

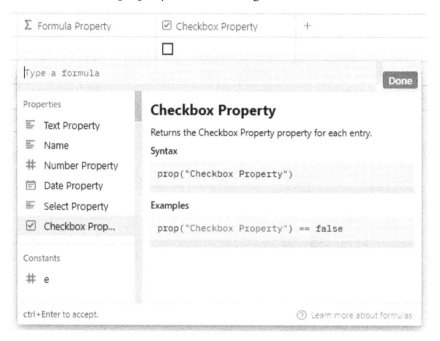

Figure 5.4 – The Formula input window showing each property
type icon next to the name of the property

- The icon that is next to **Text Property**, **Name**, and **Select Property** represents a text style.

- The icon that is next to **Number Property** represents a number style.

- The icon that is next to **Date Property** represents a date style.

- The icon that is next to **Checkbox Property** represents a Boolean style.

Now, each style of property allows for some changes in formatting. We will examine this in the next section.

Basic database properties

In this section, you will learn about all the basic properties that you can use inside a database. These properties include manual input properties that function in the same way as blocks on a page but are inserted into the metadata of the page in the database. They also include some automatic properties that, after inclusion, don't require any manual work.

Understanding all of these options will give you flexibility later on when you are looking to view the information in different database views. These properties can also be used to filter and sort information for personalized and contextual database views.

The Text property

The **Text** property is a simple text editor that allows you to enter any text style such as letters, numbers, symbols, and emojis. You can start a new line by using *Shift + Enter* while typing, giving you a different aesthetic in the property:

> **Note**
> When using the *Shift + Enter* aesthetic, the lines will make the table look longer unless you wrap the table view, as shown in *Figure 5.5*. When the size of the column is increased and decreased, the sentence length will be adjusted automatically if it is all on one line.

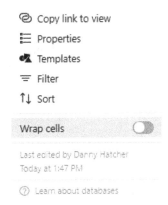

Figure 5.5 – The drop-down menu found from the ... menu in the upper-right corner of a database, showing the Wrap cells toggle

Despite the option to add numbers into a text property, there are benefits to using the number property. We will cover them next.

The Number property

The **Number** property only allows for number inputs. This property does allow for formatting options that automatically change how the number is viewed using numbers with commas, percentages, and a wide variety of currencies:

Figure 5.6 – The drop-down menu for every number property accessed
using the 123 buttons in the number property cell

Even though you can write date information in the text property, there are property types specific for dates that give added functionality.

The Date property

The **Date** property opens up a date picker window, as shown in *Figure 5.7*. You can type out a date, search through the arrows by month, and use shortcuts in the text field to find a date for selection:

- **T** is today.
- **Y** is yesterday.
- **M** is Monday of the current week.
- **Tu** is Tuesday of the current week.
- **W** is Wednesday of the current week.
- **Th** is Thursday of the current week.
- **F** is Friday of the current week.

- **Sa** is Saturday of the current week.

- **S** is Sunday of the current week.

- **L** is one week in the past from the present day.

- **N** is two weeks in the future from the present day:

> **Note**
> The shortcuts work both for lowercase letters and uppercase letters.

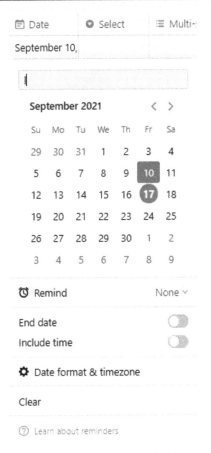

Figure 5.7 – The date picker window using the l (lowercase L) shortcut in the text search to go back one week, giving September 10 as the result

In addition to the picker and shortcuts, the date property allows for reminders to be added, which will give a push notification. The **End date** toggle can be added, giving a date range. The **Include time** toggle allows hours and minutes to be added. All of this will be shown in the date property. Alongside this, the **Date format & time zone** option allows the viewing of the date property to be changed depending on all the other settings.

In *Figure 5.8*, the **Date** property is showing a red reminder, as the start date was in the past (September 10), and the reminder was given **1 hour before 1 AM**. It also shows the end date (September 24) with a time of **2 PM**. The date property is in 12-hour format showing AM and PM, with the relative date setting giving an output of **Last Friday** instead of the date and **Next Friday** instead of the date, in the **BST** time zone:

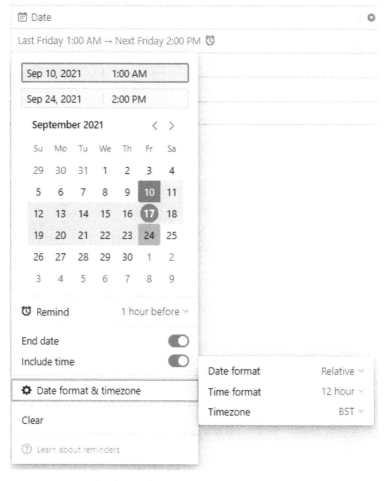

Figure 5.8 – The date picker showing the settings of a date selection
from September 10 to September 24, while the present day was September 17

The Select property

The **Select** property functions in the same way as the **Text** property with the input, but it makes each input a selection option in a drop-down list. Each option will be given a color background, which can be changed alongside the text after entering an option. You can only select one option to be shown. Additionally, the drop-down menu order can be changed by dragging the options using the :: icon found in the edit window, as shown in *Figure 5.9*:

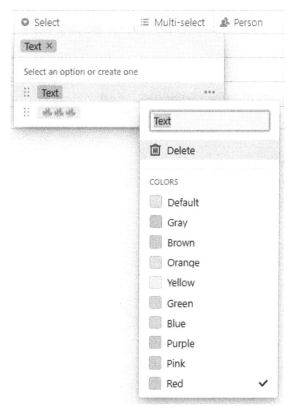

Figure 5.9 – The Select property window after selecting
the ... menu to edit the text and background color

Note
This property is often used to organize the **Board** view in databases.

The Multi-select property

The **Multi-select** property functions in the same way as the **Select** property, except you can have more than one selection shown. When you enter a new option into either of these properties, you will make a selection and then have to go back into the property to add another entry. A quick way to enter lots of options at once is to write them in a **Text** property using , to separate the options. Then, change the property into a select or multi-select property, as shown in *Figure 5.10*, *Figure 5.11*, and *Figure 5.12*:

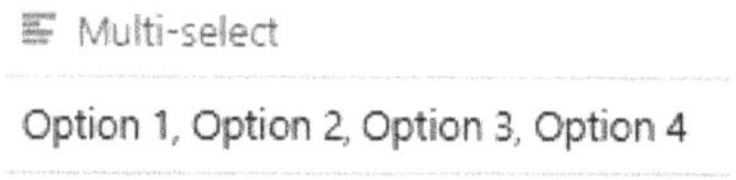

≡ Multi-select

Option 1, Option 2, Option 3, Option 4

Figure 5.10 – A text property with four options separated by ,

Figure 5.11 shows the menu that opens after clicking on the property name and by selecting the property type:

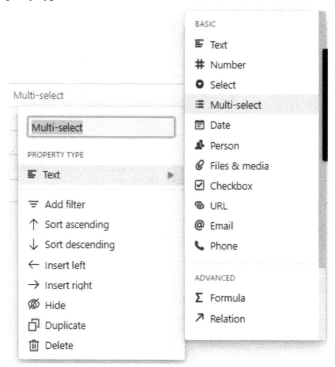

Figure 5.11 – Clicking the property title showing the property edit window, and then selecting the Property type to change the current property type from Text to Multi-select

Once you have selected the **Multi-select** option, it will change all of the words in the text property to the selections in the drop-down menu, as shown in *Figure 5.13*:

Figure 5.12 – The resulting Multi-select property with all four options as part of the drop-down selection

Other properties

Here is a list of a few other properties that can be added with unique features:

- The **Person** property allows you to select any account that has access to the page. It functions in the same way as the **Multi-select** property.

- The **Files & Media** property functions in the same way as the embed block, allowing an upload or an embed link to be used, showing the result in the property. This property can be useful for customizing the view of each page of the database when creating personalized or contextual views.

- The **Checkbox** property works in the same as the checkbox block and can be selected on or off. For changing multiple checkboxes at once, you can highlight the cells by clicking and dragging over them with the mouse and pushing *Enter* on your keyboard to toggle them all on or off, as shown in *Figure 5.13*

Figure 5.13 – The highlighted checkbox cells for toggling on or off using Enter

- The **URL** property is for adding URL links to a page that can be clicked on for quick navigation if the link is successfully active, as shown in *Figure 5.14*:

Figure 5.14 – Showing the URL property with a successful link with
a pencil to edit the website and an unsuccessful link with no edit pencil

- The **Email** property works in the same way as **URL** but instead, it directs you to your email service after clicking on an email account that has been entered.

- The **Phone** property functions in the same way as **URL** and **Email** but instead, it works for a phone number.

With all of these basic properties, there needs to be a manual input from a user or some interaction with a filtered view, which will be covered in *Chapter 7, Database Features and Functions*. However, some properties do automatically get added or changed just by being active inside the page.

Automatic properties

In this section, you will learn about the properties that, once created, automatically fill with information. These properties can be useful for filtering and sorting, but often, they are more useful in a team or collaborative setting to check who made the action and when it was taken.

Figure 5.15 shows all four of the automatic properties:

⏱ Created time	👤 Created by	👤 Last edited by	⏱ Last edited time
August 19, 2021 3:51 PM	🌐 Danny Hatcher	🌐 Danny Hatcher	September 18, 2021 8:35 AM
August 19, 2021 3:51 PM	🌐 Danny Hatcher	🌐 Danny Hatcher	September 17, 2021 2:47 PM
August 19, 2021 3:51 PM	🌐 Danny Hatcher	🌐 Danny Hatcher	September 17, 2021 2:36 PM

Figure 5.15 – The four automatic database properties

Each column in *Figure 5.15* is a different page with unique metadata:

- The **Created time** property automatically shows the date the page was created.

- The **Created by** property automatically shows the account that created the page.

- The **Last edited by** property automatically shows the account that last edited the page.

- The **Last edited time** property automatically shows the time the page was last edited.

> **Note**
>
> Each of these properties has information that is saved as soon as a page is created. This means if you have not got the property in the database, add the pages, and then create the property, the data will still be inputted and correct.

Understanding what each property can do is just part of the power of databases. When combining these functions with other features, the database can become the most powerful aspect of your workspace. So, understanding how to view the information inside properties is important to get to the important information.

Viewing database properties

In this section, you will learn how to view the various database properties and alter their appearance on each page. Understanding where and how to view properties will become useful when working out the workflow of everyone in the workspace.

Some people prefer an overview of information so that they can view lots of information at once, whereas other people prefer specific information being shown. Another use case when considering workflows is that properties also appear on each page as metadata, which also impacts workflow.

> **Note**
>
> The screenshots that are in this section are from the table view, but all of the functions mentioned are available across the database view options, which will be covered in *Chapter 6, Database Views*.

Figure 5.3 shows all the basic property types with a symbol next to each type. That symbol will remain the same in all the views of the database that show the symbol. The symbol and type of property will also remain the same unless they are manually changed by an individual who has editing privileges to the database.

Each property can have a unique name with text, numbers, symbols, and emoji icons for easy identification or explanation of what is included in that property. You cannot have two properties with the same name. There must be either a case-sensitive difference or an additional letter, number, or symbol to make each property unique, as shown in *Figure 5.16*:

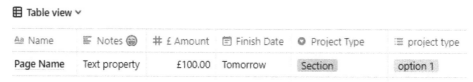

Figure 5.16 – An example page with different property names

Each property has the option to be hidden or made visible by using the properties menu, which can be accessed by the **…** menu in the upper-right corner of the database view, as shown in *Figure 5.20*:

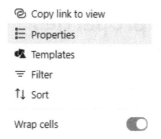

Figure 5.17 – Using the … menu in the upper-right corner of the
table database view to access property vision

Alternatively, you can click on the property and select **Hide** from the drop-down menu, as shown in *Figure 5.18*:

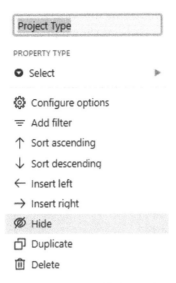

Figure 5.18 – The action drop-down menu highlighting the option to hide the property

As each entry into a database is a page, the properties are treated as metadata for each page. This means that when accessing a page inside a database, you will be presented with each property at the top of the page, as shown in *Figure 5.19*:

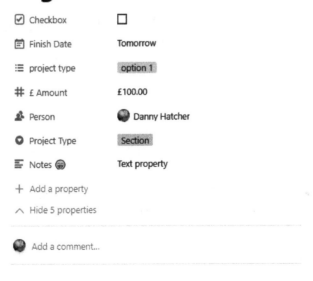

Figure 5.19 – A page in a database showing all of the property information

There is the option to hide properties inside this view as well. This can be done by selecting the property and selecting **Hide**, as shown in *Figure 5.17*, or by going to the **...** menu in the upper-right corner of the page and selecting **Customize page**, as shown in *Figure 5.20*.

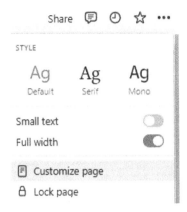

Figure 5.20 – Showing the page drop-down option with the Customize page button

As mentioned in *Chapter 2, Workspace Navigation, Sharing, and Appearance*, the properties on a page in a database have multiple viewing options that will affect its appearance. However, when these properties are hidden, the order in which they appear cannot be changed.

Properties in each database view will be viewed differently depending on the database settings, which will be covered in the next chapter.

Summary

In this chapter, we examined all the property options that you can include in a database and how they can store and show information specific to a page entry. This is useful for filtering, sorting, and surfacing specific information when viewing information in database views.

Additionally, you learned how metadata can be manually or automatically included on a page and how to change the name and viewing option of each property.

In the next chapter, we will cover more specific details about each database view and how the property type can impact the information you can see.

6
Database Views

Databases inside Notion can be as simple or as complex as you want to give you the option to view, filter, sort, and manage information in various ways. A database in Notion does have different views—that doesn't affect the information in the database but does affect how you can see it.

In this chapter, we're going to cover the database views, as follows:

- The fundamental database views
- The **Board** database view
- The **Gallery** database view
- The **Calendar** database view
- The **Timeline** database view

You will learn how to use each view with their differences, and how to utilize each view for maximum benefit. Some of the views require specific properties to function, which will be covered alongside how you can interact with each property in each view.

Some views are more powerful when viewing things that are time-sensitive, such as the **Calendar** and **Timeline** views. Some views are more useful for dashboards, for viewing specific information, such as the **List** and **Gallery** views. Other views are more powerful when wanting lots of information at once in a specific pattern, such as the **Board** or **Table** views.

You will also learn how to change the look of the database by hiding and showing properties, rearranging properties, and interacting in the database views.

The fundamental database views

In this section, you will learn about the **Table** database view functions with calculations and the main views that you will see alongside the **List** views. This is important as the **Table** view is often the best view for maintenance of data, and it helps you see the most information on your screen at once, whereas the **List** view is great for seeing important information without overload.

> **Note**
>
> Every database view can be full-page or inline, both with unique differences, but all the information stored in the database is added and removed in each instance. This means that if you add something to an inline-linked view of a database, it will be added to every instance of that database.

You can create a **Table** database view by typing `/table` into a textbox and selecting **Table - Inline** for an inline view and **Table - Full page** for a full-page view. This will create a first instance of the database. The following screenshot shows the drop-down menu, which will also have all other blocks and database views available if you scroll up and down the menu:

Page

/table

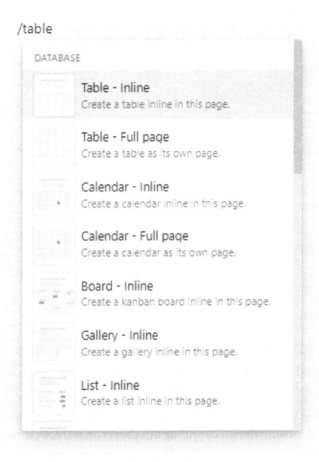

Figure 6.1: The database view drop-down menu after searching for a table

Another way to create a database is to create a new page and select the desired view in the displayed menu, as shown in the following screenshot:

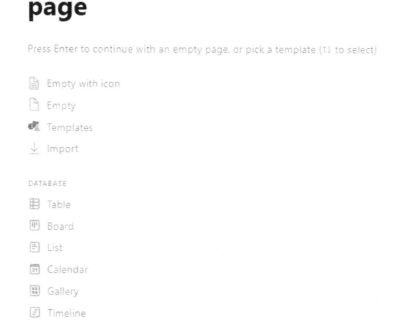

Figure 6.2: The New page menu showing the different database view options

Once you have selected the **Table** view, you will be given a database page with two default properties, as mentioned in *Chapter 5, All the Basic Database Properties*.

Each column size in a **Table** view can be adjusted in width by clicking and dragging the property title and moving the mouse in the direction you want, as shown in the following screenshot:

Figure 6.3: The blue selected line can be clicked to move left or right to adjust the column width

Each page row can also be condensed by using the **Wrap cells** option, keeping all the information on one line found in the top-right ellipsis (...) menu, as shown in the following screenshot:

Figure 6.4: The drop-down menu showing the Wrap cells toggle option

The main feature of a table database is the calculations that each property column allows. These are discussed in more detail here:

- The calculations available are dependent on the property types and number properties having **mathematical calculations**, as shown in the following screenshot:

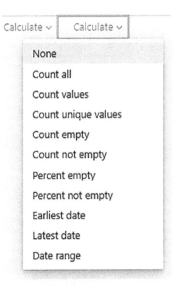

Figure 6.5: Date property calculation options

- The **date properties** having date ranges are shown in the following screenshot:

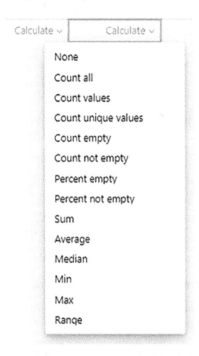

Figure 6.6: Date property with different date ranges

- The **string properties** with all the default options are shown in the following screenshot:

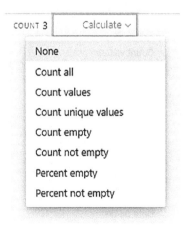

Figure 6.7: String property calculation options

- The **Boolean property** types, allowing for `true` or `false` calculations, are shown in the following screenshot:

Figure 6.8: Boolean property calculation options

- Every database view can be locked, meaning editing is disabled. Locking can be activated in the top-right **...** menu of the full-page version of a database, as shown in the following screenshot:

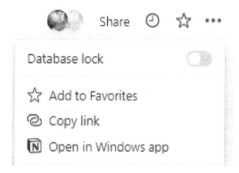

Figure 6.9: The Database lock toggle from the top-right ... menu

- The number of page rows shown can be changed in an inline database view through the **...** menu option, as shown in the following screenshot:

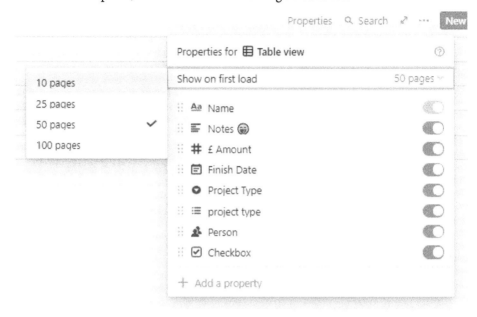

Figure 6.10: The changing number of properties shown in the drop-down menu

> **Note**
> The **Table** database view is the view that is used by default when importing information into Notion. You can also merge a **comma-separated values (CSV)** file with any database in Notion, but the **Table** view is best for checking all the imported information.

The **Table** database view is mostly for viewing lots of information at once and for simple property column calculations. The **List** view is much more minimal in terms of information but can be better suited to a dashboard.

To create a different database view, you go through any of the same methods, but instead of selecting **Table**, select another option such as **List**.

The **List** database view functions the same way but doesn't have property column calculations, the ability to highlight cells for editing, or the option to edit without entering the page. Its main use is for aesthetic change, as shown in the following screenshot:

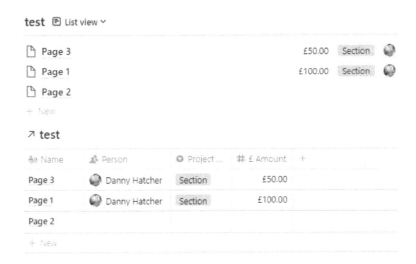

Figure 6.11: The List view of the test database with the Table view of the test database underneath

You may also notice in *Figure 6.11* that the top image has **List view** shown, and there is an arrow next to **test**, which is the name of the **Table** view database. An arrow identifies a linked database view. The database remains the same but has been shown in a mirrored location, which will be covered in the next section, alongside how to navigate the different views of a database.

Linked database views

In this section, you will learn how to create **linked database** views. A linked database view is one of the most powerful and useful features when utilizing a database inside of Notion. It allows you to take information from a database, sort, filter, and organize the information just how you want it, and display it where and how you want.

Before you can make a linked database view, you need an original database. The database can be inline or full-page, as each inline database will have a full-page version anyway. Once you have decided which database you would like to create a linked view of, you can do any of the following:

1. Use the **/Create linked database** option in a text block and search for the name of the database you want to link to.

2. Go to the full-page version of the database, go to the top-right corner **...** menu, and copy the link to paste into the desired location.

3. Click on the **::** option next to the inline database, and then in the drop-down menu, select **Copy link**.

> **Note**
>
> When you have a linked database view, you can click and hold the :: option from the inline database view and hold down the *Alt* key on your keyboard as well. While holding down on the key, you can drag your mouse to the desired location and then release the mouse, creating another linked database view, essentially duplicating the view.

Clicking on the name of the database will take you to the full-page version of the database. To clarify, when you make a database, it will have a full-page view but can also have multiple view types, multiple views, and multiple linked database views, as shown in the following screenshot:

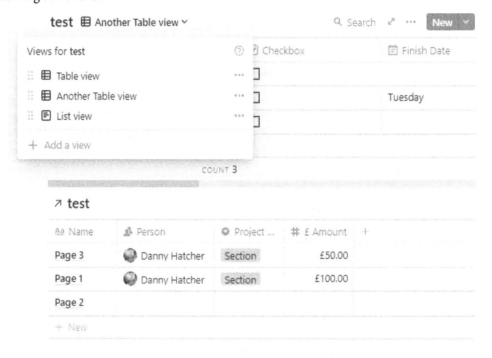

Figure 6.12: Two inline database views of the test database with the View tab open for changes

In *Figure 6.12*, there is an inline view of the **test** database at the top of the screen showing **Another Table view**, seen next to the name of the database. Underneath that, there is a drop-down menu of three different views available for that inline database, showing **Table view**, **Another Table view**, and **List view**. The **List view** option has a different icon next to the name as it is a different view type. This means there are three available views, but two available view types currently made.

Underneath the **test** database inline view, there is a linked database view of the **test** database. This view doesn't have any view option next to the name, meaning there is only one view available that is active, showing a **Table** view. When moving the mouse close to the name of the database, an option appears to create a view, as shown in the following screenshot:

Figure 6.13: The test linked database view showing the Add a view option

The views in a linked database view are not copied and cannot be seen in any other instance of the database, making the view unique to that inline database instance. The views created in the original database, which won't have an arrow next to the name, will also be seen in the full-page version, which can be accessed via the double-sided arrow seen at the top right of an inline database, as shown in *Figure 6.13*.

> **Note**
>
> It is a good practice to have the original database stored in a place that won't be forgotten, lost, or accidentally deleted as if the database is deleted, all linked versions will also be deleted. If a linked database is deleted, nothing in the main database is affected.

Now that you understand how you can create multiple views, multiple linked database views, and multiple view types, let's cover how the other view types can alter how information is viewed.

The Board database view

In this section, you will create a **Board** database view and learn which functions and features you can use that are unique to this type of view. A **Board** view is often used for task and project management, as it mimics the properties of a Kanban board, which is used in knowledge work or for manufacturing processes.

To reiterate this point, the database view still uses the same information as all the other database views if it is created from the same database. The following screenshot shows the same database as seen previously in this chapter, but shows a **Board view** option and **Board view** in the linked database:

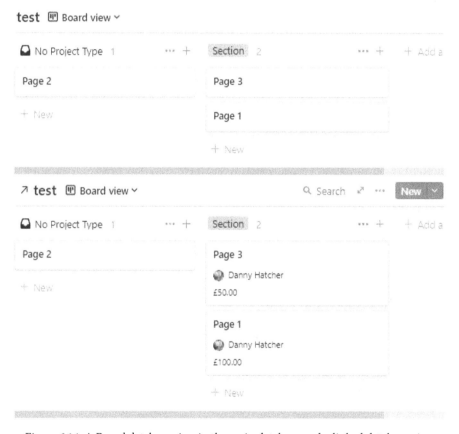

Figure 6.14: A Board database view in the main database and a linked database view

> **Note**
> There will always be a section in the **Board** view that is for no status. In the example shown in *Figure 6.14*, **No Project Type** shows the pages without any status.

Columns are created by property information that is in the database, from either a **Select** property, a **Multi-select** property, or a **Person** property that can be changed using the **Group by** setting shown in the following screenshot:

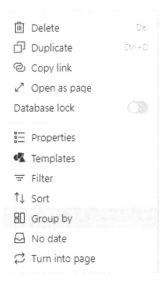

Figure 6.15: The Group by setting located in the top-right … menu at the top of the database view

As seen in *Figure 6.13*, the selected property in the **Table** view has been turned into a column in the **Board** view shown in *Figure 6.14*.

As with the **Table** view, the **Board** view can show and hide properties, but as the **Board** view shows cards of each page, the properties are shown on the cards. In *Figure 6.14*, the top **Board view** instance has all properties hidden, but the linked database view has the **Person** and **Amount** properties showing.

Adding a group

Adding a new group to the view adds a selection option to the property that the view is being grouped by. In the following screenshot example, a group is being added by clicking **Add a group**, which will then create this group in the linked database as well:

Figure 6.16: Adding a group to a Board database view

Note

You can change the grouping of the database view by going into the ... menu at the top right of the database and selecting a group by which to show the grouping options.

After adding a new group, it will be shown in every other instance of that database, as the group has been added to the property. In the following screenshot, **New Section** was added to the **Project type Select** property:

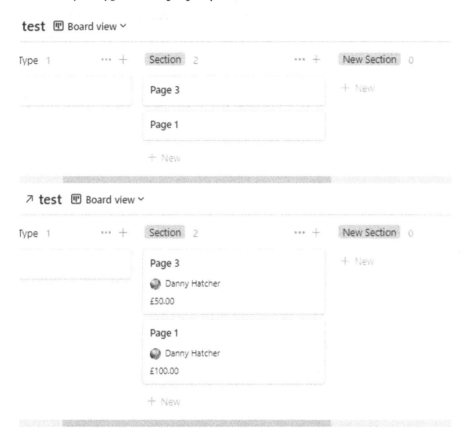

Figure 6.17: The result of adding a group to the database view

> **Note**
>
> The pages in this database view are in card format, so instead of using the ⠿ icon to move the pages, you can click and drag on any part of the card. This means you can click and drag pages across sections, which will change the property information in all the other database views.

Card preview and Card size

The **Card** view adds some customization options in the database view, such as changing the **Card size** setting with **Small**, **Medium**, and **Large** options. You can also change the **Card preview** setting, showing **None**, **Page cover**, or **Page content**. These options can be found in the **...** menu properties section at the top right of the database, as shown in the following screenshot:

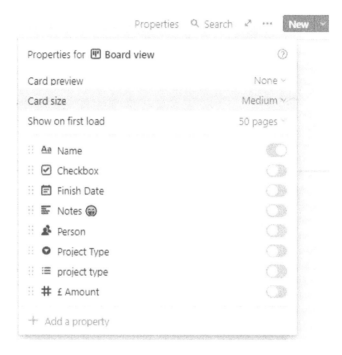

Figure 6.18: The Card preview and Card size options appearing in the property's drop-down menu

As the pages are seen in a **Card** view, the click-through options available in the **Table** view are unavailable, but if you show the properties, all interactions remain the same.

Checkbox property

Here, we are showing the **Checkbox** property, as a card allows itself to be checked or unchecked from the **Card** view.

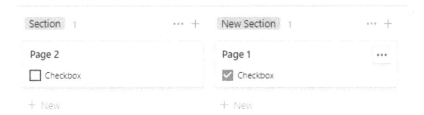

Figure 6.19: A Board database view showing a Checkbox property being checked from the view

Most uses for the **Board** view are for status checking, using a **Select** property to identify what stage a particular page is at, which will be covered further in *Chapter 12, Note Taking, Knowledge Management, and Wiki Example*. The **Gallery** database view also uses cards as page views, but has more flexibility with the organization.

The Gallery database view

In this section, you will learn about the **Gallery** database view, which has lots of similarities with the **Board** database view but does not use groupings in the view. This database view can be useful for a more visual aesthetic and can be used as a horizontal or vertical button display, allowing for better customization of showing information.

The **Gallery** view works with each page as a card, which is viewed in a grid display, as shown in the following screenshot:

Figure 6.20: Two Gallery database views

> **Note**
>
> Every **Gallery** view will have an empty card with + **New** in it, giving the option for a new page to be created. There is no way to remove this from the view.

As seen in *Figure 6.20*, the **Gallery** view gives you the option to show things on cards. This feature is also available in the previously mentioned **Board** view by going to the **Preview** option and selecting **Cover** or **Content**. As the page preview option for *Figure 6.20* is set to **Cover**, an additional option has appeared, giving you the option to make the image fit or not in the card, as shown in the following screenshot:

Figure 6.21: A Gallery database view drop-down menu option showing
the Fit image toggle using a files property for the card preview

> **Note**
>
> If there is a file property in the database with an image, that property will also appear as a selection option in the preview drop-down menu seen in *Figure 6.21*.

As seen in *Figure 6.20*, the **Gallery** database view will adjust the aesthetic according to the size of the column, making it more vertical the narrower the column. If the column is therefore wide, the view becomes horizontal.

All other database viewing features are available, such as hiding and showing properties, interacting with properties when shown, and dragging and dropping pages to different locations in the view. Further use cases of this view will be covered in *Chapter 12, Note Taking, Knowledge Management, and Wiki Example*, but most uses are alongside other linked database views such as the **Calendar** view, which will be covered next.

The Calendar database view

In this section, we will go over the **Calendar** database view and how it can help for planning, viewing, and adding information in the date property. This database view does have some limitations when moving across devices, but it can be very powerful when using the **Auto-add** feature.

The first thing to be aware of when using the **Calendar** view is the full-page view, which can be accessed by clicking the arrow shown in the following screenshot:

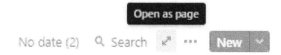

Figure 6.22: The expand arrow button to access a full-page database view from an inline database view

When you scroll down the page, it will keep moving forward into future dates, whereas if you want to visit previous dates, you need to push the backdate arrow button located next to the **Today** button, which jumps you to the current date, as shown in the following screenshot:

Figure 6.23: The backdate arrow is highlighted next to the Today button

As with the previous database views, each page is a card seen on the calendar. You can move the card by clicking, holding, dragging, and dropping the page onto a different date. This will change the corresponding date property value. A red dot on the calendar signifies the current date.

In addition to this, each property can be hidden or shown on the card just as with the other database views, allowing for interaction with the properties that have those functions, such as the **Checkbox** and **URL** properties. The following screenshot shows **Page 1**, showing the date property being moved from **September 29** to **September 30**, which is the current date, which will then change the date property once it is dropped:

Figure 6.24: A page being moved in a Calendar database view

The result of moving that page has changed the view of the calendar and also changed the information in the date property, as shown in the following screenshot:

Figure 6.25: The result of moving the page in the Calendar database view

In the example shown in *Figure 6.25*, the date property that is being shown on the page is the same date property that is being used when looking at the **Calendar by** settings accessed through the **...** menu, as shown in the following screenshot:

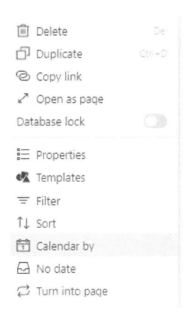

Figure 6.26: The Calendar by settings in the ... menu

You can have multiple date properties inside a database, but only one can be used in the **Calendar** view, meaning you could have a different date property being shown on a page, while it is on a different date in the **Calendar** view.

Calendar by setting

Something else that is useful in the **Calendar** view is that it accommodates all of the functions that the date property allows. The following screenshot shows a page having a start and end date, with the page spanning the time, showing the start and end times on the appropriate days. The date property being used for the **Calendar by** setting is also being shown on the page, alongside a second date property that has a relative date setting and a reminder set:

Figure 6.27: The Calendar database view with two date properties being shown over 8 days

As the **Calendar by** setting only uses date properties, it means every page that is shown in the **Calendar** database view needs to have a date value. If a page doesn't have a date value, it is moved to the **No date** section, similar to the **No status** section from the **Board** view.

> **Note**
>
> A formula property or rollup property that is formatted for a date output can also be used in the **Calendar by** settings. If you try to move the pages in the **Calendar** database view, it will move the page out of the database, as a formula and rollup date value are automatically generated, not manually inputted.

No date calendar setting

The **No date** section can be found at the top of the database, as shown in the following screenshot, and when a page is selected from that menu, it will be given the current date value and will appear in the database view:

Figure 6.28: The No date calendar setting location

The reason this view is powerful is that when you have deadlines, reminders, or information needed when planning, you can see all the information in one view. Using the **No date** view can also create a list of things you need to plan out, as seen in the following screenshot:

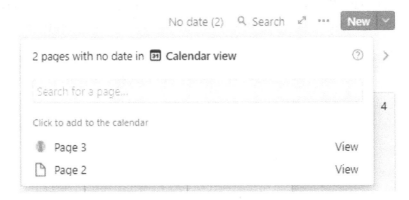

Figure 6.29: The No date expanded view giving the option to add each page to the Calendar view

The biggest limitations to the **Calendar** view come when looking at the view on different devices such as mobile and tablet, as instead of seeing the page names, you only see dots. The other limitation is that there is either the month view or full-page view, with no **Hours**, **Day**, **Week**, **Bi-week**, **Quarter**, or **Year** view, unlike the **Timeline** view, which will be covered in the next section.

The Timeline database view

In this section, we will go through the **Timeline** database view. As mentioned previously, this view has limited uses depending on the plan of the workspace, which was covered in *Chapter 3, Templates, Imports, Account Settings, and Workspace Settings*.

This view has much more flexibility when looking at the information when considering time, as it has an **Hours**, **Day**, **Week**, **Bi-week**, **Month**, **Quarter**, and **Year** view, allowing for various levels of overview, as shown in the following screenshot. This view mimics much of the Gantt chart style view you may have seen or experienced in other applications.

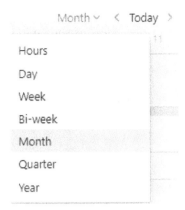

Figure 6.30: Different types of views available in the Timeline view

The view works in a similar way to the **Calendar** view in that instead of having one option in the **Calendar by** setting, there are two date properties allowed in the **Timeline by** settings, meaning you can use a **Start date** property and **End date** property. This allows for options such as an automated formula for a start or endpoint, as shown in the following screenshot:

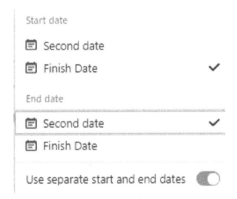

Figure 6.31: The Timeline by option menu accessed through the Properties tab in the … menu

In addition to the **Timeline** view, there is an option to show a **Table** view alongside the Gantt chart view when inside the full-page view, as shown in the following screenshot:

Figure 6.32: A full-page Timeline database view with a Table view and Gantt chart view available

All the previously mentioned features are available, such as dragging and dropping pages, interacting properties, hiding properties, database locking, **No date** options, and linked database views.

As with the **Calendar** view, you can click on the side of a page and drag the card in the direction you want the date property to change. This makes date changes quick in both the **Calendar** and **Timeline** view, as seen in the following screenshot:

Figure 6.33: The edge of the page being dragged to move the date of the property

> **Note**
>
> If the information that is being shown on a page in the **Timeline** view is longer than the page due to the **Timespan** view, then the properties will overflow outside of the page. This only affects the aesthetic, but could affect the number of properties you show, or the timespan you select.

And with the **Timeline** view covered, that is all the individual database view types you can use inside of Notion. To reiterate, a database can have all these views multiple times across multiple linked database views, all using and syncing the same data and information.

Summary

In this chapter, we learned that each database can be viewed inline, with other blocks, or in a full-page view. A database can have multiple views with six types: a **Table** view, **List** view, **Board** view, **Gallery** view, **Calendar** view, and **Timeline** view. Each database can have linked views that can be placed anywhere in the workspace using the same data and information from the original database, also allowing multiple views unique to that linked database.

Each database view has unique viewing options, often utilizing specific property types, but some property types have multiple uses, such as the relation and rollup properties affecting the filtering and sorting features of databases differently, which will be covered in the next chapter.

7
Database Features and Functions

Thankfully, the advanced properties of the Notion database help increase the features and flexibility drastically. The **relation property** combines different databases and transfers data, and the **rollup property** acts as a lookup of information from other databases.

In addition to this, the **filtering** and **sorting** options on each database view can add another level of flexibility in viewing the database brought together by the various properties.

In this chapter, we're going to cover the following:

- How to use the relation property
- How to use the rollup property
- The database sorting option
- The database filtering option
- Database grouping

You will learn how to use each of these advanced database features to your advantage, bringing together all the data from your workspace to create whatever view suits you and/or your team.

How to use the relation property

In this section, you will learn how to create, alter, and use the relation property in any database. This property is the only way to access other database information from the **Property** menu and is also required if you want to use the rollup property, which is used for calculations. This property can be a great way to show information in multiple database views, also allowing quick page navigation.

> **Note**
>
> In this section, the images will be in the table database view, but the property is applicable across the view types and linked views.

Let us see how we can use the relation property:

1. Once you have created a database, you can add a relation property, but before Notion creates the property, it will take you to an additional window that asks you to select a database, as shown in *Figure 7.1*:

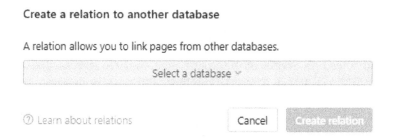

Figure 7.1 – Relation property window to select a database

2. When you click on the **Select a database** dropdown, a selection of all the databases that are in the workspace will appear, allowing for a search by name to help you find the database you are looking for, which is shown in *Figure 7.2*:

Create a relation to another database

A relation allows you to link pages from other databases.

Select a database ˅

projects

📄 Projects
   Page

Figure 7.2 – Searching for a database called Projects in the relation property drop-down window

3. Once you have selected the database you want to make the relation to, it will create the property in the database in which you made the property and create a relation property in the database you selected.

> **Note**
> The property that is made in the database that was selected will show **Related to (name of the database you made the property in)** and then, in brackets, the name of the property you created.

In *Figure 7.3*, there are two databases. **Person database** has a relation property that is called **Project Relation** and that relation property is related to the **Projects** database and creates another relation property called **Related to Person database (Project Relation)**:

Person database

A̶ Name	☰ Projects			☰ Notes	↗ Project Relation	+
Danny	Project 1	Project 2	Project 3	Some notes		
Jon	Project 1	Project 2				
Esme	Project 3					
Kim						
+ New						
	Calculate ˅					

Projects

A̶ Name	👤 Person		☷ Date	☰ Project Description	↗ Related to Person database (Project Relation)	+
Project 1	Danny Hatcher	Jonathan Stewart		A podcast Project		
Project 2	Danny Hatcher	Jonathan Stewart		A book project		
Project 3	Danny Hatcher			An education project		
+ New						
Calculate ˅						

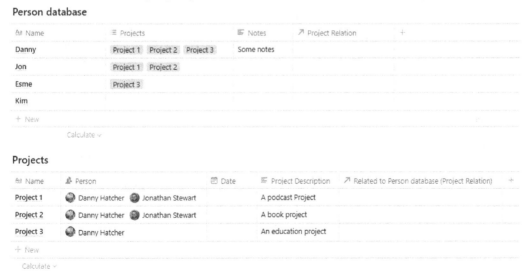

Figure 7.3 – Two databases with a relation property connecting them

In **Person database**, there are four pages representing information about people. There can be multiple properties and information on each page about that person, but in *Figure 7.3*, you can see the **Projects** multi-select property next to a **Notes** text property.

The **Projects** property is useful for viewing purposes but does not allow you to click on it for any other information as it just shows text information. The new **Project Relation** property is related to the **Projects** database, which means that when a relationship is created, you can see the information in that database.

When you click the **Project Relation** property on the **Danny** page (as per *Figure 7.3*), a search menu opens showing a list of all the pages in the related database, which in this case is the **Projects** database, as shown in *Figure 7.4*:

Person database

Aa Name	↗ Project Relation	☰ Projects
Danny	Search for a page, or create a new one...	
Jon	Aa Name	
Esme	Project 2	
Kim	Project 3	
+ New	⊕ Project 1	
Calculate		

Figure 7.4 – The search dropdown in the relation property

By clicking on a page, you will add that page to the property, and if the page is already added, you can remove it by clicking the page again, shown by the + and **x** signs next to the page.

Note

When you add a page to a relation property, the reciprocal property, the relation property linked with the one you edited, will automatically add the page relation.

In *Figure 7.5*, I have added relations in **Person database** to all appropriate projects, which are also shown in the other related property in the **Projects** database:

Person database

Aa Name	↗ Project Relation	≡ Projects	≣ Notes	+
Danny	🗋 Project 1 🗋 Project 2 🗋 Project 3	Project 1 Project 2 Project 3	Some notes	
Jon	🗋 Project 1 🗋 Project 2	Project 1 Project 2		
Esme	🗋 Project 3	Project 3		
Kim				
+ New				

Calculate ⌄

Projects + Add a view

Aa Name	↗ Related to Person database (Project Relation)	♟ Person	🗓 Date	≣ Project Description	+
Project 1	🗋 Danny 🗋 Jon	🔵 Danny Hatcher 🔵 Jonathan Stewart		A podcast Project	
Project 2	🗋 Danny 🗋 Jon	🔵 Danny Hatcher 🔵 Jonathan Stewart		A book project	
Project 3	🗋 Danny 🗋 Esme	🔵 Danny Hatcher		An education project	
+ New					

Calculate ⌄

Figure 7.5 – Two databases with relation properties now filled with information

You can see in *Figure 7.5* that the relation property is mimicking the **Person** property in the **Projects** database, but **Esme** is not a person with an account in the workspace, so she cannot be added to the **Person** property. However, it can be created as a page in a database, meaning there are no restrictions on personal information and linking information.

This relation property can be clicked on in the page view to navigate through. *Figure 7.6* shows the properties in the **Danny** page and highlights the **Project 1** page relation, which when clicked will take the user to the **Project 1** page. If the red-colored cross (**x**) is clicked, the relation will be removed rather than navigating the user to the page.

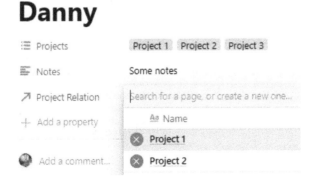

Figure 7.6 – In-page navigation through the relation property dropdown

In addition to creating relations between databases, you can also relate a database to itself. The process of creating the relation doesn't change much apart from the fact that once you have made the relationship, a second window will pop up, as shown in *Figure 7.7*. The figure shows an option to create a new property that adds two relation properties to the database, mimicking the functions previously explained, or use the same property, creating just one relation property:

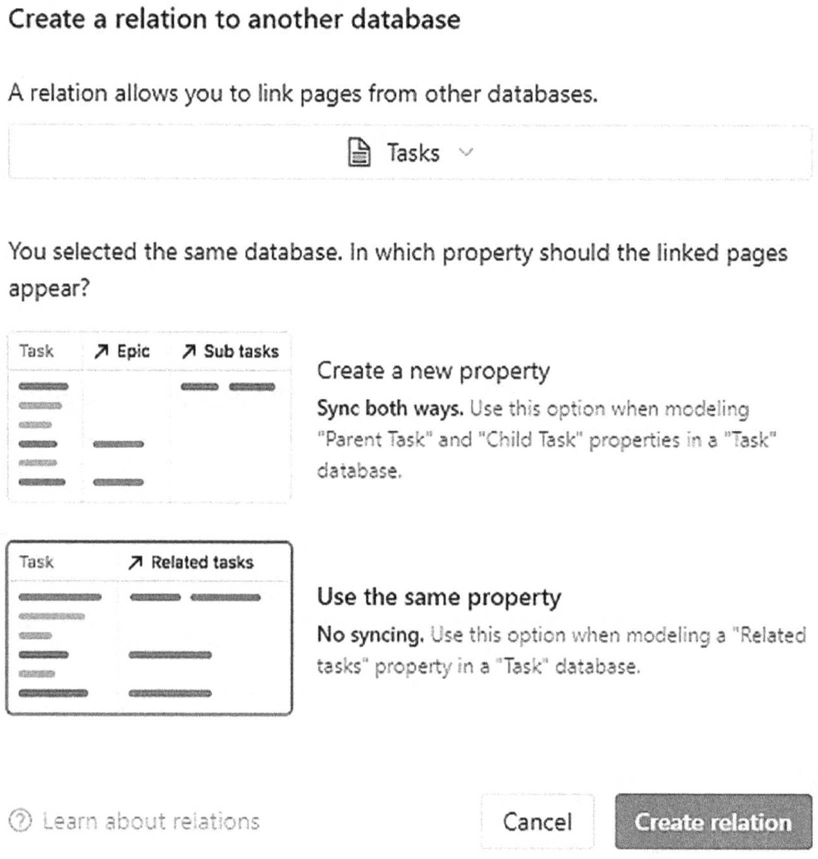

Create a relation to another database

A relation allows you to link pages from other databases.

> 📄 Tasks ∨

You selected the same database. In which property should the linked pages appear?

Create a new property

Sync both ways. Use this option when modeling "Parent Task" and "Child Task" properties in a "Task" database.

Use the same property

No syncing. Use this option when modeling a "Related tasks" property in a "Task" database.

⑦ Learn about relations   Cancel   **Create relation**

Figure 7.7 – The relation property is related to the same database

When we relate a database to itself, it is often to view information and links in different ways, which will be covered more in *Chapter 13, Other Example Use Cases*. However, the most used case for the relation property is to allow a rollup property to be used, which we will cover next.

How to use the rollup property

This section covers the rollup database property and how you can use it to get calculations from another database and use that value in various views, as well as shows us how rollups can be used to change the information you see.

The reason this property is so powerful is that it saves navigation time, helps create clear overviews, and calculates the value and numbers you are looking for.

> **Note**
> As mentioned previously, you cannot use a rollup property without a relation property in the database.

Using the same database as the previous chapter, we are going to add a rollup property showing information across databases. *Figure 7.8* shows selecting the relation property in the rollup configuration window. This drop-down menu will only show relation properties that are in the same database you are creating the rollup in:

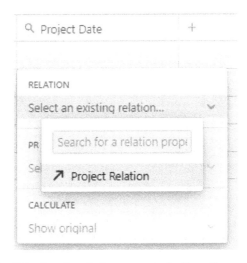

Figure 7.8 – Selecting the relation property for the rollup configuration

Once the relationship has been selected, you need to select the property of the database you want to look at; in this case, the **project relation property** is related to the **Projects** database, meaning a list of the properties available in that database will show but not necessarily in the same order, as seen in *Figure 7.9*:

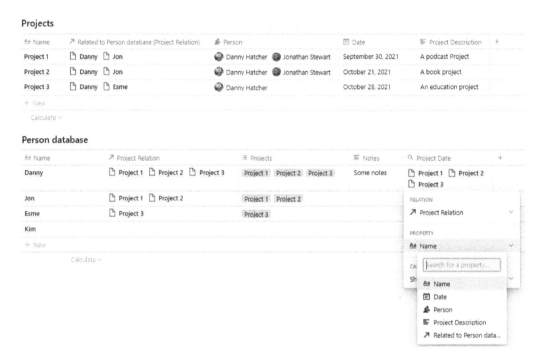

Figure 7.9 – Rollup configuration window in Person database showing
the properties in the Projects database through the relation

If you were to leave the rollup configuration there, it would look through **Project Relation** for the selected property and show that information. In the example in *Figure 7.10*, the **Date** property has been selected. For each page in the **Project Relation** property, the rollup is finding the related date and showing it in the rollup output:

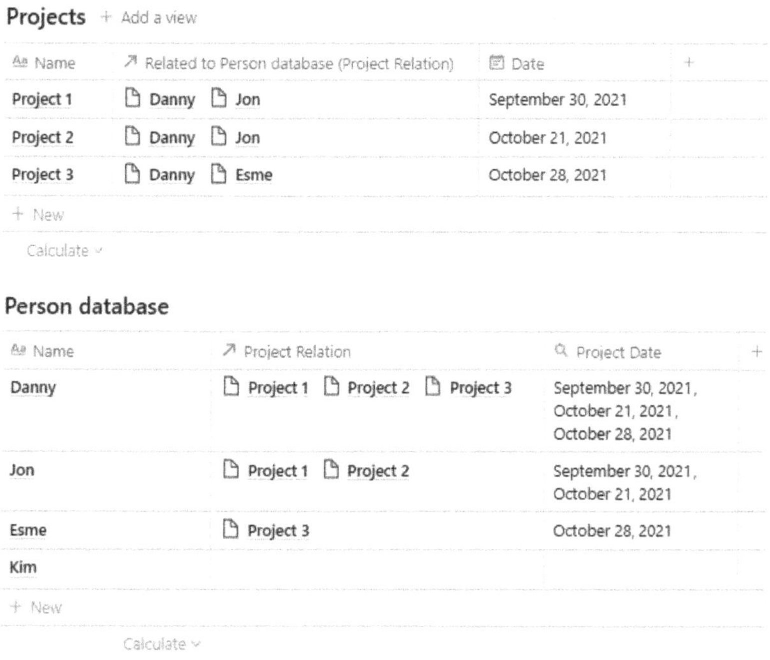

Projects + Add a view

Aa Name	↗ Related to Person database (Project Relation)	🗓 Date	+
Project 1	🗋 Danny 🗋 Jon	September 30, 2021	
Project 2	🗋 Danny 🗋 Jon	October 21, 2021	
Project 3	🗋 Danny 🗋 Esme	October 28, 2021	
+ New			

Calculate ⌄

Person database

Aa Name	↗ Project Relation	🔍 Project Date	+
Danny	🗋 Project 1 🗋 Project 2 🗋 Project 3	September 30, 2021, October 21, 2021, October 28, 2021	
Jon	🗋 Project 1 🗋 Project 2	September 30, 2021, October 21, 2021	
Esme	🗋 Project 3	October 28, 2021	
Kim			
+ New			

Calculate ⌄

Figure 7.10 – Person database rollup showing the date property information from the Project Relation property linking to the Projects database

Just like the calculations mentioned in *Chapter 6*, *Database Views*, the rollup property will work out those calculations for the information it is gathering from the relation and properties you selected.

Moving forward with this example of the date property, we are shown the date property calculations, as shown in *Figure 7.5*, which we put in the **CALCULATE** section of the configuration, looking something like *Figure 7.11*:

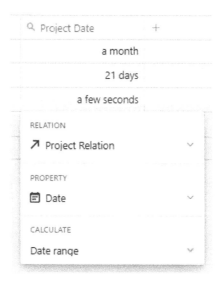

Figure 7.11 – Rollup configuration complete with date range
being calculated from the Project Date property

> **Note**
>
> The calculation that you do in the rollup will affect what the output is. It could show a string, number, date, or Boolean output, which may change how filters, sorts, and formulas work, which will be covered later in the book in *Chapter 8, Basic Formula Functions* onwards.

There is no restriction on how many rollups you can use per relation property, and no restrictions on the number of related properties you can use, so you can have multiple combinations of relations and rollups to bring various information into one database. *Figure 7.12* shows an example of multiple rollup properties doing different calculations using the same relation property:

Person database

A≠ Name	↗ Project Relation	Q Earliest Project Date	Q Latest Project Date	+
Danny	🗋 Project 1 🗋 Project 2 🗋 Project 3	7 days ago	in 21 days	
Jon	🗋 Project 1 🗋 Project 2	7 days ago	in 14 days	
Esme	🗋 Project 3	in 21 days	in 21 days	
Kim				
+ New				

Figure 7.12 – Two rollup properties doing different calculations on
the same relation property information

In the rollup configuration window, you can bring in any property type through the relation property except another relation, so the ability to roll up a rollup requires the use of the formula property, which will be covered in *Chapter 8, Basic Formula Functions*.

Apart from bringing in information into a database for viewing, that information can also be used to alter the views, as the information can be used to filter and sort the information in more desirable ways.

In the next section, we will look at how you can use property information to alter the view of the database by sorting the view.

Database sorting

Database sorting is a feature that can be accessed in every database view and in this section, we will cover how the sorting works and some ideas you could use when thinking about property use.

Sorting is useful for viewing information in more appropriate ways for the situation or context that the page is for. Some individuals may need different views from others and sorting is a great option.

The location of the **Sort** option is at the top right of the database view in the **...** menu, as shown in *Figure 7.13*:

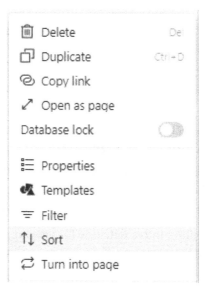

Figure 7.13 – The location of the Sort option in the ... drop-down menu

> **Note**
>
> Once you have some sorting in the database, the word **Sort** will appear when you hover over the top right of the database, so there is no need to go to the menu again.

The **Sort for** menu shows two drop-down options. The first is a list of all the properties in the database, with the second being the actions you can take. The actions list consists of **Ascending** and **Descending** options, which will be applied to the selected property, as shown in *Figure 7.14*:

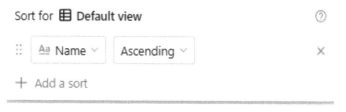

Figure 7.14 – Sorting the Name property in Ascending order

> **Note**
>
> **Text** properties are sorted alphabetically, **Number** properties are sorted numerically, but **Select** and **Multi-select** properties are sorted by the order the drop-down menu is configured. This means changing the order the options appear in the list will change the sorting priority.

When adding additional sorts, the priority is placed top down. This means that the view will be sorted by the first property and action, and then will be sorted by the second sort, and so on. You can change the order of the sort by using the :: option by the side of the sort or removing the sort by selecting the **x** icon to the right side of the sort, as shown in *Figure 7.14*.

In many cases, having a distinction between views can be useful. When combining the sorting feature and the page load limit, you can create views where the most important information is seen. The sort will put the most important information at the top of the database, with the page load limit restricting it to **10 pages** or **25 pages**, which means you can highlight the top 10 or top 25 pages needed, as shown in *Figure 7.15*:

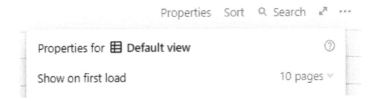

Figure 7.15 – Sort added to a database view with the page limit load set to 10 for a top 10 view

Combining the various database views and some of the additional features, such as sorting, page limits, and filtering, can allow for an almost infinite number of potential views you can create for the specific context you are working in. Filters add much more flexibility for targeting specific information, which will be covered next.

Database filtering

In this section, we will cover database filters and advanced database filters, which allow you to show or hide information specific to conditions you add to the filter of a database view. This is useful for not only hiding information you don't want to see but also showing specific information when searching for something.

In addition to this, using filters also allows some added functionality when interacting with pages in databases, using them to auto add property information, saving you time during the workflow.

> **Note**
> All of the information that was mentioned about the **Sort** option in the database remains active with any filter that you add to a view. You can have multiple sorts and filters on a single database view.

Figure 7.13 shows the **Sort** and **Filter** menus in the database view, which is accessed via the **...** menu at the top right of the database view. The difference between them becomes apparent when you access the filter as it comes up with additional options in the drop-down window, as shown in *Figure 7.16*:

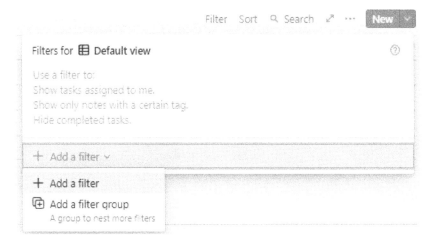

Figure 7.16 – The filter drop-down menu showing single filter and group filter options

You may notice the **Sort** option in *Figure 7.16* is blue, which indicates that there is an active sort in the database view, which is the same database sort from the previous section in this chapter.

Understanding the fundamentals of how filters work will allow you to expand out from the simple filter options and use them in groups and other added filter features, such as grouped filters, self-referencing filters in templates, and the auto filter feature.

Single filters

When creating any filter, there will be a minimum of two requirements, which will be the property and a selection. The selection options may expand to two different dropdowns, but for the example shown in *Figure 7.17*, the property selected from the database is the **Name** property and there is the **Is empty** selection, which is filtering out everything in the database that has something in the **Name** property:

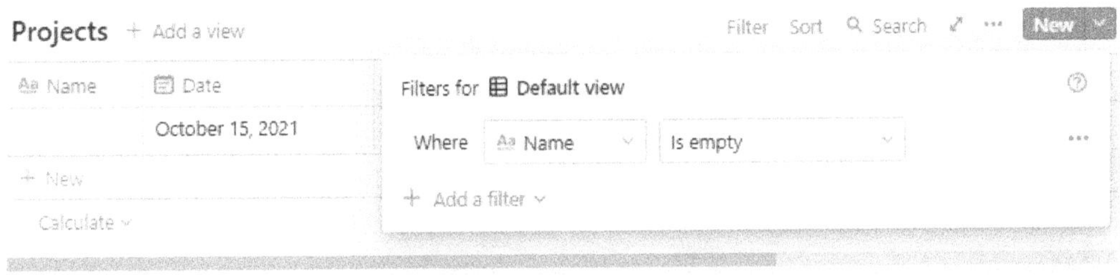

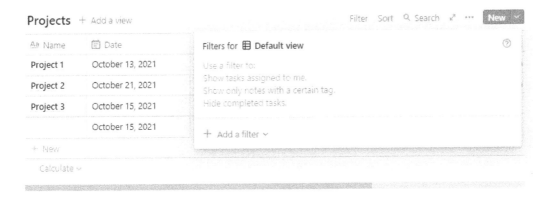

Figure 7.17 – Filtering the Projects database using the Name filter for Is empty giving one result

With the filter of the database view, other pages can be seen in *Figure 7.18*:

Figure 7.18 – The Projects database without a filter showing all four pages

So, whatever information is true according to the filter will be shown; in the case of the preceding example, every database entry that has an empty **Name** property will show.

The selection options can vary depending on the type of property. As an example, in *Figure 7.19*, whatever text you put in the **Value** box, the filter will show pages that only contain that text in the **Name** property:

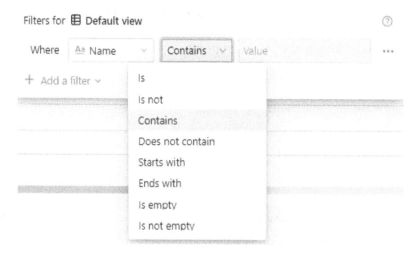

Figure 7.19 – Showing the drop-down filter options for the Aa and Text property types

As you may notice in *Figure 7.19*, there are pairs of conditions that appear in the filter dropdown that can be applied to different types of properties:

Filter Option	Properties Available
Is and **Is not** are applied to:	• **Aa** property type • **Text** property type • **Checkbox** property type • **Email** property type • **Phone** property type • **Select** property type • **URL** property type

Contains and **Does not contain** are applied to:	• **Aa** property type
	• **Text** property type
	• **Created by** property type
	• **Email** property type
	• **Last edited by** property type
	• **Multi-select** property type
	• **Person** property type
	• **Phone** property type
	• **Relation** property type
	• **URL** property type
Starts with and **Ends with** are applied to:	• **Aa** property type
	• **Text** property type
	• **Email** property type
	• **Phone** property type
	• **URL** property type
Is empty and **Is not empty** are applied to:	• **Aa** property type
	• **Text** property type
	• **Number** property type
	• **Created by** property type
	• **Email** property type
	• **Files & Media** property type
	• **Last edited by** property type
	• **Created time** property type
	• **Last edited time** property type
	• **Date** property type
	• **Multi-select** property type
	• **Person** property type
	• **Phone** property type
	• **Relation** property type
	• **Select** property type
	• **URL** property type
The $= \neq < > \leq \geq$ comparison symbols are applied to:	• **Number** property type

Table 7.1 – The filter options with the properties that the filters work with

In addition to the pairs, there is an additional list for the **Created time**, **Date**, and **Last time edited** property types, as shown in *Figure 7.20*:

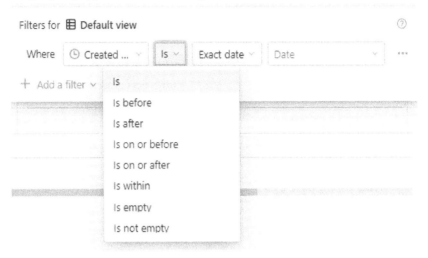

Figure 7.20 – Showing the additional drop-down menu for date-focused property types

This different list adds the option to the filter section to pick the appropriate date, which can be done by using a date picker with the **Exact date** option, shown in *Figure 7.20*, or using the **Created** drop-down list, shown in *Figure 7.21*:

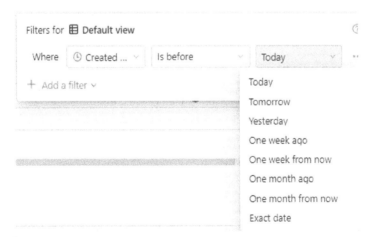

Figure 7.21 – Additional dropdown of the date selection options

The formula and rollup properties again react similarly to the calculations in that the output type will determine what options become available.

Grouped filters

Grouped filters work in the same way as the individual filters but, when you combine two individual filters, you get the option to add **And** or **Or** to the filter, whereas in groups, you are given more flexibility.

In *Figure 7.22*, there are two individual filters with drop-down options for **And** and **Or**, which will change the filtering result. The first option would be to set the **Name** property to **Is empty**, then set **And**, and then set the **Date** property to **Is before Today**, then the pages will show:

Figure 7.22 – The filter drop-down menu, which can change the filter result with and/or

The second option would be to use the **Or** option, which will show pages when the **Name** property is set to **Is not empty**, then **Or** is set, then the **Date** property is set to **Is before** and **Today**. Once the option has been selected, it will be the same going down, when adding additional conditions, as shown in *Figure 7.23*:

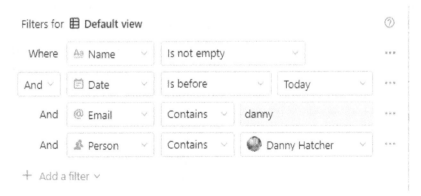

Figure 7.23 – The filter dropdown selecting And, which continues for each condition

When creating a group through the **Add a filter** button or the **...** menu next to any active filter, the **And/Or** option appears for that group. These groups can be added inside of one another, allowing you to combine filter conditions, as shown in *Figure 7.24*:

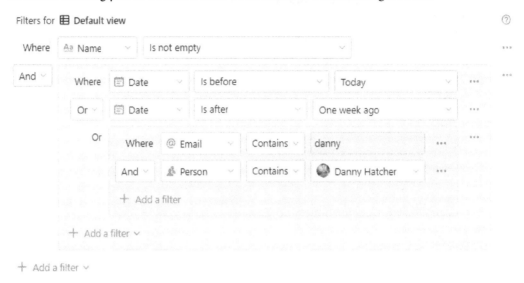

Figure 7.24 – Grouped filters with And/Or conditions in place

The example in *Figure 7.24* can be any page where **Name** is set to **Is not empty**, meaning the page needs a name. **Date** is set to **Is before** and **Today**, then **Or** is set, then **Date** is set to **Is after** and **One week ago**, meaning any date in the last week. **Or** is set, then **Where** **@Email** is set to **Contains**, then, in this example, **danny**. Then, set **And**, then **Person**, then **Contains**, and, in this example, **Danny Hatcher**, meaning that there is danny in the **Email** property and the **Danny Hatcher** account is in the **Person** property.

Multiple filters can be added to each group, with multiple groups inside a group, allowing for almost any configuration of filter that you would need.

Self-referencing filters

Self-referencing filters is a feature that is used specifically in the templates of a database, using linked database views.

> **Note**
>
> If you are not yet very familiar with linked database views and database templates, this could be confusing.

Figure 7.25 shows the **Database Template** page inside **Project database** while being edited with a linked database view of **Person database**:

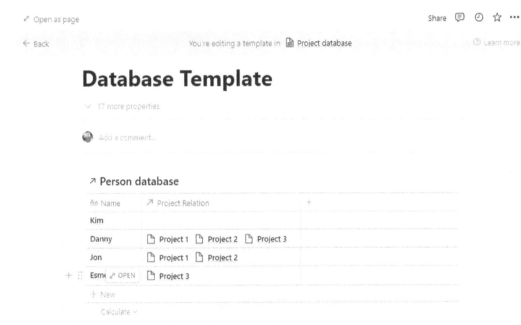

Figure 7.25 – Editing the Database Template page

When adding a filter to the linked database view of **Person database**, the selected property is the relation property called **Project Relation**, which shows the pages in **Project database**. While editing **Project database**, the **Database Template** page will appear in the drop-down menu, as shown in *Figure 7.26*:

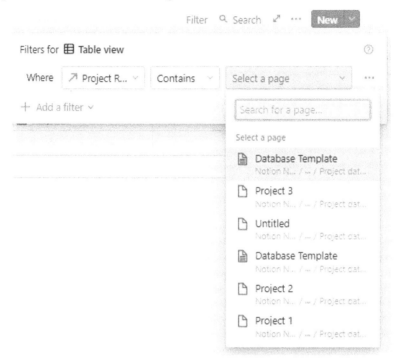

Figure 7.26 – Self-referencing the Database Template page in the person-linked database view filter

What this means is that when the template called **Database Template** is used when creating a page, the name of the page will be added to the filter. For example, if the **Database Template** page was used in a page called **Project 1**, then it would be added to the relation filter automatically, which will then filter the **Person database** linked database view for just that project, as seen in *Figure 7.27*:

Figure 7.27 – Self-referenced filter for the Project 1 page in the Person database view

When combining this self-referenced filter feature with the filter groups and other linked database views, you can create a template for a database that will generate a personalized page with automatically generated views with one click.

Auto filters

The **auto filter** features require linked database views with filters in them. Any filter that has a specific condition will add that condition to the page dragged into the view. This means the **And** condition will add the condition information to the property of the page, but the **Or** condition may not. The most notable example of when the **Or** function works is if the same property is used in the condition, in which case the top condition will be taken. This could be seen in *Figure 7.24* with the **Date** property being referenced two times with an **Or** condition.

> **Note**
> Going through each possible combination of property type, grouping situation, and condition sets is not possible in this book, so I would encourage you to experiment with this.

Creating a linked database view with a filter is all that is required to set up this feature. By dragging a page and dropping it into the view of another database, the filtered information will be changed. *Figure 7.28* shows the original view of two database views, one of them being a filtered linked database view for **Date**, which is **Today**:

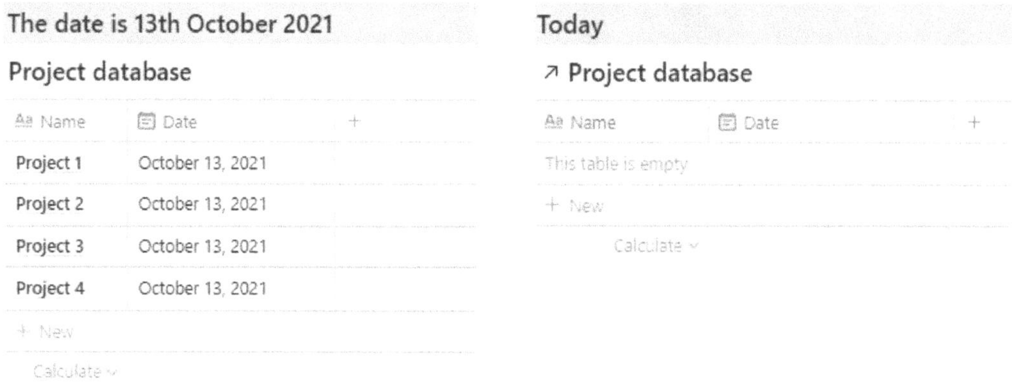

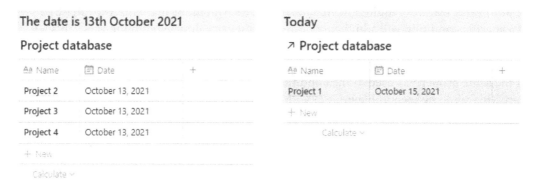

Figure 7.28 – A linked database view of Project database with a filter for the date as Today

Clicking :: on the side of the page, holding down and dragging it into the linked database view, then dropping the page into the view automatically changes the **Date** property information from **October 13, 2021** to **Today**, which at the time was **October 15, 2021**, as shown in *Figure 7.29*:

Figure 7.29 – Project 1 is dropped into the filtered linked database view

Auto filters can be used anywhere that the same database is seen in a linked database view. By combining this feature with the group filters and the self-referencing feature inside templates, workflows of creating filtered personalized views become quick and easy.

Database grouping

In this section, we will cover **database grouping**, which alters the way the database views can be seen. This feature, just like filtering and sorting, can be applied to any database view, which gives even more flexibility to how to present information.

One of the main benefits of this feature is that you can use all of the properties to group information. This allows the auto filter feature to be used without creating multiple linked databases, there is a smaller need for various database views, and it allows for subgrouping inside of the board database view.

Using **Project database** from previous sections, we have a relation between the project and a person database, and for easier viewing, we can use groups to separate each project by a person.

Going into the **...** menu at the top right of the database and clicking on **Group** brings up a grouping menu.

The **Group by** option gives you a list of all of the properties in that database, which you can select to group the information by. The **Sort** dropdown allows you to sort the groupings manually, so you can move certain sections up or down, alphabetically, or reverse alphabetically.

> **Note**
>
> The **Sort** option in the groupings section is different from the **Sort** option in the database view. The sort inside the groupings is sorting the groups, not the pages, whereas the sort in the database view sorts the pages in the groups.

The next option is the **Hide empty groups** toggle, which will hide all groups that you created that don't have any pages in. This could also be more specific using the **Visible groups** section, shown in *Figure 7.30*:

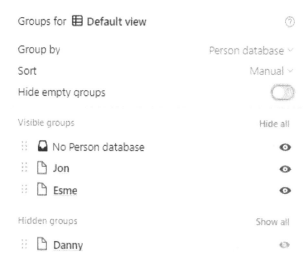

Figure 7.30 – The groups drop-down menu from a table database view using a relation property

In *Figure 7.30*, the **Group by** is a relation property called **Person database** and the **Sort** option is **Manual**, showing the :: option next to each group. Then, there are two sections, one for **Visible groups** and the other for **Hidden groups**, with an eye icon to the right of each group for toggling whether the group is hidden or visible. This then gives the view shown in *Figure 7.31*, with **1 hidden group** indicated at the bottom of the view and each grouping showing the appropriate information with the option to toggle the group shut, indicated by the ▼ symbol:

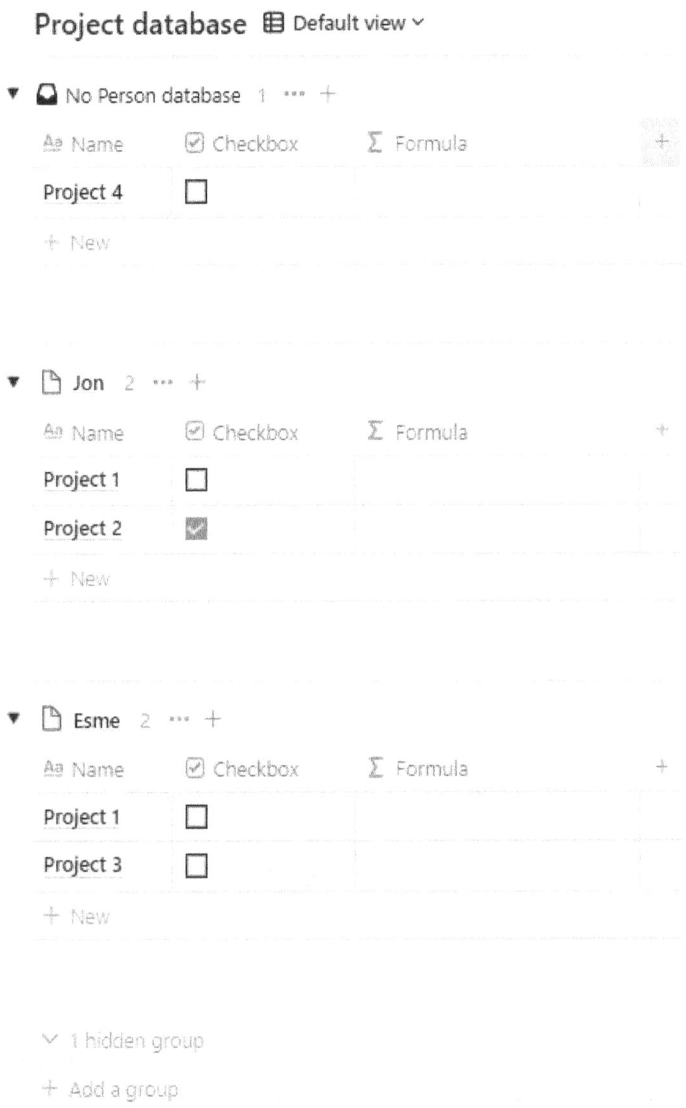

Project database ⊞ Default view ⌄

▾ ⬚ No Person database 1 ⋯ +

Aa Name	☑ Checkbox	Σ Formula	
Project 4	☐		

+ New

▾ ◻ Jon 2 ⋯ +

Aa Name	☑ Checkbox	Σ Formula	
Project 1	☐		
Project 2	☑		

+ New

▾ ◻ Esme 2 ⋯ +

Aa Name	☑ Checkbox	Σ Formula	
Project 1	☐		
Project 3	☐		

+ New

⌄ 1 hidden group

+ Add a group

Figure 7.31 – The group by option in a table view, using the relation property

This grouping feature applies to all database views except the calendar view and allows subgroups to be created in the board database view. The subgroup option is found underneath the **Group** option in the **...** menu and is viewed with the main groups functioning as a Kanban board but the subgroup functioning the same way it does with the other database views. This gives a horizontal split by the group and a vertical split by the subgroup, as seen in *Figure 7.32*:

Figure 7.32 – Group and subgroup feature being used in a board database view

When using the grouping feature alongside the filtering and sorting options, you can create a variety of views all customized to the property information that is in a database.

Summary

In this chapter, we covered how a relation property can be used to combine and transfer information between databases. We saw how the rollup property can be used alongside the relation property to bring in information from another database and use that information to create calculations and summarize information in a specific view.

The database viewing features were also covered, looking at how to sort a database view and how to use filters, grouped filters, and some of the advanced filter options, such as self-referencing filters and auto filtering. The grouping features were also covered, as well as how it can alter the view of five of the six view options.

All of these lessons can be used to create quicker, more seamless workflows when creating pages of information and creating dashboards that show specific information for contextual use cases.

There is still one more property that needs to be covered that you can use in a database, which is the formula property. As this property is so versatile, it will be covered over multiple chapters, starting in the next chapter with basic formula functions.

8
Basic Formula Functions

The **formula** property can be as simple or as complex as you want it to be, giving you the possibility to create outputs from any other piece of information from another property. The reason we are talking about this property in two chapters is due to the amount of flexibility it can give with the various functions, calculations, and combinations that can be created. Any of those formulas can be used for viewing, filtering, sorting, or for other property uses, such as database views.

In this chapter, we're going to cover the following topics:

- Formula fundamentals
- How formula constants work
- How formula operators work
- How formula functions work

You will learn how to use all the options that are in the formula property individually, with the required information regarding each option. This will enable you to create formulas in any database and generate basic outputs that can be used to change database information and views.

Formula fundamentals

In this section, you will learn the basics of how the formula property functions inside a database, what limitations it can have when using the property, and the output variations that will impact how the property can be used.

This section of the chapter is the most important to understand because each point raised will impact what functions and operators you choose to use, what information is needed, and, potentially, how using other properties may be needed for a formula to work the way you want.

> **Note**
>
> If you have previous coding experience, or experience using spreadsheet formulas and calculations, these are transferable skills that can be used. Having said that, they do not function in the same way. If you have no prior experience, the next couple of chapters will take you through each process step by step.

The first and most important thing to realize while working with Notion formulas is the properties in the database are specific to the page. This means that even in a table database view, you cannot reference something like a cell from a spreadsheet. For a formula to work, it needs to reference a piece of information stored in the page's metadata in the properties.

To explain this point further, when you create a formula property in a database and click on the property, you will be shown a formula window, as shown in *Figure 8.1*:

Figure 8.1 – The formula window

The formula window will appear similar in every database: separated into sections. On the left side of the window, there is a list with subtitles above each section of the list. The **Properties** subtitle shown in *Figure 8.1* is a list of all the other properties that are in the database the formula property is in. The preceding example shows only the **Name** property, meaning the only metadata the formula property can reference is information from that property.

The rest of the subtitles are **Constants**, **Operators**, and **Functions**, which can be used to create an output shown in the formula property, which will be covered later in this chapter.

At the top of the formula window, there is the edit panel, which is where you type and create the formula you want to apply. The *Figure 8.1* edit panel is empty, showing **Type a formula** as a cue to show you where to type.

Underneath the edit panel and to the right of the sections list there is a **Help** window. This window will change depending on what option in the list is selected and will give instructional advice and guidance about the option you currently have selected. In *Figure 8.1*, the **Name** property is highlighted, so it gives guidance on how the **Name** property can be used.

At the bottom of the window in *Figure 8.1*, there is the text that says **ctrl+Enter to accept**, which will change as you type out a formula. The *Ctrl + Enter* keypress will enter and execute the formula, giving you output, but if the output isn't shown there will be an error code instead, as shown in *Figure 8.2*:

Figure 8.2 – An error code at the bottom of the formula window

The error code could be due to missing information or incorrect syntax, which is like punctuation for the formula. The syntax of a formula for **Constant**, **Operator**, or **Function** can be found in the **Help** window when you select it in the list menu, as shown in *Figure 8.3* for the if operator:

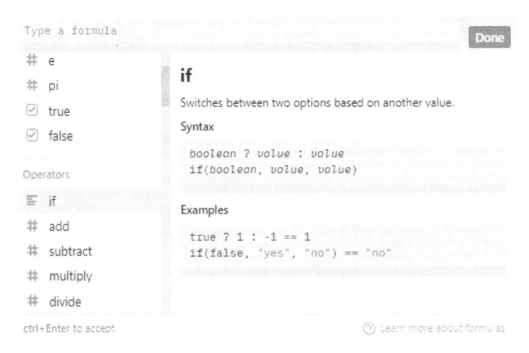

Figure 8.3 – The if operator help window showing the expected syntax and examples of use

In *Chapter 5, All the Basic Database Properties*, the different types of properties were covered, such as the string, number, date, and Boolean output options. The formula property can produce any of these types of output depending on the formula that is created, but it can only output one type of information. This means if the output has numbers and letters in it, it can only output as a string, as letters can't be numbers. This will be demonstrated throughout this chapter, but some constants can be used without needing them in a property, which will be covered in the next section.

Constant options

In this section, you will learn about the **constants** that you can use inside a formula property. Constants are not used often inside formulas, but knowing what is available without needing to create a property can help reduce database size and formula size, which makes formulas much easier to create.

> **Note**
>
> Some of the constants are numbers and some are Booleans. Boolean constants are most likely to be used, but if you require a constant to calculate something, number constants can be useful.

The e constant is the base of the natural logarithm. This means when you are creating equations inside a formula using any log functions or operators, this can be put in to create the intended output. The **Help** window shown in *Figure 8.4* shows how it can be used. It demonstrates how to get a result by using two = signs in a Notion formula property:

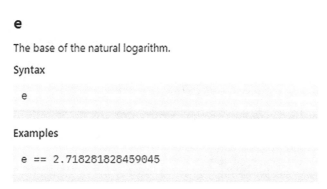

e

The base of the natural logarithm.

Syntax

```
e
```

Examples

```
e == 2.718281828459045
```

Figure 8.4 – The e constant help window

The pi constant works in a very similar way, giving you the mathematical value of pi, which again can be used in calculations.

The `true` and `false` constants work with Boolean logic. This means that they are like answers to a question that you ask using a formula. Because they are answers, to use them you need to create a question. Otherwise, if left alone they will output either a `true` or `false` result shown in Notion as a checkbox, as in *Figure 8.5*:

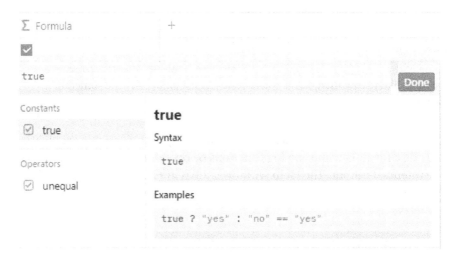

Figure 8.5 – A true formula is shown in the formula box as a checked checkbox

In *Figure 8.5* you can also see the **Help** window showing an example of how the `true` constant can be used.

The example is answering `true` for the question `yes` or `no`. The ? and : operators in the syntax are an abbreviation for an `if` operator, which will be covered further later in this chapter. The == operator in the example is showing the output of the example, which is what the formula property will show.

The `if` operator works in three sections:

- The question
- The `true` answer
- The `false` answer

Because the `true` constant is being used in the question section, the answer has to be `true`, which is the part after ?, which is `yes`. If the question section was using the `false` constant, the answer would be `false`, which is the second answer, the one after :, which is `no`. *Figure 8.6* shows a `true` example:

Figure 8.6 – The true constant being used in an if formula giving the true output

Constants don't do any calculations or change anything from the given information, which is why they are used inside operators, which will be covered next.

Operator options

In this section, you will learn all of the **operator** options inside the formula property. Each of these operators can be used using any constant or property from the database the formula property is made in. The operators are often used to create formulas that calculate something from input information.

The most beneficial thing about knowing the operator properties is that you can do almost any calculation you want, which might not be available using database view calculations or rollup calculations.

> **Note**
> Each operator can be written in different ways using the longhand or shorthand version of the syntax, which is shown in the **Help** window when the operator is selected.

There are different types of operators that can be used. Some are number focused, some are Boolean focused, and then there is the if operator.

Each example in this section will be using the same database with the same properties, the only difference being the operators used in the formula.

Number operators

The add, subtract, multiply, divide, pow, and mod operators function in the same way as the mathematical symbols would work if the input were a number type. If the input is a string type, they work differently. This allows you to do basic math by adding, subtracting, dividing, multiplying, doing powers of numbers, or finding the remainder of any number, and use them in any formula. It also allows shorthand manipulation of string inputs.

> **Note**
>
> This section covers how to learn how each operator works, rather than going through each one individually. This means if new operators are added in the future, you will be able to work out how they work.

In the **Help** window, when you open the formula box, you will see the operator you have clicked on, giving you the syntax and some examples. In *Figure 8.7*, the add operator is being used in the formula box:

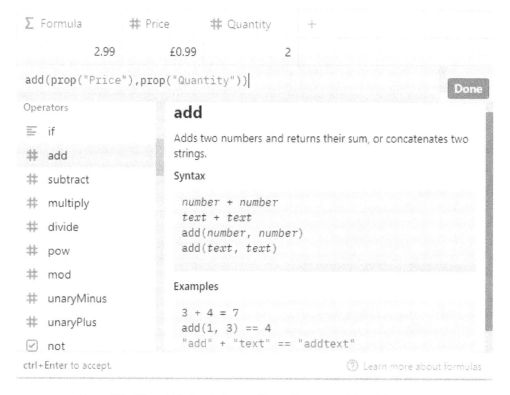

Figure 8.7 – The add help window and long-form use of the add operator

In *Figure 8.7*, the syntax shows number + number, which is being shown in the example section as 3 + 4 = 7, with = 7 showing what the output in the formula property would be.

The text + text syntax is shown in the **Examples** section as "add" + "text" == "addtext", with the " around each word telling the formula box that it is a string and not a number. So, instead of it being a mathematical calculation, it puts the words together. The == "addtext" phrase is the output in the formula property.

These two syntax examples are shorthand using the + symbol in the place of the add() operator. To write it longhand, the syntax is add(number, number) and add(text, text), which will output the same answers as the shorthand forms.

The number or text that you put into the operator can be from a constant mentioned in the previous section, something that you type into the formula on your keyboard (remembering to put "" around any text), or you could use information from a property that's already in the database.

In *Figure 8.7*, the longhand syntax is being used to add the price property and the quantity property together in the formula box, which shows the output.

In that example, we want quantity to be multiplied by the price instead of added to the price, so by using a shorthand syntax and the multiply operator we could change the property to say prop("Price") * prop("Quantity"), as shown in *Figure 8.8*:

Figure 8.8 – Using the multiply operator with shorthand syntax

You will notice that in the **multiply** help window in the **Syntax** section, there is no text option, meaning that you can't use a string input with the `multiply` operator. Once the formula is working, the **Done** button will turn bright blue and the text at the bottom of the window will show **ctrl+Enter to accept**, which will apply the formula to every row, as shown in *Figure 8.9*:

Σ Formula	# Price	# Quantity
1.98	£0.99	2
1.99	£1.99	1
60	£12.00	5

Figure 8.9 – The multiply formula being applied to each page row in the database

When looking at the **Help** window of *Figure 8.8* or *Figure 8.7*, the symbol that can be used in shorthand is shown in the **Syntax** section.

The other two operators that are number focused are `unaryPlus` and `unaryMinus`, which change a number from negative to positive or positive to negative respectively.

Boolean operators

These operators work in a similar way to the number operators but instead of the output being a number, it is a `true` or `false` statement signified by a checked or unchecked checkbox.

The `equal`, `unequal`, `larger`, `largerEq`, `smaller`, and `smallerEq` operators all have symbols that can be used for shorthand. These operators all function similarly to the number operators, doing direct comparisons of values that could be strings, numbers, or Booleans. An example is that `larger(prop("Price"), prop("Quantity"))`, which is shorthand, would look like `prop("Price") > prop("Quantity")`, both of which give the same answers, as shown in *Figure 8.10*:

Σ Formula	# Price	# Quantity
☐	£0.99	2
☑	£1.99	1
☑	£12.00	5

Figure 8.10 – Using the larger operator to compare Price and Quantity

In *Figure 8.10*, the first row shows that the **2** value in the **#Quantity** column is larger than the **£0.99** value in the **#Price** column. So, the formula prop("Price") > prop("Quantity") was false, resulting in an unchecked box.

The not, and, and or operators work differently in that they need a Boolean input to work, as shown in the syntax of *Figure 8.11*:

Figure 8.11 – The not operator help window

The example shown in the formula box of *Figure 8.11* shows the previous formula being used as a Boolean output, which is being reversed by the not operator.

The and operator combines two Boolean outputs into one. An example using this database could be that we are looking for something more expensive than £1 but something that has less than five in quantity. We could therefore use prop("Price") > 1 to find things worth more than £1 and prop("Quantity") < 5 to find things of which there are less than five in quantity. Using and between these two Boolean results would look like prop("Price") > 1 and prop("Quantity") < 5, with results shown in *Figure 8.12*:

Σ Formula	# Price	# Quantity
☐	£0.99	2
☑	£1.99	1
☐	£12.00	5

Figure 8.12 – Using the and operator to combine two Boolean answers into one output

The or operator works in the same way as and but instead of needing both |Boolean results to be true to output a true result, only one needs to be true. If we change and for or in the preceding formula, we get prop("Price") > 1 or prop("Quantity") < 5, showing the results in *Figure 8.13*:

Σ Formula	# Price	# Quantity
☑	£0.99	2
☑	£1.99	1
☑	£12.00	5

Figure 8.13 – Using the or operator to combine two Boolean outputs into one

The Boolean operators and the number operators all work with a specific type of input, but the if the operator allows all three types.

The if operator

The reason this operator has a section all of its own is that it is an operator that can use any of the three different types of information in a very free way.

The **Help** window in *Figure 8.14* shows two different syntax options that were partly explained in previous chapters, but for this explanation, there are three sections. The question is a Boolean, the `true` answer can be string, text, or Boolean, and the `false` answer can be string, text, or Boolean. The one stipulation is that the `true` and `false` answers need to be the same type.

Figure 8.14 – The if operator help window

In the **Formula** box of *Figure 8.14*, the formula is using `prop("Price")>1` as the Boolean question. The `true` text answer says `yes`, and the `false` text answer says `no`.

The `true` or `false` answers can be swapped with the constants `True` and `False`, swapped for any string of text, or swapped for any number value.

The Boolean question can also be changed to use any constant or operator that outputs a Boolean result. If, however, the `true` and `false` output in the `if` operator doesn't match, an error will appear reading **Each branch of a condition must be of the same type:**, preventing the formula from being done, as shown in *Figure 8.15*.

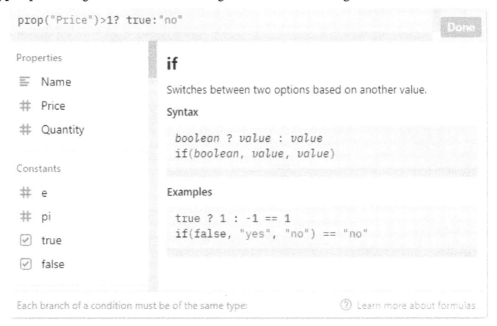

Figure 8.15 – The if operator having different types of output resulting in an error

It's important to remember that the `if` operator can be used with all types of input and output, making it one of the most flexible tools inside the **Formula** box. This operator will be expanded on in later chapters due to the wide use cases it can have. Having said that, all the operators can be used inside the functions, which will be covered next.

Function options

In this section, we will cover all the **function options** that are available in the formula property. We will see how they are similar to and different from one another regarding previous constant and operator options for potential combinations.

The function options in the formula property are often specific to a calculation or use case, making them time-consuming to remember and learn. Some of the functions can be replaced by operators in specific circumstances, but the reason learning these functions can be so useful is that they can reduce the length and complexity of the formula while giving you more flexibility at the same time.

> **Note**
>
> The most important thing to remember when learning about the formula property is to look at the type of information it uses and outputs and its syntax in the help window. Many functions can use a variety of inputs and outputs, which can make things confusing.

Once again, we will split the types of functions available into categories of type, looking into the string, number, date, and Boolean types of output. Notice that functions allow date types to be used, unlike the operators.

String functions

All these functions use a combination of inputs of the string, number, or Boolean types to create a string output.

The simplest of functions is the `id` function, which generates a unique string of numbers and letters to identify each row individually.

The most commonly used functions are the `format` and `formatDate` functions, which are used to turn numbers or dates into strings of text, as shown in *Figure 8.16*:

Figure 8.16 – Using the format function to display the number Price property
as a text string in the formula property

The `format` function is often used when creating advanced formulas and when changing a number output into text for a different function or operator to be used.

The `formatDate` function can change the look of any date, giving you the flexibility to extract the information you want for an advanced formula, or just view the date in your preferred format, with some examples shown here:

```
formatDate(now(), "MMMM D YYYY, HH:mm") == March 30 2010, 12:00
formatDate(now(), "YYYY/MM/DD, HH:mm") == 2010/03/30, 12:00
formatDate(now(), "MM/DD/YYYY, HH:mm") == 03/30/2010, 12:00
formatDate(now(), "HH:mm A") == 12:00 PM
formatDate(now(), "M/D/YY") == 3/30/10
```

The `concat` function gives you the same output as using the + symbol or the `add` operator from the previous section.

The `Join` function works in a very similar way to `concat`, but instead of putting the text together to form a long string, it uses the first argument as a separator for all the other text arguments you include.

The term *argument* is used to identify different inputs into a formula syntax. In *Figure 8.17*, in the **Examples** section, there is `"-"`, `"a"`, `"b"`, `"c"` inside the brackets, which are the four arguments that are being used in this function:

Figure 8.17 – Use of the join function and the format function while displaying the join help window

As you can see in *Figure 8.17*, the syntax of the `join` function says that it needs `text`, but as the properties in the database are numbers, we need to change how the information is being read. This is a use case for the `format` function.

The first argument is `-`, which separates the following arguments. The `Quantity` property is inside a `format` function, turning it into text, and the same is happening to the `Price` property. Now that all the arguments are text, the formula property is outputting `2-0.99`.

This example is still using three arguments in the `join` function, but two of the arguments are other functions, which in this case are the `format` function. The same can be done for all types of functions, and the `slice` function example in *Figure 8.18* is another example of this:

Figure 8.18 – The slice function and format function being used while showing the slice help window

As you can see in the **Syntax** section of the **Help** window in *Figure 8.18*, the `slice` function uses text for the first argument and then a number type for the second and third arguments.

Looking at the **Formula** box, the `slice` function is looking at the string version of the `Price` property, as that is what the `format` function is doing. It is then looking at the second character in and the fourth character in and outputting the characters in between.

£0.99 was the Price value, which was changed to 99 using the format function, and the 0. was excluded as they are index locations *0* and *1* for the slice function, which is before *2*.

> **Note**
>
> In the slice function, the numbers for the location of the string can be any formula you create with a number output.

The replace and replaceAll functions work in a similar way, with one difference. The replaceAll function replaces all instances of the located string, whereas the replace function only replaces the first instance.

In *Figure 8.19*, the **Help** window shows that the first argument can be a number, text, or Boolean, but the other arguments need to be text. This example uses the replaceAll function to look at the Price property, locate all instances of 9, and replace them with S.

Figure 8.19 – The replaceAll function being used with the help window open

The replace function would do the same action but the output would not be 0.SS; it would be 0.S9, only replacing the first instance.

Each of the output results from these functions is text, but use number, date, and Boolean for inputs. The next function's outputs are of the number type.

Number functions

All of these functions output a number, some relating directly to mathematical functions, others more specifically for traditional formula use.

The format function from the previous section turns a number into text and the toNumber function does the reverse, turning text into a number.

The length function gives the length of a string of text. Using the same database, we can change the Price property into text and then use the length function to count how many characters there are, as shown in *Figure 8.20*:

Figure 8.20 – Using the length and format functions while showing the length help window

The next few functions are likely to be used when doing a calculation in an advanced formula, or for changing the view output:

- The abs function returns the absolute value of a number.
- The cbrt function returns the cube root of a number.
- The ceil function returns the smallest integer greater than or equal to a number.
- The exp function returns E^x, where x is the argument and E is Euler's constant.
- The floor function returns the largest integer less than or equal to a number.

- The `ln` function returns the natural logarithm of a number.

- The `log10` function returns the base 10 logarithm of a number.

- The `log2` function returns the base 2 logarithm of a number.

- The `max` function returns the largest of zero or more numbers.

- The `min` function returns the smallest of zero or more numbers.

- The `round` function returns the value of a number rounded to the nearest integer.

- The `sign` function returns the sign of the *x*, indicating whether *x* is positive, negative, or `0` by displaying `1` for positive, `-1` for negative, and `0`.

- The `sqrt` function returns the positive square root of a number.

When we move to the `timestamp` function, the numbers that are being generated come from a date type instead of a number input type.

The `timestamp` function returns an integer number from a Unix millisecond timestamp, corresponding to the number of milliseconds since *January 1, 1970*. In my experience, this function is rarely used.

The `minute`, `hour`, `day`, `date`, `month`, and `year` functions all take specific parts out of a date input and give that number as output:

- The `minute` function takes the minute number.

- The `hour` function takes the hour number.

- The `day` function takes a day of the week—`0` for Sunday, `1` for Monday, and so on.

- The `date` function takes the day of the month.

- The `month` function takes the month, `0` for January, `1` for February, and so on.

- The `year` function takes the year.

As each of these functions returns a number, you can use them to calculate the difference between two dates in days, months, years, and so on. There is a function that does the calculation for you called `dateBetween`.

The dateBetween function requires two different date inputs and one text input, which is specified information shown in the **Help** window as in *Figure 8.21*:

Figure 8.21 – The dateBetween function and the help window

The example in *Figure 8.21* is using two properties in the database and is using the years text to calculate the year's difference between the two dates, which in the example is 1 year and 1 day. As the function can only output one answer, the text determines what number is shown with these options:

- dateBetween(date, date2, "years")
- dateBetween(date, date2, "quarters")
- dateBetween(date, date2, "months")
- dateBetween(date, date2, "weeks")
- dateBetween(date, date2, "days")
- dateBetween(date, date2, "hours")
- dateBetween(date, date2, "minutes")
- dateBetween(date, date2, "seconds")
- dateBetween(date, date2, "milliseconds")

You can get more flexibility with the output and the calculations and use fewer properties by using some of the date-specific functions that are covered next.

Date functions

The most commonly used **date function** is the now() function as it automatically inputs the current time and date into a formula, allowing easy date calculations and comparing other date properties to real time.

The start and end functions are often used to isolate a specific date from a date property with more than one date. As an example, in *Figure 8.22*, the Date property has a start date of October 22, 2021 and an end date of October 29, 2021. The formula is using the start function and is outputting the first date, which is October 22, 2021:

Figure 8.22 – Using the start function to isolate a date in a date property

The `fromTimestamp` function is similar to the previous `timestamp` function, but this function has a trick that can be used to help with creating formulas using the date output. This function returns a date constructed from a Unix millisecond timestamp, which means it turns a number into a date. An issue mentioned previously about formulas is that the output needs to be in the same style, but there is no way to leave a date type empty. If you use `fromTimestamp(toNumber(""))`, the formula box will output nothing as it is turning empty text into a number, which is being turned into a date type.

In *Figure 8.23*, the formula is using an `if` statement, a smaller than comparator, the `now` function, and the trick explained previously. This formula is asking if the `Start Date` value is smaller than the current date, and if it is it will return the `Start Date`, but if it isn't it will return a blank cell, using the trick explained previously. This allows the formula to be complete and work for all instances.

Figure 8.23 – Using the blank date type fromTimestamp(toNumber("")) trick in a formula

The remaining two date functions work by adding or subtracting a given value to a specified date.

The `dateAdd` and `dateSubtract` use a date, a number, and then an indicator for how much the date will be changed, as shown in the following screenshot:

Figure 8.24 – The dateAdd function being used to add one day

This leaves the Boolean functions to be covered in the next section.

Boolean functions

The `contains` and `empty` Boolean functions work the same way as the contains and empty filters in the database views: outputting a checkbox to show whether it is true or false. The `contains` function only works on text strings, whereas the `empty` function works on all types. This means the `empty` Boolean function can be used to check if all properties are full by combining the `and` and `or` functions, as shown in *Figure 8.25*:

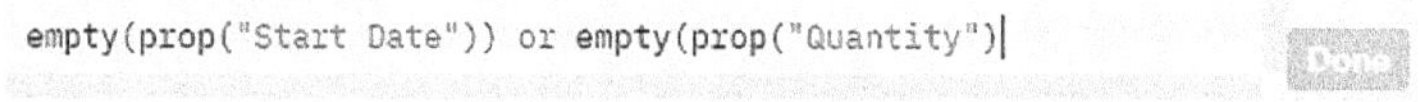

```
empty(prop("Start Date")) or empty(prop("Quantity"))|
```

Figure 8.25 – Combining multiple empty functions to check multiple properties

The `test` function works in a very similar way, searching for a specific text string inside a number, text, or Boolean output and returning a `True` or `False` result.

Summary

In this chapter, you learned the fundamentals of formulas and how the help window and formula input box work. You learned what constant, operator, and function options are available inside the formula property and how each formula uses inputs to generate a specific type of output for viewing purposes. We also covered all the tools to start building formulas inside databases.

Notion formulas can get much more complex as you start to add more advanced conditions to the properties and by manipulating the various ways of inputting information, which will be covered in the next chapter.

9
Advanced Formula Combinations

This chapter covers the advanced areas of formula creation and combination. This chapter guides you through the almost unlimited number of combinations between formula options, properties, and database input and output values to help you create solutions to your problems.

In this chapter, we're going to cover the following:

- Combined formulas

- Input and output variations

- How to create a progress bar

You will learn how to combine multiple options in formulas, using nested `if` statements and functions to create large queries or large possibilities with outputs. You will learn how to alter the properties in a database to help you calculate the information you want, and to change how a workflow operates by manipulating the input to a formula property. Then you will learn how to go about creating a formula from a problem, building it up from nothing.

Combined formulas

In this section, you will learn how you can combine various formula options into one formula and how you can then nest functions inside one another.

As demonstrated in the previous chapter, you can replace an argument in a formula with anything, including a property, function, constant, or operator. This allows you to create longer formulas such as the one shown in *Figure 8.23*.

> **Note**
>
> As long as the formula that you create has the same output type in each instance, the formula will work, just as it would with any short function.

The Eisenhower matrix

In *Figure 9.1*, you can see seven different rows in a database with various input variables from the `Priority` and `Importance` properties, which are select properties all giving different outputs in the `Formula` property from the formula box shown at the bottom of the image.

Σ Formula	● Priority	● Importance	+
DO	Urgent	Important	
DELEGATE	Urgent	Not Important	
SCHEDULE	Not Urgent	Important	
DELETE	Not Urgent	Not Important	
NEED PRIORITY		Important	
NEED IMPORTANCE	Urgent		
NEED PRIORITY AND IMPORTANCE			

```
(empty(prop("Importance")) and empty(prop("Priority"))) ? "NEED
PRIORITY AND IMPORTANCE" : (empty(prop("Priority")) ? "NEED
PRIORITY" : (empty(prop("Importance")) ? "NEED IMPORTANCE" :
((prop("Priority") == "Urgent") ? ((prop("Importance") ==
"Important") ? "DO" : "DELEGATE") : ((prop("Importance") ==
"Important") ? "SCHEDULE" : "DELETE"))))
```

Done

Figure 9.1 – The Eisenhower matrix formula with the different output variations

The **Eisenhower matrix** is something that could be used to generate a response to a possible task, and the formula in *Figure 9.1* works out the logic automatically using the information given to it by the properties.

The matrix has four corners, **do**, **delegate**, **schedule**, and **delete**, which are assigned in line with how urgent or important a task is:

- If the task is urgent and important, you do it.
- If the task is urgent but not important, you delegate it.
- If the task is not urgent but important, you schedule it.
- If the task is not urgent and not important, you delete it.

By creating two select properties inside the database, one of which is urgent/not urgent, and important/not important as the other, we can use a formula property to do the logic for us, giving us the appropriate result.

Creating individual formulas

Using the `if` statement we can ask a question with two answers, and in this case, we can use the `Priority` property and look for `Urgent`, which is in `" "` as it is a text string. The following line of code uses `yes` and `no` as text filler answers for now:

```
prop("Priority") == "Urgent" ? "yes" : "no"
```

But we also want to know what the importance status is to know which corner of the matrix we get as a result. This means we need a second question. Instead of asking the questions separately, we can combine them:

```
(prop("Priority") == "Urgent") ? ((prop("Importance") ==
"Important") ? "yes" : "no") : "no"
```

Now we are asking if the `Priority` is `Urgent`, and the `Importance` is `Important`. When comparing the two formulas, the `yes` answer in the first question has been turned into a question with two additional answers.

This means we now have three answers for two different questions. If `Priority` is `Urgent`, check whether `Importance` is `Important` and say yes or no, but if `Priority` is not urgent, output no.

Next, there need to be different answers for when the result is not urgent so we can repeat the same process as before by adding another question:

```
(prop("Priority") == "Urgent") ? ((prop("Importance") ==
"Important") ? "yes" : "no") : ((prop("Importance") ==
"Important") ? "yes" : "no")
```

Now there are yes or no answers for both select properties that we can use for the appropriate output:

```
(prop("Priority") == "Urgent") ? ((prop("Importance") ==
"Important") ? "DO" : "DELEGATE") : ((prop("Importance") ==
"Important") ? "SCHEDULE" : "DELETE")
```

This is now asking three different questions with four possible answers using the two select properties, but there are instances in a database where things may be blank or empty.

> **Note**
>
> When creating formulas, especially formulas with various variables and properties, considering each input type and output type will help avoid issues later.

The example in *Figure 9.1* has some added conditions at the beginning of the formula to account for some other results that may appear.

If any of the select properties are empty, the formula will not be able to answer, as we haven't given it anything to output. There are a variety of ways you could approach this, the simplest being to leave it empty, but if you want a message to be given you can use the same principles as before and add questions onto the formula to give some guidance as to the next steps.

Combining individual formulas

Combining the empty Boolean function and the and option, you can create a question that asks whether both Priority and Importance are empty, adding a message such as NEED PRIORITY AND IMPORTANCE if so:

```
(empty(prop("Priority")) and empty(prop("Importance"))) ?
"NEED PRIORITY AND IMPORTANCE" : "FINE"
```

The preceding code will do this individually, but to add that to the existing formula it needs to be added as a nested question just like the previous additions, but this time at the beginning rather than the end:

```
(empty(prop("Priority")) and empty(prop("Importance"))) ? "NEED
PRIORITY AND IMPORTANCE" : ((prop("Priority") == "Urgent") ?
((prop("Importance") == "Important") ? "DO" : "DELEGATE") :
((prop("Importance") == "Important") ? "SCHEDULE" : "DELETE"))
```

You may notice that the Fine answer to the question has been removed, as if there is nothing empty then we want the formula to work as we planned.

The other additions to the original formula in *Figure 9.1* are questions that are specific to just one select property being emptied, which was an unnecessary addition, but an example of how you can add questions and functions to customize the output.

Formula output variations

In this section, you will learn how to use properties to work with formula inputs to make the formula more dynamic and automatic when changing database information.

As previously mentioned, you can use property information in place of arguments in a formula, allowing you to have more dynamic formulas as shown in *Figure 9.2*.

Creating a Due Date formula

The Due Date formula looks at the Start Date property for the date argument, finding out the number argument from the Number property, then finding out the time argument from the Time property and using that information in the dateAdd function to create a due date. This means that by changing the Start Date, Number, or Time property information, the formula will automatically change.

Σ Due Date	🗓 Start Date	# Number	⏱ Time	+
November 1, 2021	October 31, 2021	1	days	
November 7, 2021	October 31, 2021	1	weeks	
November 30, 2021	October 31, 2021	1	months	
October 31, 2022	October 31, 2021	1	years	

```
dateAdd(prop("Start Date"), prop("Number"), prop("Time"))                    Done
```

Figure 9.2 – A Due Date formula using other properties in place of the formula arguments

> **Note**
>
> The dateAdd function uses a text string in the Time argument, which means the letters in the select property are case-sensitive. The number is also specific to the property being used for the number argument needs to be a number type to work.

This use of property argument substitution can be done in all of the formula options, meaning that you can use the interactive nature of the database views to change a formula output.

When viewing the database in the board view, the cards can be moved between groups, which will change the select property information and therefore change the formula output. *Figure 9.3* shows an example of this:

Figure 9.3 – All sections filled in the board view

And then *Figure 9.4* shows two pages in the **weeks** section, for which the Page 1 due date has changed from November 1, 2021 to November 7,2021:

Figure 9.4 – Two pages in the weeks section changing the due date output

Now let's see how to combine property substitutions and nested formulas.

Combining property substitutions and nested formulas

By combining property substitutions and nested formulas, you can create dynamic formulas with multiple outputs as shown in *Figure 9.5*:

Σ Due Date	🗓 Start Date	# Number	⊙ Time	+
November 7, 2021 👎	October 31, 2021	1	weeks	
November 7, 2021 👎	October 31, 2021	1	weeks	
November 30, 2021 👍	October 31, 2021	1	months	
October 31, 2022 👍	October 31, 2021	1	years	

```
format(dateAdd(prop("Start Date"), prop("Number"),
prop("Time"))) + ((dateAdd(prop("Start Date"), prop("Number"),
prop("Time")) > dateAdd(now(), 1, "weeks")) ? " 👍" : " 👎")     Done
```

Figure 9.5 – Combining nested formulas and property substitution using emoji outputs

The date calculation is the same but is being turned into text by using the `format` function in the first section of the formula, then being used a second time in the section half of the formula:

```
format(dateAdd(prop("Start Date"), prop("Number"),
prop("Time")))
```

The first section outputs the date as it did before but the + operator has been added to the second part of the formula:

```
+ ((dateAdd(prop("Start Date"), prop("Number"), prop("Time"))
> dateAdd(now(), 1, "weeks")) ? "👍" : "👎")
```

The second part asks if the new Due Date is more than one week in the future from the current day. If the new Due Date is more than a week into the future, a 👍 is put after the Due Date value and if it isn't then a 👎 is put instead.

> **Note**
>
> Due to the way the `concat` function and + operator work, there is no space put between output results, so inside the " " of the emoji result there is a space before the emoji, which shows up in the formula box changing the aesthetic. This could also be added to any formula using + " " + between results.

By changing what properties are used in a formula, you can use database functions and features to change the output of a formula, which could, in turn, affect filtered, sorted, or grouped views elsewhere in the workspace. This is where the creativity comes into using Notion databases.

By combining various property types, formula options, nested formula features, and property substitutions, along with using the various database features, you can manipulate the data in a database in an almost unlimited way, with some other more advanced examples in the next section.

Creating a progress bar

In this section, you will learn how you can use the formula property to roll up a `rollup` property and how you can use various formula options to create a variety of outputs using the nested formula and property substitution techniques.

When using the `rollup` property in a database, it can do calculations on any property type except a `rollup` property itself. This means that if you want to roll up a `rollup` property, you need to have a dynamic copy of that `rollup` property so that when the information is changed, it changes the calculation automatically.

Three-database setup

The example given in *Figure 9.6* shows three databases: a **Tasks** database, a **Projects** database, and a **Person** database.

Tasks

Aa Name	↗ Project	☑ Done	+
Task 1	🗋 Project 1	☑	
Task 2	🗋 Project 1	☐	
+ New			

Calculate ∨

Projects

Aa Name	↗ Person	↗ Task	!	Q Complete	Σ Complete No	+
Project 1	🗋 Danny	🗋 Task 1 🗋 Task 2		50%	50%	
+ New						

Calculate ∨

Person

Aa Name	↗ Project	Q Complete	+
Danny	🗋 Project 1	50%	
+ New			

Figure 9.6 – A three-database setup with a roll up of a rollup being done in the Person database

The **Tasks** database has a Done property, which is checked when a task is completed. The Task 1 and Task 2 pages are related to the appropriate Project relation, which in the example is Project 1.

The **relation** property connects the **Task** and **Project** databases so that the task completion percentage can be calculated in a rollup property called Complete, with *Figure 9.7* showing the **rollup** configuration:

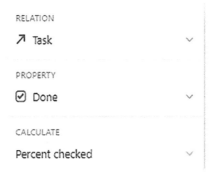

Figure 9.7 – Complete rollup configuration settings in the Projects database

This example then goes a step further and relates the **Projects** database to the **Person** database, which will allow for each person to have a rollup calculation of the projects they are working on.

The example shows Danny being related to Project 1 in the Person property of the **Project** database and in the Project property in the **Person** database. As mentioned previously, the rollup in the **Person** database cannot rollup the Complete property from the **Projects** database as it is a rollup itself, and you can't roll up a rollup.

This is where the formula property can be used by putting prop("Complete") in the formula box – it will essentially duplicate the **rollup** information from the Complete property. The formula property was then formatted to display as a percentage, using the number formatting option in the property.

Adding a relation

This new `Complete No` formula property can be used in a **rollup**, which is in the **Person** database. This also allows for other calculations to take place if more projects are added to individuals, or more tasks are added to projects, as shown in *Figure 9.8*:

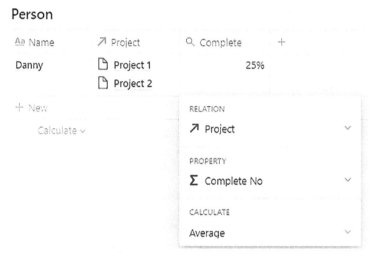

Figure 9.8 – An additional project relation being made with the rollup of a formula using the average calculation for a value

This formula can be used multiple times, duplicating information in a database to be used for other calculations for rollups or other formulas.

Visual progress bar

One example use of a rollup and formula together is in creating a visual progress bar, which is a property that uses emoji and text to help illustrate how much progress has been made as a number percentage.

Note

There are a variety of methods to create visual progress bars in a formula box giving more or fewer limitations on input and output values. The formula itself could also be done in different ways – this is just one option.

Figure 9.9 shows examples of visual progress bar options using two number properties as input values. The formulas are shown and briefly explained below with a simple step-by-step guide to a different progress bar later:

Database

Aa Name	# Done	# Total	Σ Progress Bar	Σ Progress
	10	10	☆☆☆☆☆☆☆☆☑	☑
	9	10	✖●●●●●○○●●○	◉
	8	10	✖●●●●○○●○○	◉
	7	10	✖●●●●○○○○○	○
	6	10	✖●●●●○○○○○	○
	5	10	✖●●●●○○○○○	◉
	4	10	✖●●●○○○○○○	◉
	3	10	✖●●○○○○○○○	◉
	2	10	✖●○○○○○○○○	◉
	1	10	✖○○○○○○○○○	✖
	0	10	✖✖✖✖✖✖✖✖✖✖	✖
		10	✖✖✖✖✖✖✖✖✖✖	✖
	10		✖✖✖✖✖✖✖✖✖✖	✖

Figure 9.9 – Visual progress bars being calculated from two number properties

Let's look at the formula code for the `Progress` property:

```
(prop("Total") - prop("Done") == 1) ? "●" : ((prop("Done") >=
prop("Total")) ? "☑" : (or(floor(prop("Done") / prop("Total"))
* 10) == 0, floor(prop("Done") /
prop("Total") * 10) == 1) ? "✖" : (or(floor(prop("Done") /
prop("Total") * 10) == 2, floor(prop("Done") /
prop("Total") * 10) == 3) ? "●" : (or(floor(prop("Done") /
prop("Total") * 10) == 4, floor(prop("Done") /
prop("Total") * 10) == 5) ? "●" : (or(floor(prop("Done") /
prop("Total") * 10) == 6, floor(prop("Done") /
prop("Total") * 10) == 7) ? "◌" : (or(floor(prop("Done") /
prop("Total") * 10) == 8, floor(prop("Done") /
prop("Total") * 10) == 9) ? "●" : "✖"))))))
```

The code `prop("Done")/prop("Total")` is repeated multiple times, as this is where the percentage is calculated from the two number properties, `Done` and `Total`.

The first question in the formula asks if there is 1 remaining, in which case it displays a green circle, otherwise it will ask the next question on whether the Done value is greater than or equal to the Total value, and if it is it will display a checkmark. If not, it will ask the next question. These questions continue throughout the formula until every possible situation is checked.

The Progress Bar formula code looks different in that it uses the replaceAll function instead:

```
(prop("Done") >= prop("Total")) ? "★★★★★★★★★☑" :
((prop("Total") == 1) ? "✗●●●●●●●● " :
(or(or(prop("Done") == 0, empty(prop("Done"))),
empty(prop("Total"))) ? "✗✗✗✗✗✗✗✗✗✗" :
(replaceAll(replaceAll(replaceAll(replaceAll(replaceAll(slice
("1223344556", 0, floor(prop("Done") / prop("Total") * 10)),
"1", "✗"), "2", "●"), "3", "●"), "4", " "), "5", "●") +
replaceAll(slice("9999999999", 0, 10 - floor(prop("Done") /
prop("Total") * 10)), "9", " ")))))
```

Instead of asking multiple questions and getting answers for each question, this formula has a couple of answers sliced in length to show the appropriate answer.

If Done is greater than or equal to Total it will show ★★★★★★★★★☑.
If Total is equal to 1 then it will show ✗●●●●●●●● .

If Done equals 0, or either Done or Total is empty, it will show ✗✗✗✗✗✗✗✗✗✗. The rest of the formula uses the replaceAll and slice functions, which we will go through now.

> **Note**
>
> The following example is a simplified version of the preceding example above using the replaceAll and slice functions. The preceding example also uses a rollup for the calculation instead of two number properties to make the formula shorter.

The slice function

Returning to the database from earlier in the chapter, we have Tasks and Projects with percentages of completion. To change the length of a text string we can use the slice function and create a progress bar. You can use any letter or symbol in a slice function, but for this use case, we will have ten x characters in a string, each x representing 10% as shown in *Figure 9.10*:

Projects

Aa Name	Σ Slice	↗ Task	Q Percentage
Project 1	xxxxxxxxxx	🗋 Task 1 🗋 Task 2	50%
Project 2	xxxxxxxxxx	🗋 Task 3	0%
+ New	slice("xxxxxxxxxx", 0)		

Figure 9.10 – The slice function creating a progress bar using x characters

So, at this point, there is a string of ten x characters in a formula box, and a relation property called `Task` from the `Projects` to the `Tasks`, which is being used to create a rollup property called `Percentage` that calculates how many tasks have been completed.

The 0 in the `slice` formula is where the text string is going to start being shown, and a second number will show where it ends. In this case, we only need one number to show the percentage of completion in 10% intervals.

rollup property

`50%` is shown in the rollup and half of our progress bar will contain 5 x characters as we used 10 x characters in the `slice` function. This means that the number in the `slice` function should be five, which we can put in using the property information, but as the rollup is in percentages it will be inputted as 0.5, so we need to *10 to get the number 5 that we need. This is shown in *Figure 9.11*, displaying five x characters for `Project 1` due to the 50% in the `Percentage` property.

Projects

Aa Name	Σ Slice	↗ Task	Q Percentage
Project 1	xxxxx	🗋 Task 1 🗋 Task 2	50%
Project 2	xxxxxxxxxx	🗋 Task 3	0%
+ New	slice("xxxxxxxxxx", prop("Percentage") * 10)		

Figure 9.11 – Using the rollup property in the slice function

replaceAll function

To change the look of the progress bar we can use the `replaceAll` function to replace all of the x characters in the bar with something else. Alone, the code would show `replaceAll(prop("Percent"), "x", "●")`, which would work in a separate formula property, but we want it all together, so we can combine it as shown in *Figure 9.12*:

Projects

Aa Name	Σ Slice	↗ Task	Q Percentage	+
Project 1	⦾⦾⦿⦾⦾	🗋 Task 1 🗋 Task 2	50%	
Project 2	⦾⦾⦿⦾⦾⦾⦾⦾⦾⦾	🗋 Task 3	0%	
+ New	replaceAll(slice("xxxxxxxxxx", prop("Percentage") * 10), "x",			
Calculate ∨	"●")			Done

Figure 9.12 – Using the replaceAll and slice functions together

Progress bar with a percentage

This section helps to create a progress bar for the percentage of project completion. To create the progress for the percentage that has been completed, we need to take the percentage value away from 100%, which in this progress bar is 10. *Figure 9.13* shows the completed percentage in red and the percentage left in green:

Projects

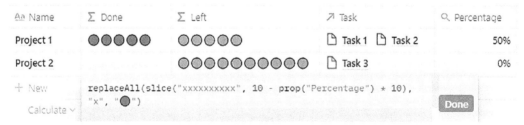

Aa Name	Σ Done	Σ Left	↗ Task	Q Percentage
Project 1	⦾⦾⦿⦾⦾	⦾⦾⦿⦾⦾	🗋 Task 1 🗋 Task 2	50%
Project 2		⦾⦾⦿⦾⦾⦾⦾⦾⦾⦾	🗋 Task 3	0%
+ New	replaceAll(slice("xxxxxxxxxx", 10 - prop("Percentage") * 10),			
Calculate ∨	"x", "●")			Done

Figure 9.13 – Completed and remaining percentage calculations in different formula boxes

When combining the two sections and adding the `Percentage` value on the end in text format with a space beforehand and a `%` sign afterward, you get the progress bar shown in *Figure 9.14*:

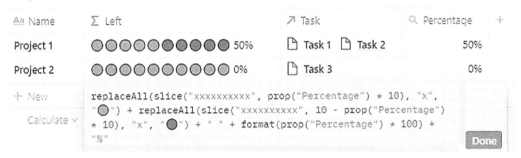

Figure 9.14 – Progress bar with percentage formatting on the end

As you can see, there are various ways to get a similar output in a formula property using multiple questions, various formulas, and different input values. The use of the formula property can therefore be as simple or as complex as you want.

In the next chapter, the techniques explained in this chapter will be used and combined with the principles of creating contextual dashboards to build an integrated and advanced formula.

Summary

In this chapter, you learned how to combine different formula options to create nested formulas with a variety of questions giving multiple output answers. You used different property options to change the input options and interaction of information with the formula property. And you learned how to create a visual progress bar using a formula property in three different styles using different input values, formula options, and formula techniques.

Now that you can create pages and databases and use advanced database features when working inside a Notion workspace, it is time to talk about strategies for creating Notion workflows in the next chapter.

Section 3: Creating Advanced Workflows

In this section, you will learn how to create fully functioning workflows in your Notion workspace. This section contains the following chapters:

- *Chapter 10, Creating an Action Management Contextual Dashboard and Workflow*
- *Chapter 11, Using API Integration and Add-On Options*
- *Chapter 12, Note Taking, Knowledge Management, and a Wiki Example*
- *Chapter 13, Other Example Use Cases*

10
Creating an Action Management Contextual Dashboard and Workflow

In this chapter, we will look at how to create pages in Notion that can be used as dashboards to show specific information in linked database views with formulas relating to task and project management. This can then extend into other pages in the workspace to provide high-level contextual dashboards and lower-level dashboards for various users.

In this chapter, we're going to cover the following topics:

- Master databases
- Contextual dashboards

- Using database templates in workflows
- Creating an advanced countdown formula

You will learn about the best practices for creating and storing information in databases while creating views from that stored data. You will learn how to combine the principles of pages aesthetics, linked database views, and database template features to create quicker workflows. Finally, this chapter will teach you how to take a contextual dashboard, isolate an issue, and use a formula to solve the issue.

Master databases

In this section, you will learn how the use of master databases can save time, increase efficiency, and save a lot of headaches when the workspace starts to increase in size or increase in user numbers. This section will be mostly directed toward the philosophy and framework of use, rather than functional features, and gaining an understanding of this Notion terminology alongside the database features will be helpful.

> **Note**
> There are nuances that have been laid out in the upcoming sections, but these guidelines can be used for the majority of use cases.

When creating databases in Notion, one of the first questions you will need to answer is whether to create multiple databases for the information you want to store. For example, if you are looking to keep track of tasks, actions, tickets, or issues for yourself or members of the business/team, you could take various approaches.

Some of the common options are to create a database per team member, a database per department, a database per type of issue, or a database per group of tasks. When considering the amount of metadata that would be included in the properties of those databases, you could find that much of it will be duplicated, meaning that the information could be put into one overall database that contains different metadata.

A master task database example

A good example of this is a master task database. The master database refers to one database that holds all of the information of that type and then uses linked database views with filters, sorts, and groups to make the view specific to your needs. *Figure 10.1* shows an example of a master task database with various property types to help you to identify tasks with contextual metadata:

Tasks

Aa Name	📅 Due Date	Q Project Due	⚓ Person	☑ Done	↗ Project	Q Project Manager	Q Department	Σ Countdown
Record Video	October 27, 2021	November 7, 2021	🔵 Danny Hatcher 🔵 Jonathan Stewart	✅	📄 Video Project	🔵 Danny Hatcher	Marketing	🔵 ON TIME
Edit Video	October 30, 2021	November 7, 2021	🔵 Jonathan Stewart	☐	📄 Video Project	🔵 Danny Hatcher	Marketing	🔵 ON TIME
Send proposal	November 8, 2021	November 14, 2021	🔵 Danny Hatcher	☐	📄 Client Proposal	🔵 Danny Hatcher	Sales	🔵 OVERDUE
Interview	November 2, 2021	November 8, 2021	🔵 Jonathan Stewart	☐	📄 Recruitement	🔵 Jonathan Stewart	HR	🔵 ON TIME

Figure 10.1 – A master task database showing different property types

The task database is for all task-related information, including any small action that needs to be taken:

- The **Name** property describes the task.

- The **Due Date** property gives a date for the task to be completed.

- The **Project Due** property is a rollup property from the **Project** relation property, which shows when the project that the task is related to is due.

One example, as shown in *Figure 10.1*, is the Record Video task, which is related to **Video Project** in the **Project** relation property; the **Project Due** column is showing **November 7, 2021**, as that is when the Video Project task is due.

As it is a rollup property, that particular date is coming from the related database, which is shown in *Figure 10.2*:

Projects   + Add a view

Aa Name	📅 Date	Σ Countdown	⚓ Project Manager	Σ Progress	⊙ Department	↗ Task
Video Project	October 29, 2021 → November 7, 2021	1 W 2 D ✖	🔵 Danny Hatcher	🔵🔵🔵🔵🔵🔵🔵🔵🔵🔵 50%	Marketing	📄 Record Video 📄 Edit Video
Client Proposal	October 11, 2021 → November 14, 2021	3 W 6 D ✖	🔵 Danny Hatcher	🔵🔵🔵🔵🔵🔵🔵🔵🔵🔵 0%	Sales	📄 Send proposal
Recruitement	November 8, 2021	Tomorrow ⚠	🔵 Jonathan Stewart	🔵🔵🔵🔵🔵🔵🔵🔵🔵🔵 0%	HR	📄 Interview

Figure 10.2 – A master projects database showing different property types

From the preceding screenshots, notice the following:

- The **Person** property in the **Tasks** database is showing who is responsible for that task.

- The **Done** checkbox indicates whether the task has been completed or not.

- The **Project Manager** and **Department** properties are both rollup properties from the **Projects** database going through the **Project** relation property.

- The **Project Manager** person property in the **Projects** database is being rolled up in the **Tasks** database through the relation property, in the same way as the **Department** select property.

The **Tasks** database also has a formula, `(now() < prop("Due Date")) ? "`⬤`"` `OVERDUE" : "`⬤` ON TIME"`, which offers a visual aid to help you with prioritization. It shows you whether the task is overdue or on time in the **Countdown** property.

There is also a formula in the **Projects** database, called **Progress**, which is very similar to the advanced formula shared earlier. It uses a rollup property of the **Done** checkbox from the **Tasks** database to calculate how close to completion the project is.

Figure 10.2 indicates that the `Video Project` task has been **50%** completed in the **Progress** property. Additionally, in *Figure 10.1*, `Video Project` appears in the **Project** relation property for `Record Video` and `Edit Video`, with `Record Video` being completed, as signified by the checked **Done** property.

So, one out of two tasks has been completed, with 50% showing in the **Progress** property, which is correct.

Using these two master databases, one for tasks and one for projects, any large or small action can be accounted for.

A **task** instance can be added with or without a date, project relation, or any piece of property information. All of it will be stored in the same database, meaning that it can be found in any linked database view.

A **project** instance can be added with or without tasks. However, when tasks are added, all the project information can be seen through the relation and rollup combination. This means that departments can have filtered views of their projects, but project managers can still keep track of all necessary projects. Top-level views and granular views can be made without the worry of losing or duplicating information.

Creating these powerful contextual dashboards is now much easier with the master databases set up.

Contextual dashboards

In this section, you will learn how to utilize the master database setup to create customized contextual dashboards using linked databases. There will be various examples shown using various filters, sorts, groups, and viewing differences to illustrate some of the combinations that are available. This is useful to understand, as each person is likely to have different needs from the information that is stored, and learning how to create contextual dashboards will open up much of Notion's database power.

A potential setup configuration

Using the same master databases from the previous section, *Figure 10.3* shows a potential setup configuration:

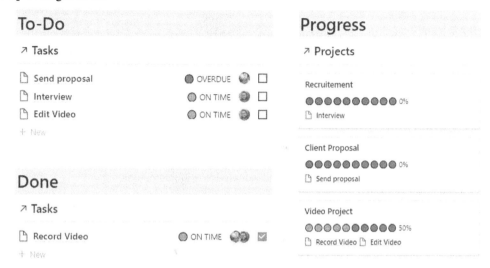

Figure 10.3 – A list and gallery contextual dashboard

As linked database views don't allow for a name change, the **Tasks** database can be seen twice in *Figure 10.3*, as there are two different linked database views on the same page, with one linked database view of the **Projects** database.

The **To-Do**, **Done**, and **Progress** sections are heading blocks with an orange-colored background:

1. The **Tasks** view underneath the **To-Do** heading is a linked database view with a filter for the **Done** property, to show items that are unchecked. Additionally, it sorts those pages for the **Due Date** property in descending order. This information can be viewed in *Figure 10.1* showing the property metadata. This particular view is in a list view that only shows the **Countdown** formula property, the **Person** property, and the **Done** checkbox property. In this view, the checkbox can be clicked on, meaning that the page will disappear due to the filter, which is where the **Done** view comes into use.

2. Underneath the **Done** heading, there is a second linked database view of the **Tasks** database, which is also in the list view showing the same three properties, sorted in the same way. Here, the difference is that the filter for that view is for the **Done** checkbox property to be checked. This means that when a task is checked, it will appear in the **Done** filtered view and will disappear from the **To-Do** filtered view. As the checkbox can be unchecked, you can move a task from **Done** to **To-Do** by simply clicking on the box.

The reason this becomes extremely powerful is that all the information is from the same master database. This means that you can have various versions with different filters, sorts, and groups, but if the task is checked anywhere, the views will respond appropriately.

3. The **Progress** heading can be found above the **Project** linked database view. This is a gallery database view with no filters or sorting options. The gallery has no card preview and shows the **Progress** formula property, the **Task** relation property, and the **Name** property, which can be seen in *Figure 10.2*.

> **Note**
>
> A linked database can be deleted with no repercussions to any other view or piece of information. This means that as long as the master database (that is, the original database) is stored in the workspace, a linked database can be deleted and recreated at any time.

The dashboard after completing the Interview task

The database properties can interact within the list view by simply clicking on a **Done** checkbox in the **Tasks** database. When I signify that I have completed a task, which will automatically update the page, information will be sent from the relation property to the rollup property in the **Projects** database, updating the formula property. This action of clicking on a checkbox will lead to *Figure 10.4*:

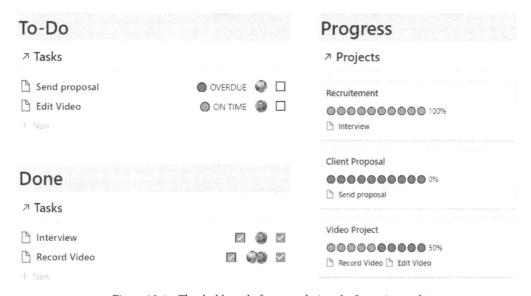

Figure 10.4 – The dashboard after completing the Interview task

Now, as you can see in *Figure 10.4*, there are two pages in the **Done** section and two pages in the **To-Do** section. Additionally, note that the progress bar of the **Recruitment** project has gone up to 100%, as the information is updated automatically. There was also a small change made to the formula's **Countdown** property to show a green checkmark when a task is completed by using an `if` statement: `prop("Done") ? "✅" : ((now() < prop("Due Date")) ? "🔴 OVERDUE" : "🔴 ON TIME")`.

Example 1 – two linked database views

The example in *Figure 10.5* uses the calendar and table database view combination. Note that the table's **To-Schedule** section, which is filtered by **Due Date**, is empty. This allows us to see a list of tasks that we need to schedule. We can remove the task from the table list, and drag it onto the calendar to automatically add the date:

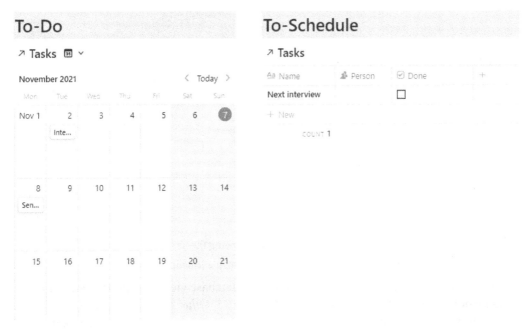

Figure 10.5 – Two linked database views of the Tasks database, one as a calendar and the other as a table

Now, let's explore another example.

Example 2 – two linked database views

A different example in *Figure 10.6* shows the **Tasks** database in a board database view filtered by unchecked tasks, showing the **Name** property, the **Done** checkbox property, and the **Due Date** property while being grouped by the **Person** property. The **Projects** database view uses the timeline view to see when a project will be finished, showing the **Name** property, the **Department** select property, the **Percentage** rollup property, and the **Project Manager** person property:

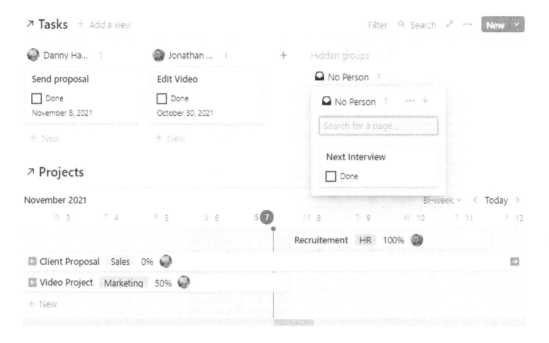

Figure 10.6 – Two linked database views, showing the Tasks database in
a board view and the Projects database in a timeline view

There is an almost unlimited combination of linked database views, properties, and filters, with some popular examples being shared in *Chapter 13, Other Example Use Cases*. Some of the dashboards that we have just explained are useful because of how they can be used in a workflow. Templates inside a database can also be manipulated in a similar way to create contextual workflows. This will be covered next.

Using database templates in advanced workflows

In this section, we will go through some important topics such as using templates in a database and creating contextual dashboards inside a database template (to help with the creative workflow). In this section, we will use the auto-filter feature, the linked database feature, and the self-referencing filter. Additionally, we will require some backend knowledge that will be introduced later in this section.

Database template configuration can be extremely powerful when used in certain use cases, as it can save time when creating dashboards and pages but also remove some of the human errors that could appear when adding in new information.

> **Note**
>
> In this section, the techniques that I have used are not necessarily needed for using templates in Notion. I have used these techniques to demonstrate a use case that combines many database features.

Using the same **Projects** database and **Tasks** database as the previous sections, a database template can be created in the **Projects** database, as shown in *Figure 10.7*:

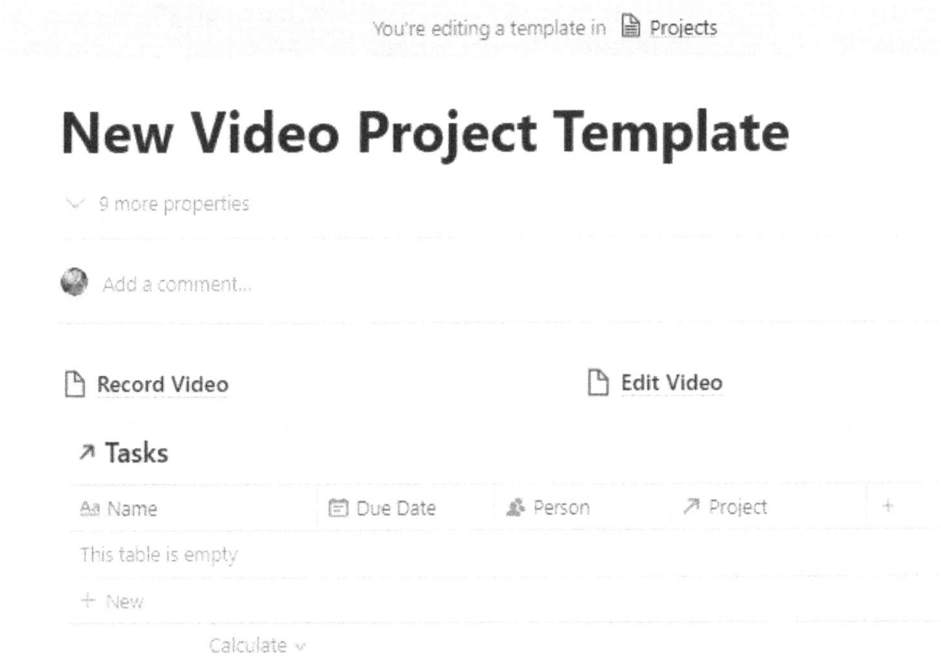

You're editing a template in 📄 Projects

New Video Project Template

⌄ 9 more properties

🌐 Add a comment...

📄 **Record Video**   📄 **Edit Video**

↗ **Tasks**

Aa Name	📅 Due Date	👤 Person	↗ Project	+
This table is empty				
+ New				

Calculate ⌄

Figure 10.7 – A database template page in the Projects database

The new database template page still has all the properties, but they are just hidden (as indicated by the **9 more properties** toggle). There is also a linked database view of the **Tasks** database on the page, which has been filtered with a self-referencing filter using the **Project** relation property, as shown in *Figure 10.8*:

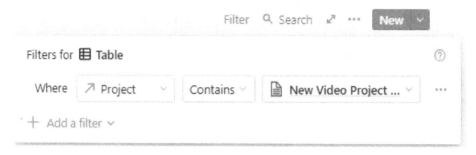

Figure 10.8 – The self-referencing filter in the task-linked database view

Therefore, the **Tasks** database is showing that it is empty, as the filter is only for the template page. In addition to the linked database view, there are two blank page blocks called **Record video** and **Edit video**.

The reason they are called pages is so that when the template is used, we can drag and drop the pages into the linked database, turning those blank pages into blank database pages. This is useful because they are already named, and with the automatic filter feature, when the template is used, the linked **Tasks** database will be filtered by the new project (meaning that the tasks will filter automatically and add a relation).

A new database page example

To demonstrate an example of this, *Figure 10.9* shows a new page in the **Projects** database using the **New Video Project Template** option:

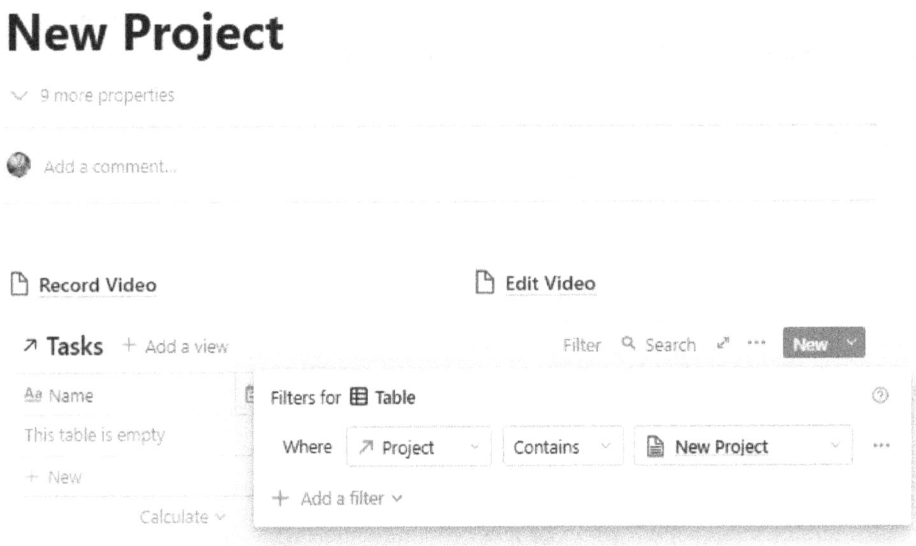

New Project

⌄ 9 more properties

🔵 Add a comment...

📄 Record Video   📄 Edit Video

↗ **Tasks** + Add a view   Filter 🔍 Search ⤢ ··· **New** ⌄

Aa Name   📋 Filters for ⊞ Table   ⓘ

This table is empty   Where ↗ Project ⌄   Contains ⌄   📄 New Project ⌄ ···

+ New

        Calculate ⌄   + Add a filter ⌄

Figure 10.9 – A new database page in the project database after using
the New Video Project Template option

As you can see in *Figure 10.9*, the filter is automatic for the **New Project** page due to the
self-referencing filter. The **Record Video** and **Edit Video** pages are there to be dragged in,
as shown in *Figure 10.10*:

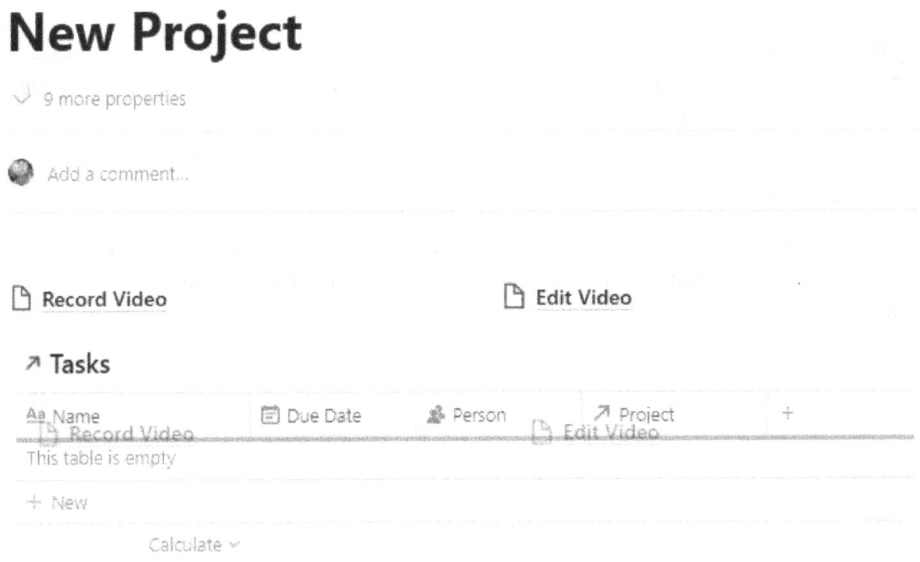

New Project

⌄ 9 more properties

🔵 Add a comment...

📄 Record Video   📄 Edit Video

↗ **Tasks**

Aa Name   📅 Due Date   🐾 Person   ↗ Project   +
   📄 Record Video   📄 Edit Video
This table is empty

+ New

        Calculate ⌄

Figure 10.10 – After highlighting the two pages with the mouse,
they are being dragged into the linked database view

Once they have been dropped into the database, the auto-filter feature will create a relation from both tasks to the **New Project** page, as shown in *Figure 10.11*:

New Project

ⵠ 9 more properties

🔵 Add a comment...

↗ **Tasks**

Aa Name	📅 Due Date	👤 Person	↗ Project	+
Record Video		🔵 Danny Hatcher 🔵 Jonathan Stewart	📄 New Project	
Edit Video		🔵 Jonathan Stewart	📄 New Project	
+ New				

Calculate ⌄

Figure 10.11 – The auto-filter feature creating the project relation for both of the task pages

This means that as the relation has automatically been created, the progress bar formula property and all the other rollup properties will work as soon as the pages are dragged into the database. This also allows multiple relations to be made at once.

You might also notice, in *Figure 10.11*, that the **Person** property has been automatically populated. This is because, during the process of creating the template, the pages were moved into the database. Property information was added, which, in this case, consisted of the people in the **Person** property. Then, the pages are taken out of the database as blank pages again, but the property metadata information was saved to the page.

In *Figure 10.12*, you can see that some of the pages have metadata inside them, as they have been added to the database, while others don't due to the lack of saved metadata within the page:

New Video Project Template

∨ 9 more properties

🌐 Add a comment...

↗ **Tasks**

Aa Name		📅 Due Date	👤 Person	↗ Project	+
Record Video			🟢 Danny Hatcher		
Edit Video			🟢 Jonathan Stewa		
Edit Video	↗ OPEN		🟢 Jonathan Stewa	📄 New Project	
Record Video			🟢 Danny Hatcher	📄 New Project	
Next Interview					
Interview		November 2, 2021	🟢 Jonathan Stewa	📄 Recruitement	
Send proposal		November 8, 2021	🟢 Danny Hatcher	📄 Client Proposal	
Edit Video		October 30, 2021	🟢 Jonathan Stewa	📄 Video Project	
Record Video		October 27, 2021	🟢 Danny Hatcher	📄 Video Project	

+ New

Figure 10.12 – A database template page with a linked database

In *Figure 10.12*, you will see **Record Video** and **Edit Video** listed in the database twice. One version of these pages will have information in the **Project** relation property going to the **New Project** page, which are the pages that we just created. The other two pages don't have any relation as there is no filter on this database. Once all the property information has been added to the pages, you can drag them out of the database view using the ⁞⁞ menu option.

Note

There is no restriction on the number or types of filters you can add to the linked database view, nor is there a limit to the amount of property information that you can add to each page.

Once you have dragged the pages out of the linked database view, they will look like regular pages, as shown in *Figure 10.13*, if you put them into columns:

New Video Project Template

⌄ 9 more properties

⬤ Add a comment...

📄 Record Video   📄 Edit Video

↗ Tasks

Aa Name	📅 Due Date	👥 Person	↗ Project	+
Edit Video		⬤ Jonathan Stewa	📄 New Project	
Record Video		⬤ Danny Hatcher	📄 New Project	
Next Interview				
Interview	November 2, 2021	⬤ Jonathan Stewa	📄 Recruitement	
Send proposal	November 8, 2021	⬤ Danny Hatcher	📄 Client Proposal	
Edit Video	October 30, 2021	⬤ Jonathan Stewa	📄 Video Project	
Record Video	October 27, 2021	⬤ Danny Hatcher	📄 Video Project	

Figure 10.13 – A database template page with a linked database and two blank pages

After adding the filter once the pages are out, the template is set up and ready to use.

This type of configuration can be useful for repeated tasks that you do for a project, a repeated set of actions, or repeated pages that need to be created with information added.

One thing to bear in mind is that you can also have different database views, sorts, groups, and additional property information in the template This means that you could set up a template that plans out a month in advance by dragging some pages into a set of filtered database views.

Now that there are master databases with linked database views being used in the database templates with self-referencing automatic filters, we can start to further customize the created contextual dashboards with more specific formulas.

Creating an advanced countdown formula

In this section, we will go through an advanced formula countdown that has various elements in which to show specific information. This section will illustrate how granular you can go with the formulas you use and how you can use some of the known mathematical functions to create an output that can be customized to your needs.

> **Note**
>
> This formula is an expanded version of the one shown in the task database from the previous section. This demonstration is only for explanation purposes and is not needed in your workspace to use Notion effectively.

Figure 10.14 shows a date property, called **Date**, and a formula property, called **Deadline**, in the **Projects** table database view:

Projects

Aa Name	🗓 Date	Σ Deadline
Video Project	October 29, 2021 → November 7, 2021	4 D ✖
Client Proposal	October 11, 2021 → November 14, 2021	3 D ☑
Client Proposal	November 11, 2021 → December 15, 2021	4 W 6 D ☑
Recruitement	November 8, 2021 → November 11, 2021	Today ⚠
Video Project	November 1, 2021 → November 12, 2021	Tomorrow ⚠
Article Project	October 30, 2021 → November 10, 2021	Yesterday ⚠
📄 New Project		Date Needed ❗

Figure 10.14 – The projects database view with the date and formula properties

The formula in the **Deadline** property signifies whether the end date of the date property is before today by displaying an ✕ emoji or after today's date by displaying a ✅ emoji with the calculated number of weeks and days remaining. Additionally, it shows a ⚠ emoji with either the text of **Today**, **Tomorrow**, or **Yesterday** to signify the relative deadline. Then, it gives a **Date Needed** ❗ warning if the **Date** property is empty. When changing the formatting in the **Date** property to relative, as shown in *Figure 10.15*, the dates change. However, they don't give a countdown, which some people might want, which is where the formula property comes in handy:

Projects

Aa Name	🗓 Date	Σ Deadline	+
Video Project	October 29, 2021 → Sunday	4 D ✕	
Client Proposal	October 11, 2021 → Next Sunday	3 D ✅	
Client Proposal	Today → December 15, 2021	4 W 6 D ✅	
Recruitement	Monday → Today	Today ⚠	
Video Project	November 1, 2021 → Tomorrow	Tomorrow ⚠	
Article Project	October 30, 2021 → Yesterday	Yesterday ⚠	
📄 New Project		Date Needed ❗	

Figure 10.15 – The Projects database with the date property format changed to relative

The preceding formula uses no new techniques or functions, but it does introduce you to different combinations. The first thing we want to do is have a message when the **Date** property is empty, which can be done using the `empty(prop("Date"))  ?  "Date Needed❗"   :` code followed by what to do when there is a date in the property.

> **Note**
>
> Each section of code will be left with an open argument, as all the sections will be put together in the end to create one long formula. This means that if you want to check any part of the formula, you can put something after the `:` character in `""`, making sure that it is a text string output.

Selecting the date formula output

As there is an extremely large number of dates that can be put into the date property, I prefer to address the outputs in groups. Before we start creating the output, we need to decide what input we want to use, as this date property has two different dates. In this case, we want to use the second date as that is the deadline, so we will use the `end()` function instead of just `prop("date")`.

As the `now()` formula includes a timestamp, we can't use that for comparison against the date property directly, so we will use the `formatDate()` formula to make the date property and the `now()` formula look the same for an accurate comparison.

In this example, I am using DMY to output the dates by day, month, and year:

```
(formatDate(end(prop("Date")), "DMY") == formatDate(now(),
 "DMY")) ? "Today !" :
```

With yesterday's and tomorrow's calculations, we need to look at a comparison from the date property and `now()`, and determine whether it is one day before or one day after today. The code for yesterday, `(dateBetween(end(prop("Date")), now(), "days") == -1) ? "Yesterday !" :`, is looking for a difference of -1, as that is one day before today. The tomorrow code is slightly unexpected, as it needs to look for 0:

```
(dateBetween(end(prop("Date")), now(), "days") == 0) ?
 "Tomorrow !" :.
```

This is because the `dateBetween` formula is looking at the days. But the `now()` formula is also outputting a timestamp, as the day cut-off is 00:00. The additional time during the day is making the formula remove the current day from the calculation as it is not a full day, making each calculation off by 1 for this specific countdown.

Due to this little difference in calculations using the `dateBetween` formula, the overdue and upcoming sections will need to be separated.

To start the upcoming section, we need to check whether the date is before today's date using this code: `(dateBetween(end(prop("Date")), now(), "days") > 0) ?`. If it is false, it will direct the formula to the overdue section.

If the date is before today's date, we need to work out what sort of output we are looking to show, and for this formula, we want the difference in the number of days and weeks to be displayed with an emoji. This means that instead of showing 7 days, we want to show 0 days and 1 week, as they will be outputted together.

We can check the difference in days, and see whether it is 7 days, in which case, we can give an output of 0, as follows:

```
(dateBetween(end(prop("Date")), now(), "days") % 7 >= 6) ? 0 :
```

Here, % is giving remainders after dividing by 7. This means that if the remainder is 6, it will be on the same day of the week, as the timestamp pushes that day forward.

If the day is the same, then we want the number of weeks to be shown, so we ask the following question:

```
(dateBetween(end(prop("Date")), now(), "days") % 6)) == 0) ?
```

Then, we give the difference in the number of weeks using this formula:

```
(dateBetween(end(prop("Date")), now(), "weeks") + 1)
```

If the difference in the number of weeks is 0, then we don't need a week value as there will be a day value that is calculated using this formula:

```
dateBetween(end(prop("Date")), now(), "weeks")) == 0) ? "" :
```

This means that if there is a difference of 0 weeks, no number for this will be displayed, but it will still show the difference in the number of days.

Now that we have the outputs for whether there are 0 days or 0 weeks, we can use some of the formulas again to create an output for all other instances where there is a day value. This is formatted in a text string format, as follows:

```
((((dateBetween(end(prop("Date")), now(), "days") % 6 >= 6)
? 0 : (dateBetween(end(prop("Date")), now(), "days") % 6)) ==
0) ? (dateBetween(end(prop("Date")), now(), "weeks") + 1) :
 dateBetween(end(prop("Date")), now(), "weeks"))
```

This is so that it can be combined with + " W " afterward as a visual aid.

Following this, we need to add the day's calculation, and as this goes beyond 1 week, we can't use %6 anymore. Now we need to use %7, which would have worked earlier on in the formula, but the additional length wasn't necessary. That is a decision you will need to make when creating formulas with calculations: what numbers to use, what syntax to use, and how you want the formula to be laid out.

So, again, you can check for the same day. This time, use %7 with the following code:

```
(dateBetween(end(prop("Date")), now(), "days") % 7 + 1 >= 7) ?
0 :.
```

So, if the number of days is the same, it will output nothing. However, if the number of days is different, it will output the difference in days using this code:

```
(dateBetween(end(prop("Date")), now(), "days") % 7 + 1)) == 0)
? "" : (format((dateBetween(end(prop("Date")), now(), "days")
% 7 + 1 >= 7) ? 0 : (dateBetween(end(prop("Date")), now(),
"days") % 7 + 1))
```

At this point, we can add the d + " D")) and the + " ✅") emoji, which completes the upcoming section:

```
(dateBetween(end(prop("Date")), now(), "days") > 0) ?
((((((dateBetween(end(prop("Date")), now(), "days") % 6 >= 6)
? 0 : (dateBetween(end(prop("Date")), now(), "days") % 6)) ==
0) ? (dateBetween(end(prop("Date")), now(), "weeks") + 1) :
dateBetween(end(prop("Date")), now(), "weeks")) == 0) ? "" :
(format((((dateBetween(end(prop("Date")), now(), "days") % 6 >=
6) ? 0 : (dateBetween(end(prop("Date")), now(), "days") % 6))
== 0) ? (dateBetween(end(prop("Date")), now(), "weeks") + 1) :
dateBetween(end(prop("Date")), now(), "weeks")) + " W ")) +
((((dateBetween(end(prop("Date")), now(), "days") % 7 + 1 >= 7)
? 0 : (dateBetween(end(prop("Date")), now(), "days") % 7 + 1))
== 0) ? "" : (format((dateBetween(end(prop("Date")), now(),
"days") % 7 + 1 >= 7) ? 0 : (dateBetween(end(prop("Date")),
now(), "days") % 7 + 1)) + " D")) + " ✅") :
```

The upcoming section doesn't have any issues with `dateBetween`, making this section much shorter, and it doesn't need to account for anything upcoming.

In this check for the same day, `((dateBetween(end(prop("Date")), now(), "weeks") == 0) ? (format(abs(dateBetween(end(prop("Date")), now(), "days") % 7)) + " D")` :, we are being asked if there is no week difference, and if there isn't, it will output the day difference.

If the week difference is 0, then it will output the difference using this code:

```
((dateBetween(end(prop("Date")), now(), "days") % 7 == 0) ?
(format(abs(dateBetween(end(prop("Date")), now(), "weeks"))) +
" W").
```

If the difference doesn't equal 0, then a new piece of code

`((format(abs(dateBetween(end(prop("Date")), now(), "weeks"))) + " W ")` is added to the days difference, which is `format((dateBetween(end(prop("Date")), now(), "days") % 7 + 1 >= 7) ? 0 : abs(dateBetween(end(prop("Date")), now(), "days") % 7)) + " D")))`. This is displayed with the cross at the end, `+ " ✖":`

```
((dateBetween(end(prop("Date")), now(), "weeks") == 0) ?
(format(abs(dateBetween(end(prop("Date")), now(), "days") % 7))
+ " D") : ((dateBetween(end(prop("Date")), now(), "days") % 7
== 0) ? (format(abs(dateBetween(end(prop("Date")), now(),
"weeks"))) + " W") : (format(abs(dateBetween(end(prop("Date")),
now(), "weeks"))) + " W " + format((dateBetween(end(prop
("Date")), now(), "days") % 7 + 1 >= 7) ? 0 : abs(dateBetween
(end(prop("Date")), now(), "days") % 7)) + " D"))) + " ✖"
```

Figure 10:16 shows the **Upcoming** formula, the **Overdue** formula, and the completed **Deadline** formula separated for reference if the **Upcoming** formula has "no" at the end:

Projects

Aa Name	🗓 Date	Σ Overdue	Σ Upcoming	Σ Deadline
	December 2, 2021	2 W 0 D ✖	2 W ☑	2 W ☑
	November 25, 2021	1 W 0 D ✖	1 W ☑	1 W ☑
	November 21, 2021	1 W 2 D ✖	1 W 3 D ☑	1 W 3 D ☑
	November 20, 2021	1 W 1 D ✖	1 W 2 D ☑	1 W 2 D ☑
	November 19, 2021	1 W ✖	1 W 1 D ☑	1 W 1 D ☑
	Next Thursday	6 D ✖	1 W ☑	1 W ☑
	Next Wednesday	5 D ✖	6 D ☑	6 D ☑
	Next Tuesday	4 D ✖	5 D ☑	5 D ☑
	Next Monday	3 D ✖	4 D ☑	4 D ☑
	Next Sunday	2 D ✖	3 D ☑	3 D ☑
	Saturday	1 D ✖	2 D ☑	2 D ☑
	Tomorrow	0 D ✖	no	Tomorrow ⚠
	Today	0 D ✖	no	Today ⚠
	Yesterday	1 D ✖	no	Yesterday ⚠
	Tuesday	2 D ✖	no	2 D ✖
	Monday	3 D ✖	no	3 D ✖
	Sunday	4 D ✖	no	4 D ✖
	Last Saturday	5 D ✖	no	5 D ✖
	Last Friday	6 D ✖	no	6 D ✖
	Last Thursday	1 W ✖	no	1 W ✖
	November 3, 2021	1 W 1 D ✖	no	1 W 1 D ✖
	November 2, 2021	1 W 2 D ✖	no	1 W 2 D ✖
	November 1, 2021	1 W 3 D ✖	no	1 W 3 D ✖
	October 28, 2021	2 W ✖	no	2 W ✖
	October 21, 2021	3 W ✖	no	3 W ✖

Figure 10.16 – All sections of the formulas displayed with varying output results

The completed **Deadline** formula has the appropriate syntax in place:

```
empty(prop("Date")) ? "Date Needed !" :
((formatDate(end(prop("Date")), "DMY") == formatDate(now(),
"DMY")) ? "Today !" : ((dateBetween(end(prop("Date")), now(),
"days") == 0) ? "Tomorrow !" :
((dateBetween(end(prop("Date")), now(), "days") == -1) ?
"Yesterday !" : ((dateBetween(end(prop("Date")), now(),
"days") > 0) ? ((((((dateBetween(end(prop("Date")), now(),
"days") % 6 >= 6) ? 0 : (dateBetween(end(prop("Date")), now(),
```

```
"days") % 6)) == 0) ? (dateBetween(end(prop("Date")), now(),
"weeks") + 1) : dateBetween(end(prop("Date")), now(), "weeks"))
== 0) ? "" : (format((((dateBetween(end(prop("Date")), now(),
"days") % 6 >= 6) ? 0 : (dateBetween(end(prop("Date")), now(),
"days") % 6)) == 0) ? (dateBetween(end(prop("Date")), now(),
"weeks") + 1) : dateBetween(end(prop("Date")), now(), "weeks"))
+ " W ")) + ((((dateBetween(end(prop("Date")), now(), "days") %
7 + 1 >= 7) ? 0 : (dateBetween(end(prop("Date")), now(),
"days") % 7 + 1)) == 0) ? "" :
(format((dateBetween(end(prop("Date")), now(), "days") % 7 + 1
>= 7) ? 0 : (dateBetween(end(prop("Date")), now(), "days") % 7
+ 1)) + " D")) + " ✅") : (((dateBetween(end(prop("Date")),
now(), "weeks") == 0) ?
(format(abs(dateBetween(end(prop("Date")), now(), "days") % 7))
+ " D") : ((dateBetween(end(prop("Date")), now(), "days") % 7
== 0) ? (format(abs(dateBetween(end(prop("Date")), now(),
"weeks")))) + " W") : (format(abs(dateBetween(end(prop("Date")),
now(), "weeks")))) + " W " +
format((dateBetween(end(prop("Date")), now(), "days") % 7 + 1
>= 7) ? 0 : abs(dateBetween(end(prop("Date")), now(), "days") %
7)) + " D"))) + " ❌")))))
```

So, if you want to use this formula, you could type it out by hand. You will only need a formula property and a date property, called **Date**.

This is just one example of how you can use formulas to show the information in a way that suits you. One thing to remember is to combine multiple property outputs into one formula. This gives you a percentage, countdown, and value calculation output all inside one property.

Summary

In this chapter, we learned why a master database setup is useful and how it can be used in combination with linked database views to create contextual dashboards. Additionally, we discovered how to use automatic filters, self-referencing filters, and metadata page storage in database templates to create more advanced workflows. Then, we looked at an advanced formula that could be used as a visual aid in a contextual **dashboard** to reduce the usage of property in views. In the next chapter, we will look at the API integration and other Notion add-ons.

11
Using API Integration and Add-on Options

In this chapter, we will look at the **application programming interface** (**API**) that Notion utilizes alongside other applications. The API allows Notion to talk to other applications, which can push information to another tool from Notion or bring information from another tool into Notion. With Notion recently acquiring **Automate.io**, not only can we use examples from that interface but also other tools such as **Zapier** or **Integromat**. Additionally, we will cover some third-party add-ons that can alter the way Notion functions or add new features that are unique to that particular add-on.

In this chapter, we're going to cover the following topics:

- How to set up the API
- The risks and limitations of the API
- API integration examples
- Notion add-on options

You will learn how to set up the API, create multiple integrations, and understand some of the risks and limitations that surround these integrations. Additionally, you will learn how to create specific integration examples using **Automate.io** and **Typeform**.

How to set up the API

In this section, we will cover how you can connect Notion with other tools using the API and how that will look on the Notion side. This will be useful when connecting to tools outside of Notion, as you will be able to check whether the integration has worked or not, what access the integration has, and where to go to find out the status of the workspace.

> **Note**
> This book won't cover how to create an API or look at how to develop an integration. This book's focus is on those who want to use Notion as a no-code tool.

As shown in *Chapter 3, Templates, Imports, Account Settings, and Workspace Settings*, in the **Settings & Members** option inside the sidebar, there is an option at the bottom of the menu called **Integrations**, as shown in *Figure 11.1*:

Figure 11.1 – The location of the Integrations tab

Inside this section, you will be shown all of the current integrations that are in the workspace you are in. Integrations work in the same way as user accounts. That is, they need to be granted access to pages. As explained in earlier chapters, the page privileges apply in the same way from top to bottom. For those who want to develop their integration, there is an option called **Develop your integrations**, which can be seen in *Figure 11.1*. This will take you to a page that will enable you to develop your integration. In *Figure 11.2*, you can see that there is an integration that has been made but is not connected to anything:

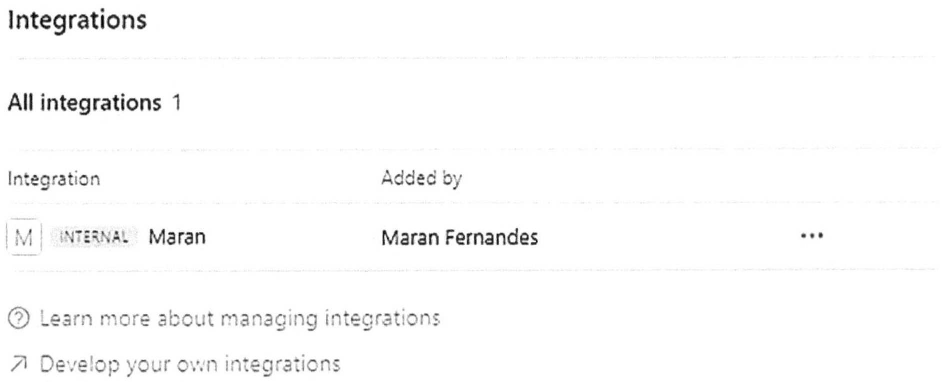

Integrations

All integrations 1

Integration	Added by	
M INTERNAL Maran	Maran Fernandes	•••

⑦ Learn more about managing integrations

↗ Develop your own integrations

Figure 11.2 – A developed integration in the Integrations tab

When creating an integration with another application, it should be done with the application you are going to connect to. For example, if you are using **Automate.io**, you can search for it on Google (`https://automate.io/`), create an account, and then click on **Create a Bot**, as shown in *Figure 11.3*:

Figure 11.3 – The Create a bot option in Automate.io

Once you are inside the menu, you will need to select whether you want Notion to trigger an action or if you want Notion to be the app that does action. When you go into the **Select Action app** option, you can type in notion, as shown in *Figure 11.4*:

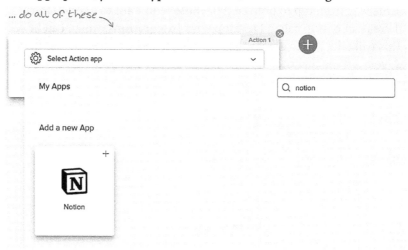

Figure 11.4 – Searching for the Notion app integration in Automate.io

Then, once you have selected Notion, you will need to authorize the integration, as shown in *Figure 11.5*:

Figure 11.5 – Checking for authorization of the Notion integration

Once the authorization process has gone through, you will need to set up the integration and its permissions. *Figure 11.6* informs you of the actions that Automate.io can take:

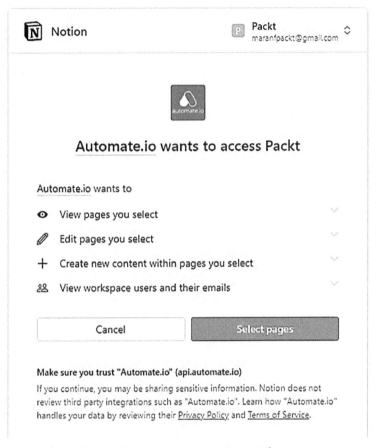

Figure 11.6 – Automate.io action privileges

Following this, *Figure 11.7* gives you the sharing privileges of the bot, which can be changed within Notion, just like the user accounts that are in the workspace:

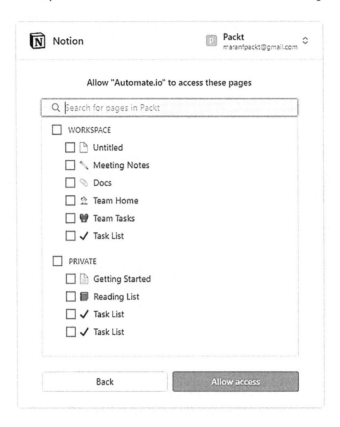

Figure 11.7 – The bot page privileges menu

Once you have allowed access, there will be an action menu that appears that explains each action you can take with the bot. Every action will then take you to a **Settings** page for the action or the trigger.

> **Note**
>
> As there are endless combinations of triggers and actions with various settings for each, there will be some examples given later in this chapter. However, they will not cover every use case.

Once you have selected a trigger, there might be some information that is then required in the action on the Notion side, which will mean that certain database properties will be needed for the integration to work.

In addition to this, in Automate.io, you can add multiple actions after a trigger. For example, you could use your email as a trigger to create a page in one database and delete a page in a different database using the same automation.

> **Note**
> If you want the bot to trigger or action a database, it needs access to the page that the original version of the database is in, not a linked database view.

When you have configured the settings for your automation, Automate.io will ask you to turn the bot on. Then, it will take you to a test trigger, as shown in *Figure 11.8*:

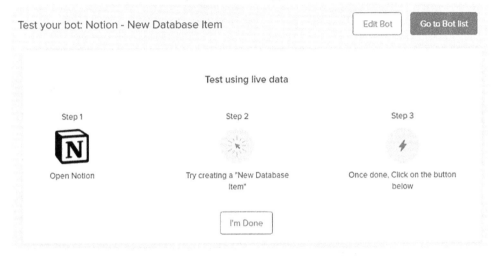

Figure 11.8 – Automate.io and Notion bot trigger testing

If the integration is successful, you will see the result of the integration in your Notion workspace and get a **Congratulations!** message from Automate.io, as shown in *Figure 11.9*:

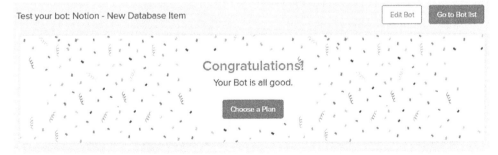

Figure 11.9 – A successful bot integration

Now let us look at the next section where we will learn the Notion view of the integration.

The Notion view of the integration

On the Notion side of this example integration, I have a database with an empty multi-select **Tags** property and three empty pages. Earlier, when the integration asked me to create a test event to test out the bot, I created a page called **New page**. Following this, a page with content was created due to the integration bot, as shown in *Figure 11.10*:

Projects

Automation Database ⊞ Default view ⌄

Aa Name	≡ Tag
1	
2	
3	
Test Event	
🖹	
+ New	

Figure 11.10 – The Notion side of the new bot integration

When looking at the sharing options on the page, there is a bot account listed there called Automate.io, as displayed in *Figure 11.11*:

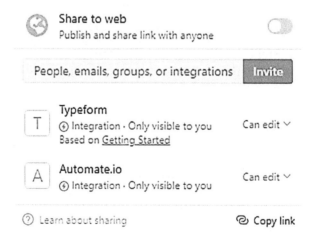

Figure 11.11 – The page privileges sharing options showing the Automate.io bot

This can also be seen in the integrations tab, as shown in *Figure 11.12*:

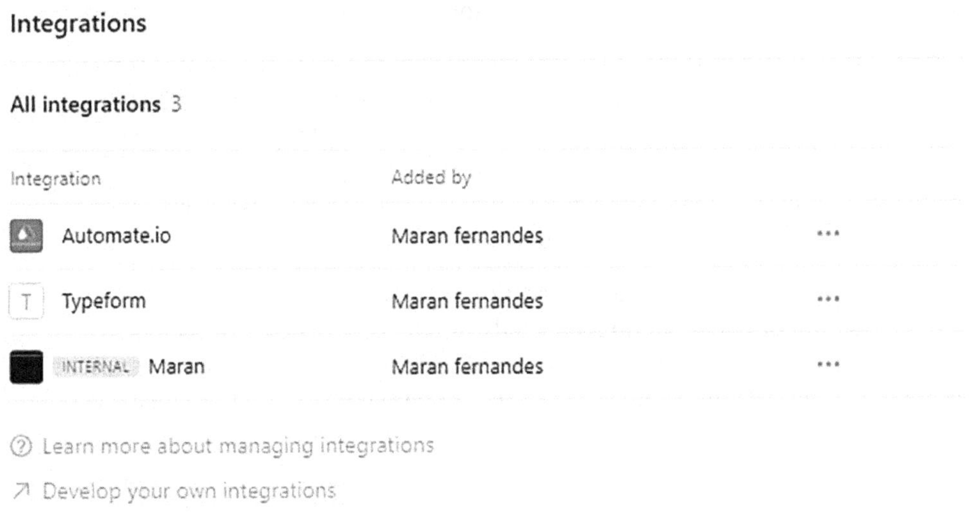

Integrations

All integrations 3

Integration	Added by	
⬟ Automate.io	Maran fernandes	...
T Typeform	Maran fernandes	...
⬛ INTERNAL Maran	Maran fernandes	...

ⓘ Learn more about managing integrations

↗ Develop your own integrations

Figure 11.12 – The integrations tab showing the Automate.io bot

Now that you know how to connect the API to another application, there are some limitations and risks associated with these integrations that you should be aware of.

The risks and limitations of using the API

In this section, we are going to go over some of the risks and limitations that using the API might have on your personal use cases. Reading this section will give you a better idea as to how you can use the integrations in your space and if you want to use them in your workspace at all.

Risks

The first and most apparent risk when using an API is that you are linking your Notion workspace to another application. This means that depending on the link and permissions you have given the app, the information in your Notion workspace can be edited, changed, and deleted. Therefore, if someone accesses the integration outside the linked app, they will be able to alter the information inside your Notion workspace. This also means that if something is changed in the outside linked app, it will change what is going on inside your Notion workspace.

In most cases, this will mean that you will need to monitor, to some extent, the automation that you create, and keep an eye on what is going on in your Notion workspace, which could add some unwanted responsibilities.

The second risk to mention is that because you are relying on an outside app to trigger and action aspects of your Notion workspace if something goes wrong (for instance, the trigger doesn't work, the action doesn't work, or there is a long delay or even an application outage), you will not be notified in the Notion application. Therefore, if you are relying on certain information in your Notion database to be correct, which depends on the automation, there might be some inaccuracies with the data.

The final risk that we will mention in this section is human error. It might sound obvious, but if an automation has been set up incorrectly or adjusted incorrectly, then, again, the only way to solve the error would be in the outside connected app, but it would be noticeable in Notion, which could take time and, potentially, lead to more mistakes.

Limitations

As the outside connection is a separate application, it will have its own pricing plans and limits to triggers and actions. This means that if you are relying on automation to happen quite frequently, the price of those triggers would mean you will need to pay more for the plan. Therefore, this might limit how many automations you want to use in a month to reduce costs, which could limit the type and frequency of automation used.

The next limitation that should be mentioned is that several different apps might have the automations you are looking for. This could mean you have multiple integrations doing various automations, which isn't limiting, but it can increase the likelihood of risks. These are likely to increase your responsibility to check whether each automation is functioning correctly or not. This can take time, and cost resources if there are issues to fix. Now that is it for the main risks and limitations, but there are some other things to be aware of.

One small, but noticeable, issue that some people might have is that some automations require certain properties to be in a database, which could add up quickly. This could lead to a larger database, which can make editing, altering, and moving information a little more complicated for those who are unfamiliar with the tool. This is more likely to be a concern for those with various team members who are not familiar with the software. This issue is likely to fade over time, but it can make the onboarding process more complex.

If you are using a trigger and an action from the same database, you could end up with circular automation. This means that, at the end of one automation, the automation will be triggered again. This can lead to reaching the automation limit unintentionally, which could cost money, lead to moving plans, or cost time due to the manual input needed later on.

Most of these limitations and risks revolve around access to your Notion workspace and checking each automation is functioning as it should, which could also take considerable time.

API integration examples

In this section, we will go through an integration example using Automate.io, between Google Calendar and Notion, and a **Typeform** integration with Notion. These are two of the most common integration uses and will give you some practical use cases for when and how the API can be used.

The Notion and Google Calendar integration

Just like at the beginning of this chapter, you will need to set up the bot in Automate.io, which permits you to use your Google Calendar account and your Notion account.

Once permission has been granted, we need to add a trigger and an action. In this example, we will use adding a Google Calendar event as the trigger and adding a database item as the action. This bot aims to create a page in a Notion database when an event is added to a specific Google Calendar trigger.

As you can see in *Figure 11.13*, there is one required field in the Google Calendar trigger section and one required field for the Notion database action section:

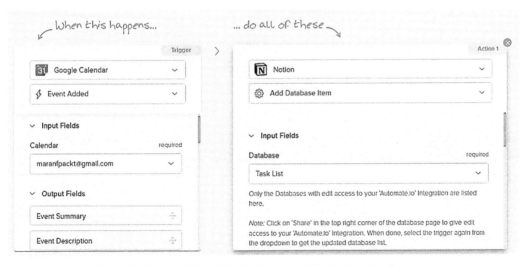

Figure 11.13 – The Google Calendar and Notion integration bot setup

The **Calendar** field that is in the trigger section is the Google Calendar called **Notion Calendar**, which in your Google Calendar, might be called something else. The drop-down menu will show a list of all available calendars, but if you add a calendar and it isn't appearing, then you might need to click out of the drop-down menu to allow Automate.io to update the list. A drop-down list will also be shown for the Notion database on the page that the Automate.io bot is shared on, as shown in *Figure 11.14*:

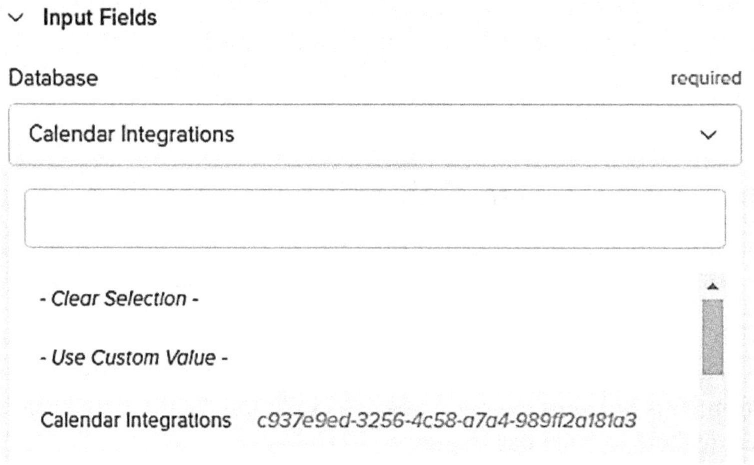

Figure 11.14 – The Notion database drop-down list for the Automate.io bot

Once the calendar and database have been selected, all of the other settings can be adjusted to your preferences, but the bot will function.

> **Note**
>
> The long string of numbers and letters next to the calendar or the database is the integration key that you should keep private unless you want to give other people access to that calendar or database.

Once you have selected the **Save** button, you will be taken to a test run-through where you will be given instructions in which to test out the bot you have created, as shown in *Figure 11.15*:

Figure 11.15 – The Google Calendar and Notion integration bot test

This particular bot features **Event Description** information from the Google Calendar event, which is shown within the Notion page content as a paragraph, as shown in *Figure 11.16*:

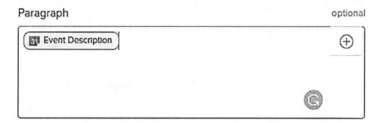

Figure 11.16 – Event Description information being added to Notion page content

The **Start Date** section in the Notion page is the **Event Begins** information from the Google Calendar event, as shown in *Figure 11.17*:

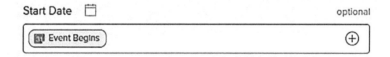

Figure 11.17 – Event Begins information being added to Notion Start Date property

The **Name** section in the Notion page is the **Event Summary** information from the Google Calendar event, as shown in *Figure 11.18*:

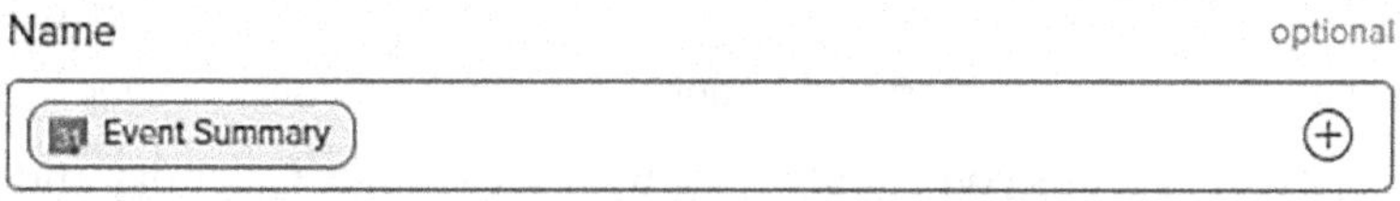

Figure 11.18 – Event Summary information being added to the Notion Name property

So, when testing this bot, the event was added to the calendar with the name **Test Event**, a description that read **This is the description of the event.**, and the date of the event, **Tuesday, November 23**, as shown in *Figure 11.19*:

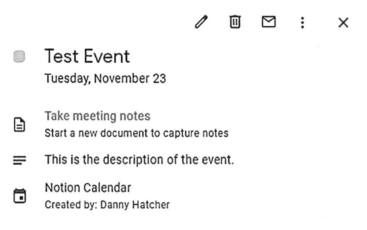

Figure 11.19 – The new calendar event in Google Calendar

This is due to the bot creating a page in the Notion database, as shown in *Figure 11.20*:

Figure 11.20 – The newly created Notion page from the Automate.io bot

This is just one of many settings you could create with the Google Calendar and Notion integration. Each time you alter the bot, Automate.io will ask you to go through and test the bot. If you are using a different application for the integration, the process might look a little different, such as when using Typeform.

The Notion and Typeform integration

Typeform is an application that allows you to publish forms and collect information from questions. Using the API to integrate with Notion, the responses of the questions can be stored and then sorted inside Notion.

Just like with Automate.io, when connecting Typeform to Notion, there is an onboarding process. First, you need to connect the apps, as shown in *Figure 11.21*:

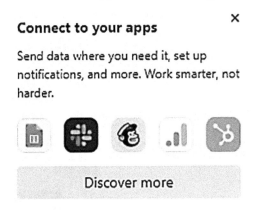

Figure 11.21 – The Typeform application connection window

If Notion isn't showing, click on the **Discover more** option from *Figure 11.21* to find Notion. You will then be shown what the integration does and some information about what can happen. After clicking on the **Add** button, you will be taken to a screen to select the Typeform you want to connect to Notion, as shown in *Figure 11.22*:

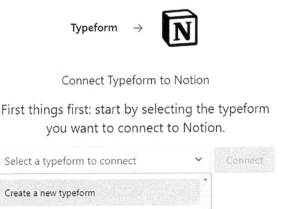

Figure 11.22 – The Typeform selection window to connect with Notion

If you already have a Typeform, it will be listed in the drop-down list, for example, **My typeform** is being displayed in *Figure 11.22*. If not, you can **Create a new typeform** from the drop-down list.

Creating a new Typeform

When creating a new Typeform, you will be asked to name the Typeform and give a reason for creating the form, as shown in *Figure 11.23*:

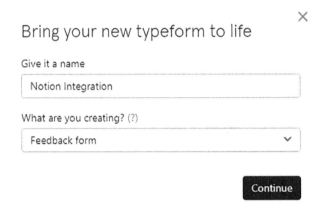

Figure 11.23 – The name and reason for creating the new Typeform

You can then create the form with all of the appropriate questions.

> **Note**
>
> This book will not cover how to use Typeform or go over any of the features available in the application.

Once the form has been created, it is time to connect it to Notion.

Connecting a Typeform to Notion

At this point, there should be a Typeform ready to connect to Notion. This is so that when you go to connect the applications, there is at least one form in the drop-down list. Select the form you want to connect with, or navigate to the **Connect** section in the form edit window, as shown in *Figure 11.24*:

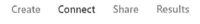

Figure 11.24 – The Typeform edit menu Connect section at the top of the screen

Once the connection has been made, it needs to be authenticated by selecting the ... menu next to Notion, as shown in *Figure 11.25*:

Figure 11.25 – The Notion and Typeform connection edit option

When you are in the **Edit** area, you need to authenticate the Typeform account, the Notion account, and then map the Typeform fields to Notion, as shown in *Figure 11.26*:

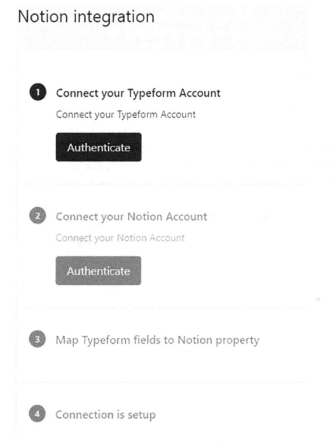

Figure 11.26 – The Typeform and Notion authentication settings

Once you have completed all four sections, you can check whether the Typeform has been shared; otherwise, you will need to go back to the integrations section and make the Typeform public from the **Create** section, as shown in *Figure 11.27*. In this example form, there are three questions mapped to three text properties inside the Notion database, as detailed in *Figure 11.27*:

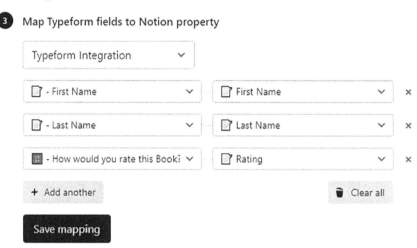

Figure 11.27 – The Typeform property settings showing the questions to the property links

Once the form has been completed and connected to the Notion database, you can test out the form in **Section 4** of the connection setup or by accessing the form through a share link. After completing the form, the results will appear in the Notion database you have connected it to, as shown in *Figure 11.28*:

Figure 11.28 – The Notion and Typeform integration results database

This information can be checked in Typeform by going to the results section of any form, as shown in *Figure 11.29*:

Big picture

| All devices | Desktop | Mobile | Tablet | Other |

Views	Starts	Responses	Completion rate	Average time to complete
1	1	1	100%	00:11

Figure 11.29 – The Typeform result section for the connected form

Additionally, these forms can be adjusted in various ways using different property types, such as multiple databases with multiple forms, which can all be included in a specifically created workflow. Combining these API databases with the concept of contextual dashboards can create some useful views for understanding the information that might be coming in through forms, events, or any other integration that you might need or want.

The Notion add-on options

In this section, you will find out about some external embed options, alongside other tools that can be used to enhance your experience with Notion. These add-on options can be free or paid options with similar risks to the API integrations.

> **Note**
> This book will not go through how to use every add-on option listed, but it will cover the most common uses and processes to activate the majority of tools.

The first add-on to mention has been built by the team at Notion, which is the web clipper. This add-on, alongside many of the add-ons available, is a browser extension. This means that some extensions will only be available on certain browsers, which is important to bear in mind when working as a team.

> **Note**
> The following instructions are for the **Google Chrome** browser. The instructions will be similar across browsers if the extension is available.

After searching in the **Google Search** bar for Chrome extensions, assuming you are using Chrome, there will be the option to go into the Chrome Web Store. Once you have entered the store, search for `notion web clipper`, and all of the related extensions will appear, as shown in *Figure 11.30*:

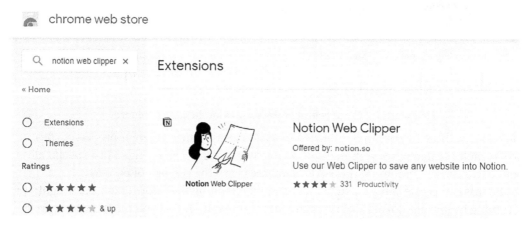

Figure 11.30 – Search result for the Notion Web Clipper Chrome Web Store extension

After clicking on the **Notion Web Clipper** extension, you will be given the option to **Add to Chrome**, which will add the extension to your browser, showing the information pop-up box from *Figure 11.31*:

Figure 11.31 – The Notion Web Clipper pop-up box containing installation information

Each Chrome extension has a dedicated keyboard shortcut that can be changed in the Chrome browser settings. The default Notion web clipper for Windows is shown in *Figure 11.31*. The appropriate shortcut will be displayed for the device you are on when installing the extension.

Once the extension has been installed, there will be an option to pin the web clipper to the top of your browser, as shown in *Figure 11.32*:

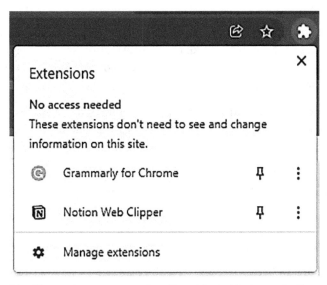

Figure 11.32 – The Chrome browser extensions list with the Notion web clipper being pinned

What this allows you to do is create a page in a database with a link to the website you are on. Now that the web clipper can be easily accessed, when you are on any web page, you can click on the Notion icon and a pop-up window will appear. You can select the database or the page in the **Add to** section, the **Workspace** section, and the name of the page, as shown in *Figure 11.33*:

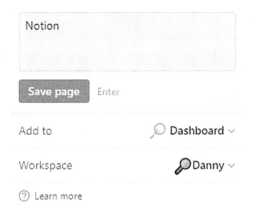

Figure 11.33 – The Notion web clipper pop-out box

Once you select the **Save page** button, as shown in *Figure 11.33*, a page will be created in either the page you selected in the **Add to** section or the database you selected with a link to the clipped website.

This extension will allow you to change the name of the page you have created and will save the website URL. But if you would like more information saved when clipping information, there is a different add-on, called **Save to Notion**. This is also an extension, but it has not been made by the Notion team.

Evergreen Notes (for Notion) is another extension that may be of use. It brings up a side panel with added page navigation and information. **Notion Boost** is an extension that offers more customization to the aesthetics of the app, with an outline option, small text setting, and more.

Other add-on options can enable icon options, such as the following:

- **The Notion VIP website**: `https://www.notion.vip/`
- **The Favicon Icons website**: `https://icons8.com/icons/set/favicon`
- **The Notion Icons website**: `https://www.notion.vip/icons/`

This is alongside many more places that can be found via Google Search. Some add-ons give more embed options, such as the following:

- **The Indify website**: `https://indify.co/`
- **Notion Chilipepper forms**: `https://www.notioneverything.com/tools/chilipepper`
- **Notion metrics**: `https://notionmetrics.com/`

Again, many more options can be found via Google Search. Some add-on websites allow you to create a website built from Notion, such as **Super** (`https://super.so/`).

For those of you who are interested in more changes to the aesthetics of Notion, there is a project on GitHub called **notion-enhancer** (`https://github.com/notion-enhancer/desktop`), which you can use and contribute to.

> **Note**
>
> Notion Web Clipper is the only add-on that has been built by the Notion team. The rest of these options are all open to the risks mentioned in *The risks and limitations of using the API* section. So, before using any of the add-on options, try and find out from an online Notion community if they are still working and don't cause any issues. The most popular communities are the Facebook group **Notion Made Simple**, the **Notion** subreddit, or the Discord Community's **Tools For Thought**. Alternatively, you can reach out to the Notion team themselves via email or through the **Send us a message** option in the **?** menu in the lower-right corner of the tool.

Summary

In this chapter, we covered how to set up the API inside a Notion workspace and how the API bot is shared to a page giving it privileges like any other user account. We looked at the risks and limitations of using the API with other tools. We went through some use case examples, integrating Google Calendar and Typeform with Notion. Then, we looked at the Notion-made add-on and some other add-on options that could be used to alter the functions and aesthetics of your Notion workspace.

In the next chapter, we will look at how to use the information captured by integrations and ensure the information is organized so that it can be accessed in a productive way.

12

Note Taking, Knowledge Management, and a Wiki Example

In this chapter, we will look at using Notion for notetaking and wiki management. We will combine concepts such as contextual dashboards, master databases, and how to use the web clipper to create a flexible system that can be altered to create a process for capturing, organizing, processing, and sharing information.

In this chapter, we're going to cover the following topics:

- How to capture information in Notion
- How to organize information in Notion
- How to share information in Notion

You will learn how to bring information into the Notion application in a quick, organized, and convenient way. Following this, you will learn how to maintain a good level of organization with that information using database features. Then, you will look at how to process that information so that it can be applied in practice rather than stored and forgotten about. You will also learn how to share the information with a team or with other people that you are collaborating with.

Capturing information

In this section, you will learn how to put new information into Notion in a quick, convenient, and organized way to help speed up the capture stage of note-taking. This is important to prevent information from being lost or forgotten about while keeping the process quick enough to not be an irritation.

One key aspect of capturing information is that is it easy to do. On the web, this is easy to do using the web clipper, which was covered in the previous *Chapter 11, Using API Integration and Add-on Options*. Once you have created a database inside Notion, you can clip web pages to the database, as shown in *Figure 12.1*:

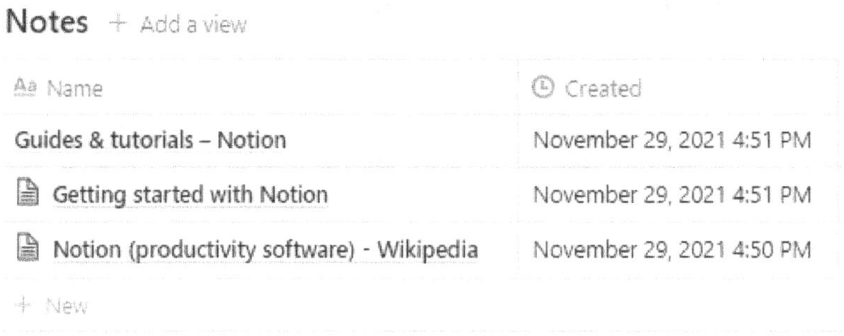

Figure 12.1 – The Notes database with web clipper results as pages

Figure 12.1 shows three different web pages that have been clipped into a database, called **Notes**. They were done only a minute apart, as clipping is so quick, and can be seen in the **Created** property, which is a created time property type. There is a difference in the clipped web pages: two of the pages have information that was clipped alongside the name, and the URL of the site is indicated by the icon next to the name.

Page property and page information

When opening the **Getting started with Notion** page, some properties can be seen at the top of the page, including the URL link that was automatically added and a **Task** relation property, which was created manually before clipping. Then, inside the page, there is the content of the original web page, as shown in *Figure 12.2*:

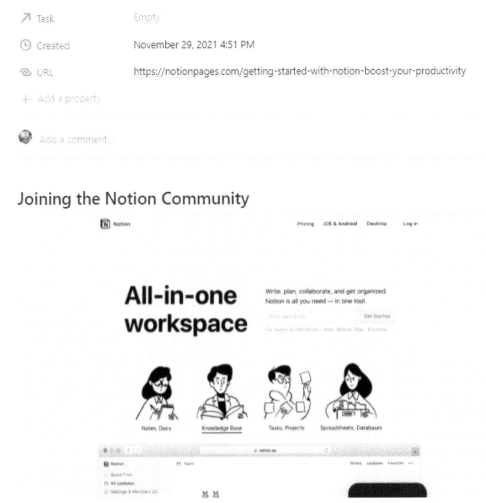

Figure 12.2 – The page property and page information from the clipped page

However, if the information you want to capture is not a web page that can be clipped on the browser and you are on a different device, you can share the web page with Notion, as shown in *Figure 12.3*:

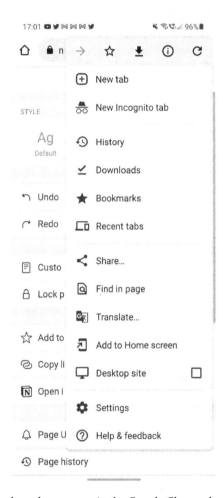

Figure 12.3 – The drop-down menu in the Google Chrome browser on a mobile

Figure 12.4 shows the available options after pressing the **Share** button:

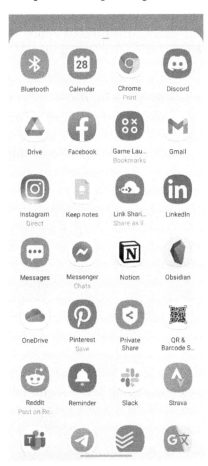

Figure 12.4 – The applications on a mobile device with the sharing to Notion option available

Alternatively, you might have something you have thought of that you would like to capture on a page or in a database. In this case, using a contextual dashboard will be useful.

Contextual dashboards

The contextual dashboard can include any of the features and functions that were previously covered in this book. However, the simplest option would be a database, preferably a linked database view, which is filtered by something that would be useful when capturing those types of notes.

For example, having a linked database view of the master notes database on a page that is filtered for notes that have only been created today, will remind you of things that you already thought of on that day. Potentially, this will allow you to add more information or new thoughts, too. *Figure 12.5* shows this example using the previously used database with the clipped information:

Figure 12.5 – An example of a contextual dashboard with a filtered linked database view

The reason for putting the clipped information and thoughts into a database is that it allows easier organization later on during the note-taking process, which we will cover in the next section.

Organizing information

In this section, we will cover some options for organizing the notes inside databases and on pages. This can help you keep up to date with information, prevent forgetting information, and avoid things being lost.

> **Note**
>
> In this section, the example that is used utilizes the same database setup from previous chapters alongside the contextual dashboard concept.

The formatting of a page can help with organizing information and notes on a page. By combining the toggle blocks, pages, and columns, you can create a storage system for any block, page, or database that might store information. When using the web clipper with a page, you can move the page or any note into a column, under a toggle, as shown in *Figure 12.6*:

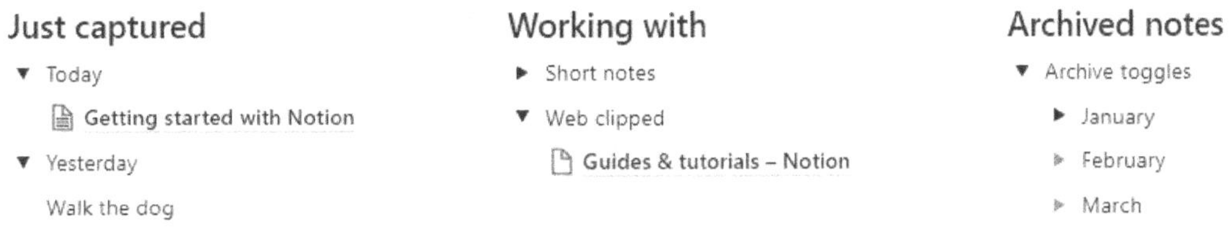

Just captured
- ▼ Today
  - 📄 Getting started with Notion
- ▼ Yesterday
  - Walk the dog

Working with
- ▶ Short notes
- ▼ Web clipped
  - 📄 Guides & tutorials – Notion

Archived notes
- ▼ Archive toggles
  - ▶ January
  - ▶ February
  - ▶ March

Figure 12.6 – Organizing a page using columns and toggles

Each page can have various combinations of toggles, columns, and linked databases with multiple color combinations. This style of organization is more manual than using databases and requires a little more maintenance work, but it is great for simple organization.

When organizing information in databases, using filters, sorts, and linked databases can help create various folder-like structures and layouts. The example view from *Figure 12.5* shows that a filter is used with the `created` property. But for further organization, other properties can be added, such as a `multi-select` property for tagging, a `relation` property for attaching notes to tasks or projects, or a `checkbox` property for a checked update, as shown in *Figure 12.7*:

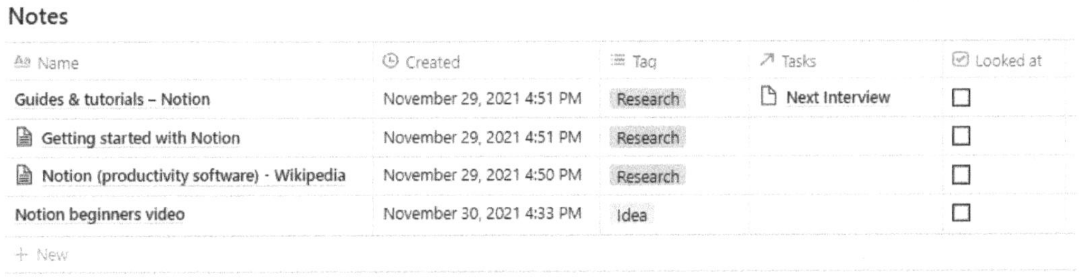

Notes

Aa Name	⊙ Created	☰ Tag	↗ Tasks	☑ Looked at
Guides & tutorials – Notion	November 29, 2021 4:51 PM	Research	📄 Next Interview	☐
📄 Getting started with Notion	November 29, 2021 4:51 PM	Research		☐
📄 Notion (productivity software) - Wikipedia	November 29, 2021 4:50 PM	Research		☐
Notion beginners video	November 30, 2021 4:33 PM	Idea		☐
+ New				

Figure 12.7 – A Notes database with various properties for the organization

These properties can be used to create linked database views next to one another for contextual viewing. If used with filters, information can quickly be tagged or related by dragging and dropping the page into a different view.

An example setup might have a filtered linked database view with new notes and no tag showing. It can have a linked database view next to it with a filter for **Research** and a different one for **Idea**. Then, when organizing the notes, you can drag the pages into the appropriate database to tag the page, and they will then appear in the linked database view in the respective contextual dashboard elsewhere in the Notion workspace. This example is presented in the following screenshots, starting with *Figure 12.8*:

Just captured (no tag)				Research notes				Idea notes		
↗ Notes				↗ Notes				↗ Notes		
Aa Name	☰ Tag	+		Aa Name	☰ Tag	+		Aa Name	☰ Tag	
Getting started with Not				Guides & tutorials – Notion	Research			Notion beginners video	Idea	
+ New				Notion (productivity sof	Research			+ New		
Calculate ∨				+ New				Calculate ∨		

Figure 12.8 – A three-column linked database view setup with filtered views for each tag

Figure 12.9 shows the dragging of an untagged page to one of the filtered database views:

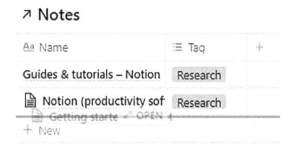

Figure 12.9 – Dragging the untagged page into the Research notes filtered linked database view

After each note has been organized and tagged with appropriate information using the properties that you have added to the database, you can filter for what note you need, as shown in *Figure 12.10*:

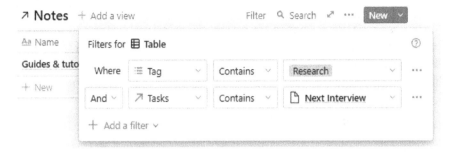

Figure 12.10 – A contextual dashboard using filters with organized notes

In the contextual dashboard, the filter includes the relation property, so only notes that are classed as research and are related to the next interview will appear. As more research notes are added into the database, the **Notes** database will increase in size, but only information that is specific to the next interview will appear in that contextual dashboard view.

> **Note**
> This example only uses two properties to categorize and organize any database. However, all property types could be used, with various filters and sorts to create the views that are being looked for.

As database views are automatic, once you have added the **tag**, they will appear in all of the appropriate places with the linked database, displaying the notes in all of the pages that you need them in. This also means that any change you make to the note will be seen wherever the note is linked, such as a linked database view, unlike when writing notes inside a block on a page, unless you put notes into a synced block.

Tagging information

When attaching information to a note in a database, the properties you use can be limiting depending on the type you use. For example, if you use a `select` property or a `multi-select` property for tagging information, and all of your notes are in one database, the list of tags can get extremely long. This might lead to multiple tagging properties or elaborate linked database views to make tagging information easier.

Unlike other note-taking tools such as **Evernote**, **Obsidian**, and **Roam Research**, Notion doesn't have global tag features, but this can be somewhat recreated using a master tags database. This involves using the idea of a master database specifically for tags, but this idea can be extended to a variety of other options.

One benefit of having a tags database is that a relation property is **searchable** (allowing you to have an almost unlimited list of tag options). Additionally, it allows for further specifications with the tags using a different property in the database for status. In addition to this, as each tag is a page in the master tag database, you can view all the tasks, projects, or pages that are related to that tag. This means you can see all of the clients, projects, tasks, notes, and employees that relate to a specific tag. *Figure 12.10* shows an example linked database view using the **Notes** database with a grouping for the **Tags** relation property to the master tag database:

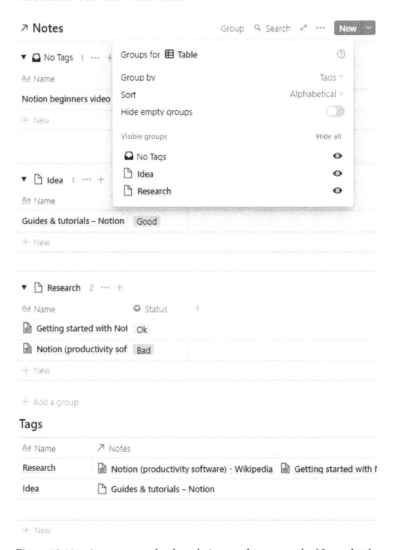

Figure 12.11 – A master tag database being used to group the Notes database

When viewing a master tag database with the various types of information in it, it can be used with any filter, sort, or grouping that suits your needs in the specific contextual dashboard you are making.

In the next section, we will cover different ways of sharing the information across your workspace for team use.

Sharing information

In this section, we will cover some dashboards that can be used to make sharing information easier for the disseminator and the consumer. This will be helpful if you are collaborating with someone unfamiliar with Notion or with a team that has multiple people with various responsibilities and needs for information.

The first thing that helps when organizing a workspace for collaboration is to have a home dashboard that can help with orientation. This would be a top-level page that can be accessed by all individuals in the workspace. From this page, there can be links to contextual dashboards, potentially for specific groups of people, or you can have contextual dashboards showing specific information, allowing for quick navigation back to the home dashboard. This not only makes navigation quicker, but it also makes sharing information easier, as each piece of information has a place.

The home dashboard doesn't need to be overly complex with various linked database views, it could just be a list of pages such as *Figure 12.12*:

Figure 12.12 – An example home dashboard space

Figure 12.12 shows an **Onboarding Guide** space, which can be a page filled with a list of resources about how to use Notion for beginners, information about the workspace setup, and any other onboarding information that might be needed for individuals who will be using the workspace. Having a go-to help page such as this can make sharing information easier, as people will know where to go to find what they are looking for.

The **Client list** page is likely to be a contextual dashboard that could be a friends list, an employee list, or a company list. The dashboard would include a linked database view of information that is specific to that contextual dashboard with the main database being stored elsewhere for safety and to prevent unintentional deletion.

The **Active projects** and **Task list** pages can be similar to the **Client list** page and be contextual dashboards. Alternatively, they can be the main database with filtered views, which could be more convenient for some users. When using the person filter and filtering for **Me**, this page could then become everyone's task list and active projects list, as it is filtered for the user viewing the database, as shown in *Figure 12.13*:

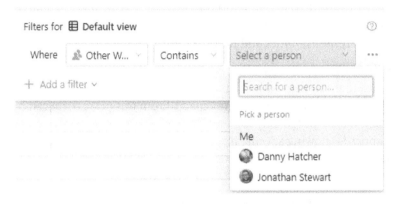

Figure 12.13 – The Person property filtered for Me

The **Resources** section, as shown in *Figure 12.12*, can be a list of pages that are frequently used. **Ideas** and **Conversations** are useful for sharing thoughts about future projects or goals alongside meeting notes.

Having a **Directory** page can be a good way to give a short introduction to people who are new to the team. This page could have a database of each member alongside some information about who they are, their journey in the group, the team they are part of, the company they work for, and some things they are interested in, to help new members or potential clients understand the people they could be working with.

The **Event calendar** page demonstrates how using the API and Google Calendar could be useful, by creating a calendar that everyone can see while working inside Notion, instead of having to open up a specific calendar or, potentially, multiple calendars.

A **standing operating procedure (SOP)** page can be useful for sharing policies and procedures with other team members. A common use case is when a team member is off sick or requires someone else to complete a task. As the SOP is in the Notion workspace, anyone can access the page, given that the correct privileges are given through the sharing features. This is so they can follow the step-by-step instructions without needing help from the original worker. Another example could be when hiring or delegating a job to someone else.

When creating lists of things for others to do, using callout blocks, headings, and embedded videos inside a page in a database allows for the most flexibility. The database of SOPs can be searched and filtered through for easy navigation and the page can be simple to follow, allowing you to navigate from **Step 1** to the end, as shown in *Figure 12.14*:

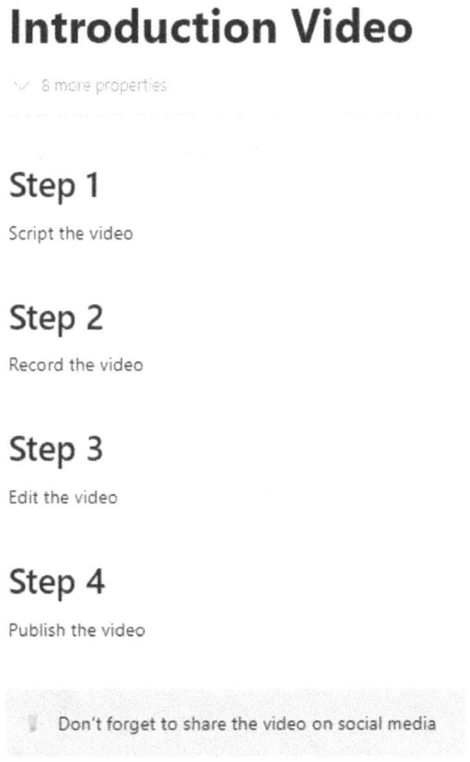

Introduction Video

∨ 8 more properties

Step 1
Script the video

Step 2
Record the video

Step 3
Edit the video

Step 4
Publish the video

    Don't forget to share the video on social media

Figure 12.14 – An example SOP to produce a video

The example in *Figure 12.14* is very bare, but that might be all the information needed.

One important element of sharing information inside a Notion workspace is the sharing privileges that are available, which were covered in *Chapter 2*, *Understanding Workspace Navigation*, and the ease of navigation around using contextual dashboards and a home dashboard, which people can navigate back to for orientation.

Summary

In this chapter, you learned how to capture information quickly in Notion using the web clipper with a page or database for storage. You learned how to organize the information stored in databases using properties, filters, sorts, and the master database concept to create a master tag database. Additionally, you learned some methods to make the process of sharing information easier for others who enter the workspace. This will help with clearing your mind of thoughts, as they can be easily captured in Notion for later use. Also, you can ensure that when you are looking for an old idea or note, you know where to find the information.

In the next chapter, we will look at how you can combine these note-taking tips with concepts such as contextual dashboards and master databases to create use case templates and entire workspace systems.

13

Other Example Use Cases

In this chapter, we will look at a variety of Notion use cases, ranging from basic to advanced templates for students, business owners, and everyday individual uses. This chapter will inspire ideas and open your mind on how to use Notion in your work as well as in your personal life. The examples shown in this chapter are from my own personal experience and other Notion ambassadors that aim to help users get the most from the app.

In this chapter, we are going to cover the following topics:

- Planning dashboards
- Tracking dashboards
- Popular workspace systems

You will learn how dashboards are used for a variety of use cases. You will also learn how to start building out your workspace and get directions to other resources that you can use to kick-start your Notion journey.

Planning dashboards

In this section, you will see lots of dashboard combinations that are used to help with planning tasks, projects, notes, and events. These examples will use the master database concept, contextual dashboard concept, and other database and page features, which will be explained.

Note

Each template in this section is either created by me or by other Notion ambassadors that are happy to share their work as examples. The example is briefly explained with a link for you to follow if you would like further details on the specifics.

Student Workspace

When thinking about creating a page for planning, considering all the elements that are included in the planning is the first step. For most people, tasks will be something to keep track of, alongside events. But for students it may look like *Figure 13.1*, with tasks and lectures alongside other important planning elements:

Figure 13.1 – Student Workspace template with four list database views and a calendar view

When you look at *Figure 13.1*, you may notice that the linked database view underneath the **Upcoming Lectures** heading and the **Calendar** heading are both from the same database, but they are in different views, with different filters and sorts.

> **Note**
>
> Also note that the images next to the headings are underlined, indicating that there is a link on them, meaning that if they are clicked, the image will function as a hyperlink and take you to the page it is linked to.

My Notion Workspace

Another option for linking pages (in the same way) using images with links is to put them in a synced block (which can be placed on each page in the workspace) and use it as a navigation bar at the top of the page, as shown in *Figure 13.2*:

My Notion Workspace

Figure 13.2 – My Notion Workspace template with a navigation bar at
the top with linked databases on the main page

In *Figure 13.2*, the titles are inline math that allows different colors and fonts to be used for the aesthetic of a different arrangement of linked databases. The **Tasks** database underneath the **Today Tasks** heading shows the project relation next to a checkbox, indicating there is another database elsewhere in this workspace, which is located in the **Review** page, next to the navigation at the top right of *Figure 13.2*.

In the preceding screenshots, the calendar view is used to give an overview of the upcoming tasks and a list view for today's tasks, but some prefer a week view, which can be achieved by using blocks in a page or using the board view, as shown in *Figure 13.3*:

Weekly Agenda

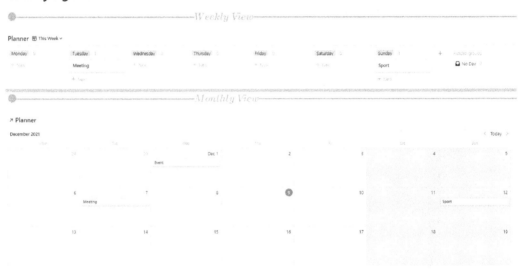

Figure 13.3 – Weekly Agenda template with a board and calendar view of the same database

The dividers shown in *Figure 13.3* are alternative ways of using inline math to create an aesthetic on the page. The **Planner** database is used twice on this page with a board view showing the current week, and the calendar view showing the month. As these views are from the same database, as tasks are moved in the board view, they will also move in the calendar view.

> **Note**
> This database setup uses formulas to calculate *what week the task is on* and *what day to show the task on* on the calendar. This means the calendar view can't be used to move tasks unless the calendar by value is changed from the formula property to the date property.

Starter Space

Any aspect from a dashboard is taken and used differently, as shown in *Figure 13.4*:

Figure 13.4 – Starter Space template using various linked database views and inline math dividers

Moving beyond tasks, notes, and projects for individual or team use cases, there are areas brought up in *Figure 13.4* to categorize certain areas of life or work. It is a database where each page is a contextual dashboard that allows easy navigation to a specific area for certain information.

An example use case for the database could be for content management as a marketing business or content creator. Each page can be a contextual dashboard for content, as shown in *Figure 13.5*:

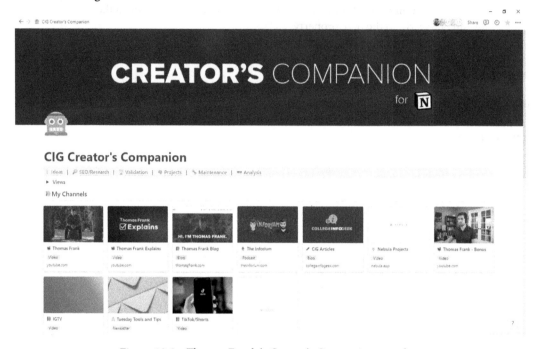

Figure 13.5 – Thomas Frank 's Creator's Companion template

Figure 13.5 shows a gallery database view with each channel of content being shown as a page as a way to access a contextual dashboard for that channel. This template expands into a much deeper system, which will be explored later in the chapter, but a few words from Thomas first:

> *I use Notion to organize my entire life, but the main thing I (and my team) use it for is managing our content production process. We use a system I've called Creator's Companion, which keeps all our content in a master database and helps us manage it throughout every stage of the process – idea generation/validation, research and writing, editing, and publishing. I spent most of my career as a YouTuber juggling several apps to manage this process – Evernote for ideas and writing, To-do list for task management, and Google Sheets for other things. I love how Notion lets me do all of this in one tool now.*
>
> *– Thomas Frank*

CRM System

An example area in a business workspace could be for client relationship management. Information about each deal, each client, and the associated numbers with each deal can be presented in a database view with information feeding in from action databases and other information databases storing client, company, and contact information, as shown in *Figure 13.6*:

Figure 13.6 – CRM System template with linked database views

Figure 13.6 shows how you can use a formula property and the board database view calculations to give you all the information you may need briefly without needing to go into each page. The **Actions** database has been linked in the view twice for upcoming tasks and completed tasks, which is common to see in dashboards as a safety procedure.

Recurring tasks

Let's understand the tasks one by one:

1. Notion doesn't have a traditional way of performing recurring tasks, which can make the method for getting repeated tasks into Notion a problem with various solutions. The easiest solution is to use a `select` property that tags a task repeatedly, using a linked view, as seen in *Figure 13.6*, that is filtered for the recurring tasks. Alternatively, you can use a template button to generate each recurring task and then drag it onto a calendar view, as shown in *Figure 13.7*:

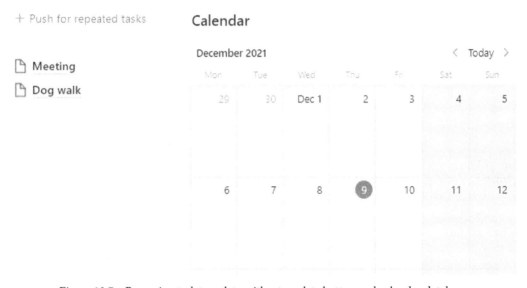

Figure 13.7 – Recurring task template with a template button and calendar database

With the various database features and page blocks, there are almost endless possibilities for solving the recurring task issue, but for most people, a tag or duplicate page works wonders.

Buffer's OKRs

Alongside the CRM system, goal setting, *key performance indicator (KPI)*, and *objectives and key results (OKRs)* tracking can be useful, with an example template shown in *Figure 13.8*:

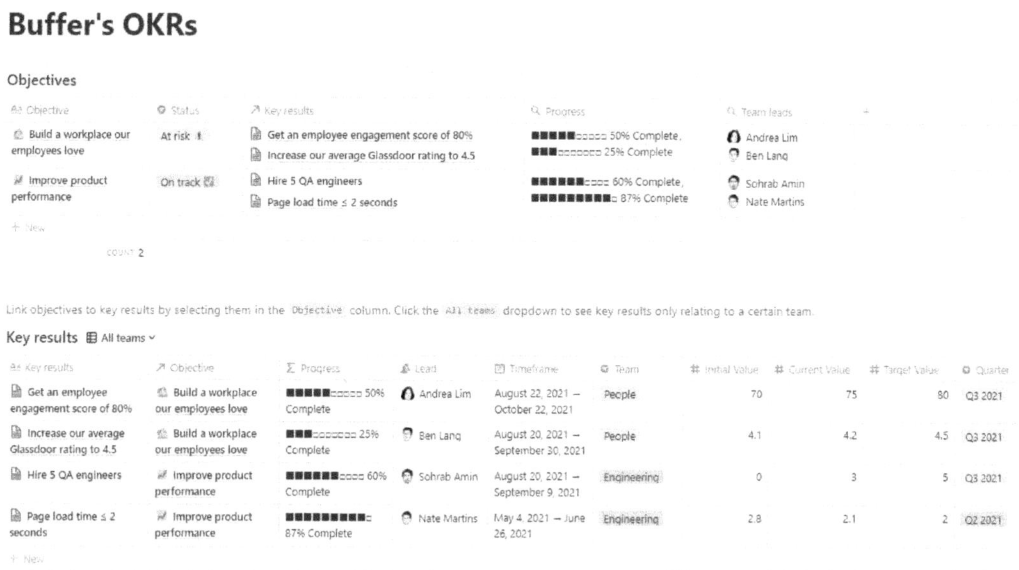

Buffer's OKRs

Objectives

Aa Objective	◎ Status	↗ Key results	○ Progress	○ Team leads	+
◎ Build a workplace our employees love	At risk ‼	📄 Get an employee engagement score of 80% 📄 Increase our average Glassdoor rating to 4.5	▰▰▰▰▱▱▱▱ 50% Complete, ▰▰▱▱▱▱▱▱ 25% Complete	🐱 Andrea Lim 😐 Ben Lang	
∥ Improve product performance	On track ☑	📄 Hire 5 QA engineers 📄 Page load time ≤ 2 seconds	▰▰▰▰▰▰▱▱ 60% Complete, ▰▰▰▰▰▰▰▱ 87% Complete	😐 Sohrab Amin 🐱 Nate Martins	

+ New

count 2

Link objectives to key results by selecting them in the `Objective` column. Click the `All teams` dropdown to see key results only relating to a certain team.

Key results ⊞ All teams ∨

Aa Key results	↗ Objective	Σ Progress	👤 Lead	📅 Timeframe	◎ Team	# Initial Value	# Current Value	# Target Value	◎ Quarter
📄 Get an employee engagement score of 80%	◎ Build a workplace our employees love	▰▰▰▰▱▱▱▱ 50% Complete	🐱 Andrea Lim	August 22, 2021 – October 22, 2021	People	70	75	80	Q3 2021
📄 Increase our average Glassdoor rating to 4.5	◎ Build a workplace our employees love	▰▰▰▱▱▱▱▱ 25% Complete	😐 Ben Lang	August 20, 2021 – September 30, 2021	People	4.1	4.2	4.5	Q3 2021
📄 Hire 5 QA engineers	∥ Improve product performance	▰▰▰▰▰▰▱▱ 60% Complete	😐 Sohrab Amin	August 20, 2021 – September 9, 2021	Engineering	0	3	5	Q3 2021
📄 Page load time ≤ 2 seconds	∥ Improve product performance	▰▰▰▰▰▰▰▱ 87% Complete	🐱 Nate Martins	May 4, 2021 – June 26, 2021	Engineering	2.8	2.1	2	Q2 2021

+ New

Figure 13.8 – Buffer's OKR template located in the Notion template gallery

Figure 13.8 shows the use of visual progress bars, person properties, select properties, and number properties to display information with many other combinations available.

Kitchen

In a similar sense, planning and organizing meals can be done in databases, as shown in *Figure 13.9*:

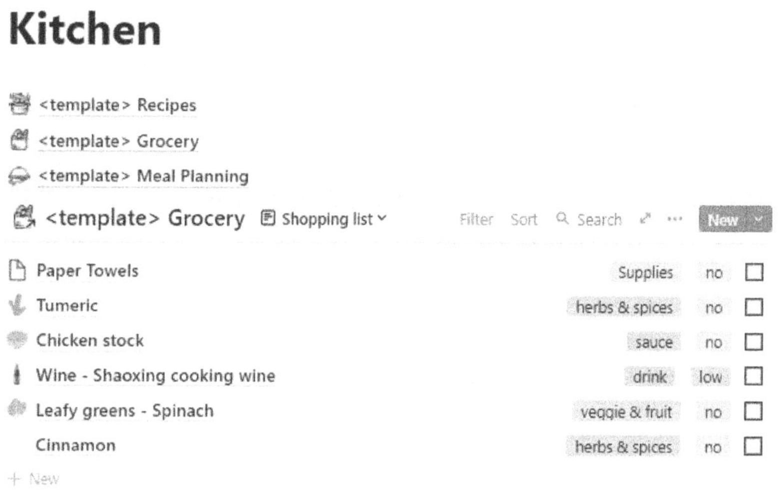

Kitchen

📋 \<template\> Recipes

📑 \<template\> Grocery

🥄 \<template\> Meal Planning

🛒 \<template\> Grocery ⊞ Shopping list ∨   Filter   Sort   🔍 Search   ↗   ⋯   **New** ∨

📄 Paper Towels	Supplies	no	☐
🌿 Tumeric	herbs & spices	no	☐
🍲 Chicken stock	sauce	no	☐
🍶 Wine - Shaoxing cooking wine	drink	low	☐
🥬 Leafy greens - Spinach	veggie & fruit	no	☐
Cinnamon	herbs & spices	no	☐

+ New

Figure 13.9 – Kitchen template located in the Notion template gallery

Figure 13.9 shows the use of filters, sorts, and linked databases to create meal planning dashboards that can generate shopping lists from planned recipes.

Travel Planning

Planning trips or events can be done using an agenda-style layout for the database, as shown in *Figure 13.10*:

Travel Planning

Travel Dates

04/30/19 - 05/05/19

Type '/' for commands

Schedule ⊞ Full Schedule ⌄   🔍 Search ⤢ ⋯   **New** ⌄

Aa Activity	🗓 Date	≣ Location	📎 Files	🔗 URL	≣ Notes
✈ Departing Flight	Apr 30, 2019	SFO, Terminal 1			
Airbnb 1	Apr 30, 2019 → May 03, 2019				Find key in lockbox, code 567.
Sagrada Familia Tour	May 01, 2019	Carrer de Mallorca, 401, 08013 Barcelona, Spain			Starts at 2 pm.
Teleferic Ride	May 01, 2019				
Miro Museum	May 02, 2019	Parc de Montjuïc, s/n, 08038 Barcelona, Spain		https://www.fmirobcn .org/en/	
🍽 Lunch	May 01, 2019	Viana Barcelona, Carrer del Vidre, 7, 08002 Barcelona, Spain		https://www.vianabcn .com/	Recommended by Cameron.

Figure 13.10 – Travel Planning template located in the Notion template gallery

Notice in *Figure 13.10* the use of basic properties such as **Files** and **Notes** to keep information organized. There is no need for advanced properties in some use cases.

Other planning may require more places for storing various pieces of information, which could lead to the creation of a planning dashboard. Wedding planning is an example, as shown in *Figure 13.11*:

Wedding planning

- Guest List
- Bills
- To Do List
- ? Questions to Ask
- Inspiration

- Vendors
- Contacts
- Documents
- Invoices

Figure 13.11 – Wedding planning template located in the Notion template gallery

Inside each of the pages in *Figure 13.11,* there are places for recording and sorting information for all the different areas of the event. In a similar sense, this could be used for brainstorming, daily, weekly, monthly, or yearly reviewing, and even customer journeys.

For some of the planning elements, there could be an important time element, either as a deadline or for repeated checkups. A review may require a certain frequency to make sure the task appears, or a more complex case may be flashcard spaced repetition, as shown in *Figure 13.12*:

Flashcard

Q Topic	Empty
↗ Lecture	Empty
Σ Review date	Empty
Σ Showing	☐
📅 Date wrong	Empty
⬇ Stage	1

Figure 13.12 – Spaced repetition database for a review located in the Student Workspace template

The formulas used inside **Review date** can add time for specific property information, or take time away from the review. For the example in *Figure 13.12*, the **Stage** and **Date wrong** properties are used to create the next **Review date** property.

As demonstrated in this section, planning can be done with various types of views of databases, layouts of pages, and configurations of properties, all with the flexibility to be changed at any time. Tracking has a similar level of flexibility, but a much larger set of ideas that can be used.

Tracking dashboards

In this section, we will go through some dashboards that can be used for tracking information, which can be useful (since information can be shown in various configurations).

> **Note**
> Each template in this section is either created by me or by another Notion ambassador or is located in the Notion template gallery.

The simplest type of database setup for tracking information is the one with simple property types. Using the number property, text property, date property, and checkbox property is often all that is needed to collect information while keeping it organized in storage. *Figure 13.13* shows an example of a habit tracker:

Habits

🗓 Date	☑ 🦷	☑ 🦷	☑ 🦷	☑ 🐦	Aa Notes
Today	☐	☐	☐	☐	
+ New					

Figure 13.13 – Habit tracker database filtered for today

The example shown in *Figure 13.13* is a database with checkbox properties named using emojis. There is a filter on this particular example on the **Date** property, filtering for today, which means that tomorrow, the record for today will disappear and a new page can be created with the correct date due to the auto filter feature. The **Date** property in this example is also configured to show the relative date format.

Once the information is taken, calculations can be done using either the database calculations or through the formula property. Using regular expressions inside the formula property can allow for calculations on the multi-select, person, and text properties. *Figure 13.14* shows a different version of a habit tracker using the multi-select property and a formula for a complete count:

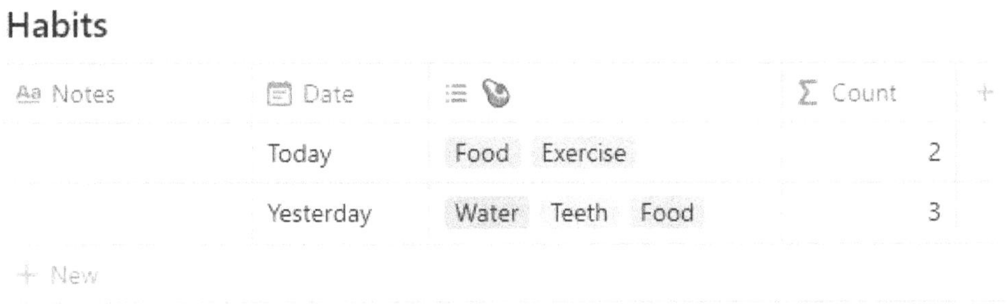

Habits

Aa Notes	📅 Date	≣ 🐚			Σ Count	+
	Today	Food	Exercise		2	
	Yesterday	Water	Teeth	Food	3	

+ New

Figure 13.14 – Habit tracker with a completion count formula

The formula for the count will change depending on the properties used, but for properties with text, *Figure 13.15* shows us one solution:

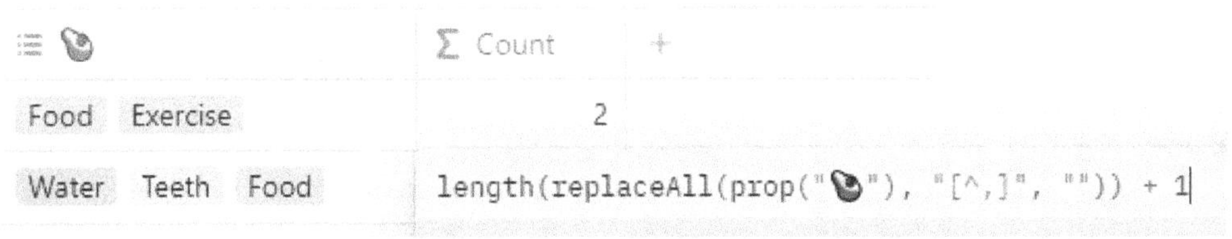

≣ 🐚			Σ Count +
Food	Exercise		2
Water	Teeth	Food	`length(replaceAll(prop("🐚"), "[^,]", "")) + 1`

Figure 13.15 – Regular expression formula for counting text

The formula in *Figure 13.15* works by removing all of the letters and numbers, leaving the , (comma). Then, the length function adds up all the commas, which are then increased by one. The reason can be seen in the first row of *Figure 13.15* – **Food** and **Exercise**, leaving one comma separating the words, but there are two words, so 1 must be added. This means that if the 🥑 property is empty, there will be a count of 1 unless the formula is adjusted to account for that situation. One solution could be `empty(prop("🥑"))` ? `0 : (length(replaceAll(prop("🥑"), "[^,]", "")) + 1)`.

Further examples could be used in shopping lists, food storage tracking, and any other nutrition-based information tracking, such as the recipes shown in *Figure 13.16*:

🍱 <template> Recipes ⊞ Details ⌄

Aa Name	☰ Tags			☰ Dish	⊘ Energy	⊘ Thoughts	Σ Planned...	Σ % In Stock	Σ N Out of Stock
📄 Savory Herb Butter Dutch Baby	Protein	Carbs		Dessert	Low	to try		92%	1
📄 Roasted brussels and squash	Veggies	Carbs		Lunch/Dinner	Medium	Go-to		88%	1
📄 White peach + rose + basil hand pies	Baking			Dessert	Medium	to try		90%	1
📄 Chunky Monkey Smoothie	Protein	Veggies	Carbs	Breakfast	Low	to try		89%	1
📄 Vegetable Lo Mein for Two	Carbs	Veggies		Lunch/Dinner	Low	Go-to		100%	0
📄 Broccoli beef	Protein	Veggies		Lunch/Dinner	Low	Go-to	Broccoli beef	100%	0
📄 Honey lemon chicken	Protein	Carbs		Lunch/Dinner	Low	tried & liked		100%	0

Figure 13.16 – Meal planning template located in the Notion template gallery

Workout trackers or exercise programs can be created, tracked, and shared through Notion, as shown in *Figure 13.17*:

Figure 13.17 – Ultimate workout system template located in the Notion template gallery

Tracking sleep, meditation, movies, and books, as shown in *Figure 13.18*, can also all be done in similar ways:

Reading list

status	headline	url	tags	category	note
	Design in Tech Report	https://design.co/design-in-tech-report-:	report tech	design	
	How to move a masterpiece: the secret business of shipping priceless artworks	https://www.theguardian.com/artanddes	art	super cool	
	The Information Diet — Future Crunch	https://futurecrun.ch/articles/the-inform;			
	Why do we work so hard?	1843	https://www.1843magazine.com/features			
	Good usability goods – UX Collective	https://uxdesign.cc/good-usability-good:			

Figure 13.18 – Reading list template located in the Notion template gallery

Medical information, health products, and skincare can also be tracked, as shown in *Figure 13.19*:

Beauty & skincare tracker

Use this database to inventory your beauty and skincare products. The type and brand boxes come pre-populated with options but you can change them or get rid of them altogether.

Figure 13.19 – Beauty & skincare tracker template located in the Notion template gallery

In addition to all of these tracking use cases, journaling, bullet journaling, investment tracking, finance tracking, roommate finance costs, subscription tracking, and plant trackers can all be added to the list of templates that have all been created ready for you to duplicate and adjust:

Plants

All plants ▦ All plants ˅

Aa Name	☰ Spot	◢ Picture	☰ Watering	☰ Misting	☰ Fertilizing	☰ Notes	🕙 Last watered	🕙 Last fertilized	☰ To do
🌿 Fiddle leaf	Kitchen, next to the window		medium	yes		Don't overwater. It likes regularity.	March 14, 2020	March 14, 2020	
Philodendron	Kitchen, next to the window		medium	yes often	medium once every two weeks		March 14, 2020	March 14, 2020	repot
Philodendron Xanadu	Living room, next to the tv		medium	yes			March 14, 2020	March 14, 2020	
Fern	Living room, next to the tv		medium	yes		Never let the soil dry.	March 14, 2020	March 14, 2020	
Pilea	Living room, next to the tv		medium	yes			March 14, 2020	March 14, 2020	repot

Figure 13.20 – Plants template located in the Notion template gallery

Essentially, any piece of information can be tracked inside a Notion database, but some trackers can be visualized differently. *Figure 13.21* shows an image property that can be used in a gallery or board database alongside the formula properties for rounded information, providing an information card view as seen in *Figure 13.21*:

Habits ▦ Gallery ˅

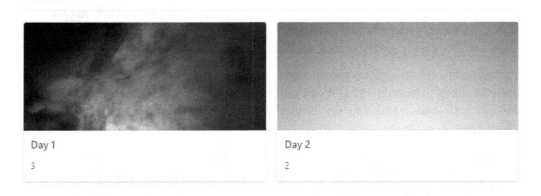

Day 1

3

Day 2

2

Figure 13.21 – Gallery database view example with the formula count property showing

Some unique use cases that have been created in the Notion community include birthday tracking, anniversary reminders, Dungeons & Dragons database setups, gaming databases for characters, shortcuts, and things to remember alongside client portals, webinar portals, and other contextual dashboard uses.

By combining these tracking database setups and views with the planning database setups and dashboards, workspace systems can be created to manage home, work, and learning life.

Popular systems

In this final section of the book, we will be covering some overarching workspace systems that use certain frameworks and methodologies to organize the entire system inside Notion. This can give you an idea of an overarching methodology that might work for you or your team.

> **Note**
>
> Each example in this section is a snapshot of a much wider system that has been built by everyone to support their work inside Notion. For further information on each system, you can find the links to their work in their respective section.

PARA system

The **PARA system** is built around a framework suggested by Tiago Forte and the work he does on his course about building a second brain. The system breaks down projects, areas, resources, and archives into separate storage silos.

This system was originally used for files and folders inside a PC in the file explorer and was then used in notetaking tools such as Evernote and then Notion.

When using PARA in Notion, the overarching theme is to silo information into master databases, such as a master projects database, master areas database, master resources database, and potentially, a master archives database.

Due to the way Notion functions, the information doesn't necessarily need to be moved between databases to be archived as it can be filtered out of the linked database view. In addition to this, a master task database is often used alongside the project's database to help with granular planning and actions.

The project database will store all the projects and larger actions that you plan to be completed. The areas database would be where you store things that don't have measurable deadlines, which could be areas of life and work. The resources database would store the notes, references, and any other information that may be needed for the projects.

> **Note**
>
> The PARA framework suggests master databases, but that doesn't mean other databases won't work.

The system has been adopted by many Notion users and it has evolved to include more databases, different names of pages, and has been used in a variety of contexts. An example dashboard is shown in *Figure 13.22*:

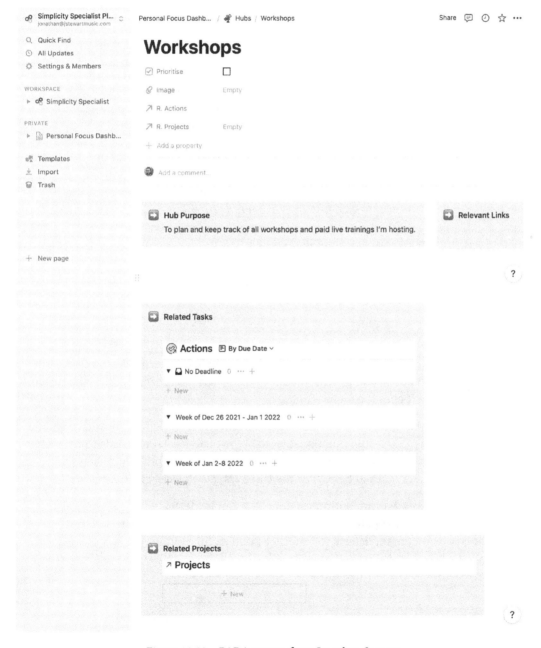

Figure 13.22 – PARA system from Jonathan Stewart

Figure 13.22 shows how simple the view can be to start with yet have all the core databases stored in the workspace. This example shows the actions or tasks database with grouped filtered views and a project database view.

Here are some words from Jonathan:

> *Notion helps me by being able to see all the moving parts of my business in multiple ways, giving me the flexibility to see everything how I need it.*
>
> *Although PARA is not just based on Notion, by using PARA, you can keep all your information across multiple tools and solutions fairly simple and minimal, but also give yourself space for flexibility when required.*
>
> *The greatest power of Notion is its flexibility, but that can also end up causing bloating within the system. If you're not sure where to get started, I always suggest starting with a PARA-style base, defining what each letter means to you, and then expanding from there.*
>
> *– Jonathan Stewart*

For more information, visit the following link: `https://simplicity-specialist.com/`.

GTD system

The **GTD system** was first suggested by David Allen in the book *Getting Things Done*. The system is focused on actions and giving context to those actions. As information comes in, there is a process that it goes through.

If the *stuff* is not actionable, then it is eliminated, included in a bucket, or moved to an area for reference later. If the *stuff* is actionable, the type of action taken needs to be decided. It could be a multi-step project, which leads to planning and then reviews for more granular action, or it could be part of the three Ds; *Do it, Delegate it, Defer it*.

If the action can be done within 2 minutes, do it. If it can be delegated to someone else, communicate for that to happen and wait for someone else to complete the action. If it requires time you don't have, defer it for another point in time, either by days or weeks in a calendar or by hours on a next actions list.

This entire system has been adapted and evolved in various ways, again with additions and subtractions depending on the user's use case and considering the tools available to the person at the time. When it comes to GTD's application in Notion, it can be taken a little further than just actions, as shown in *Figure 13.23*:

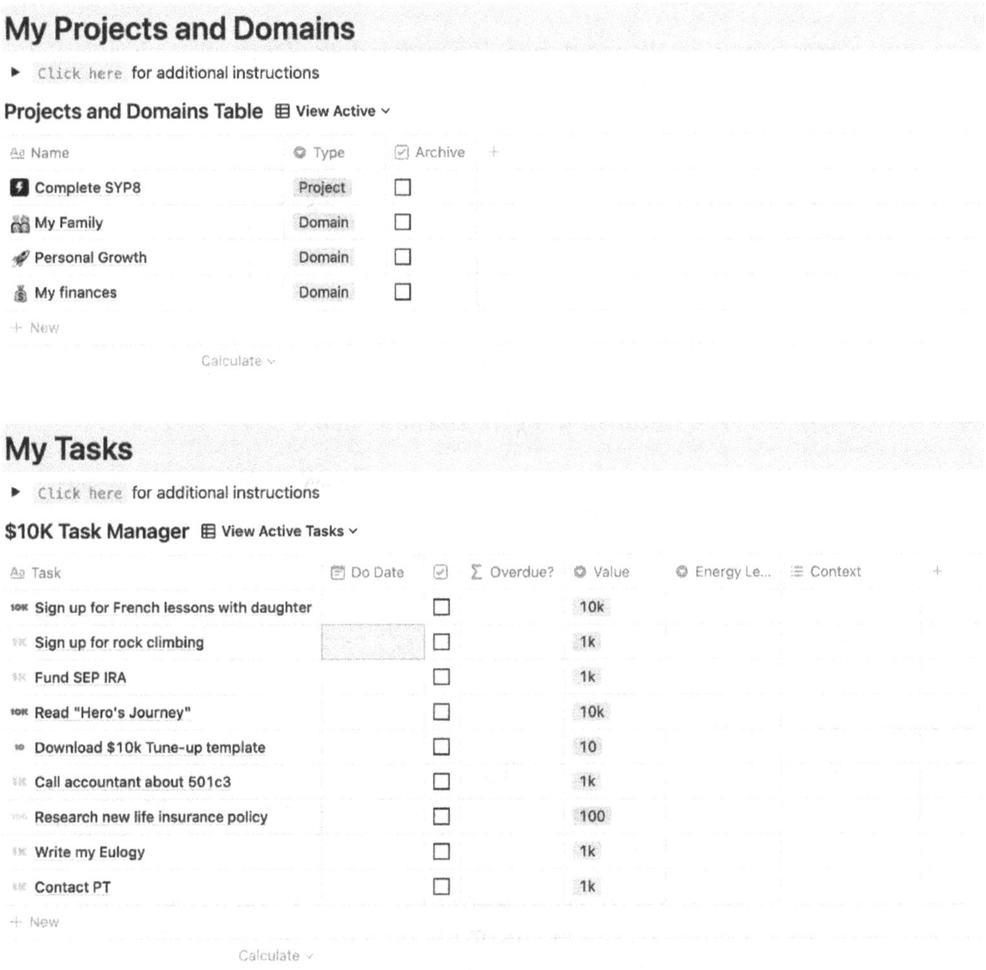

My Projects and Domains

▶ Click here for additional instructions

Projects and Domains Table ⊞ View Active ⌄

Aa Name	◉ Type	☑ Archive	+
🔋 Complete SYP8	Project	☐	
👪 My Family	Domain	☐	
🚀 Personal Growth	Domain	☐	
💰 My finances	Domain	☐	
+ New			

Calculate ⌄

My Tasks

▶ Click here for additional instructions

$10K Task Manager ⊞ View Active Tasks ⌄

Aa Task	📅 Do Date	☑	Σ Overdue?	◉ Value	◉ Energy Le...	≡ Context	+
10K Sign up for French lessons with daughter		☐		10k			
1K Sign up for rock climbing		☐		1k			
1K Fund SEP IRA		☐		1k			
10K Read "Hero's Journey"		☐		10k			
10 Download $10k Tune-up template		☐		10			
1K Call accountant about 501c3		☐		1k			
100 Research new life insurance policy		☐		100			
1K Write my Eulogy		☐		1k			
1K Contact PT		☐		1k			
+ New							

Calculate ⌄

Figure 13.23 – The Getting Things Done system from Khe Hy

Figure 13.23 shows how the **value** of an action is rated in the select property, which impacts when the action should be completed. Other properties, such as **Energy Level** and **Context**, are also included to help create a **do date** for the action. The larger projects and domains are kept in a separate table, which has a **Type** select property and an **Archive** checkbox to help with organization.

Here are some words from **Khe Hy** about the $ 10K methodology that has evolved out of GTD and was then applied in Notion:

> *The $10K work methodology evaluates tasks based on a 2x2 matrix of unique skill and leverage. By ruthlessly prioritizing activities that have leverage (a one-to-many element), you're able to achieve more while spending less time at work. Notion helps me implement the $10K methodology in the following matters:*
>
> *Stratification of tasks using different views, filters, and groupings.*
>
> *Prioritization using the calendar view.*
>
> *Reflection through the integration of pages and tasks (which are contained in tables).*
>
> *– Khe Hy*

For more information, visit the following link: `https://radreads.co/`.

PPV system

The PPV system was built by August Bradley due to the PARA and GTD systems not quite working for his personal use. There are elements of each system inside PPV, but it functions in its way, specialized to fit with Notion.

The Pillars Pipelines and Vaults system is based around zones of work, the action zone, and the alignment zone. *Figure 13.24* shows the main dashboard view with linked databases, pages, and navigation bars:

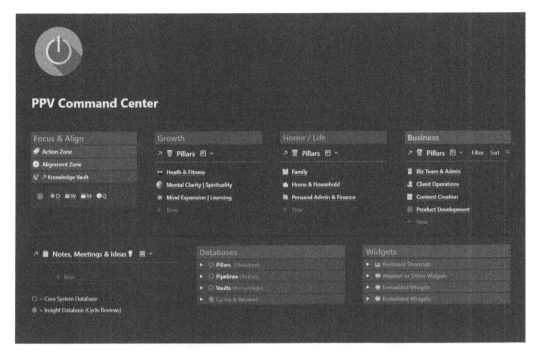

Figure 13.24 – Pillars Pipelines and Vaults system from August Bradley

The dashboard shown in *Figure 13.24* illustrates the depth of the system with the pillars database being linked and filtered in three separate columns for **Growth**, **Home / Life**, and **Business**. The main **Focus & Align** column has links to the relevant contextual dashboards, alongside a linked page to the knowledge vault. In addition to this, the **Widgets** section uses the toggle block to hide away time-specific widgets to give information showing how this has plenty of depth behind it to make navigation simple, the organization of information simple, and, most importantly, life easier to manage.

Here are some words from August Bradley about how Notion and PPV work well together and can evolve to each user's use case:

> *Notion is groundbreaking and it enables us to build our own apps and implement customized system design. In the case of PPV, it enabled building a system that directly connects one's highest-level aspiration in life straight to the daily and hourly actions needed to achieve them, ensuring that we are consistently working on the right things to achieve our highest priorities in life. By implementing with Notion, each person can then further customize their PPV system to their own needs.*
>
> *– August Bradley*

For more information, visit the following link: http://www.augustbradley.com/.

Horizons system

The Horizons system has been applied to Notion by a few users, with the most well known in the community being Marie Poulin.

Horizons uses the concept of contextual dashboards based around a timed context, as seen in *Figure 13.25*:

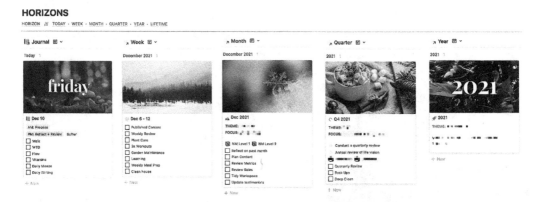

Figure 13.25 – Horizons system from Marie Poulin

Figure 13.25 only shows the high-level view of the main dashboard, but, like the PPV example, illustrates the depth to which this system goes. There is a **Journal** database view that is for daily actions and hour-by-hour work. The **Week**, **Month**, **Quarter**, and **Year** views are all linked databases in *Figure 13.25*, showing how the main storage of information is being kept in the main database with specific information being shown in this contextual view, which is based around the current point in time.

The system uses time-based contextual dashboards to reduce the amount of information in each context as goals may be less likely to be needed daily and more appropriate for other time scales. In a similar sense, daily tasks would be less useful in a larger time context, potentially due to the number of tasks that may appear.

Notion has given me a way to visualize and get a handle on
my responsibilities more clearly. It has helped me gain a sense of peace while
simultaneously giving me space to get playful and feel inspired. It's truly
my daily companion!

– Marie Poulin

For more information, visit the following link: `https://mariepoulin.com/`.

Gamification system

The **Gamification system** by Conrad Lin goes beyond simple database structures and uses a variety of relation, rollup, and formula combinations in a couple of key databases to build a workspace that tracks and grades every action, task, project, and goal you have.

The system is based on gamifying daily actions to level up your character, which is your avatar. Using badges, loot boxes, and item shops to gamify your actions further, this Notion workspace works for personal and team use, as there can be multiple avatars in one workspace, as shown in *Figure 13.26*:

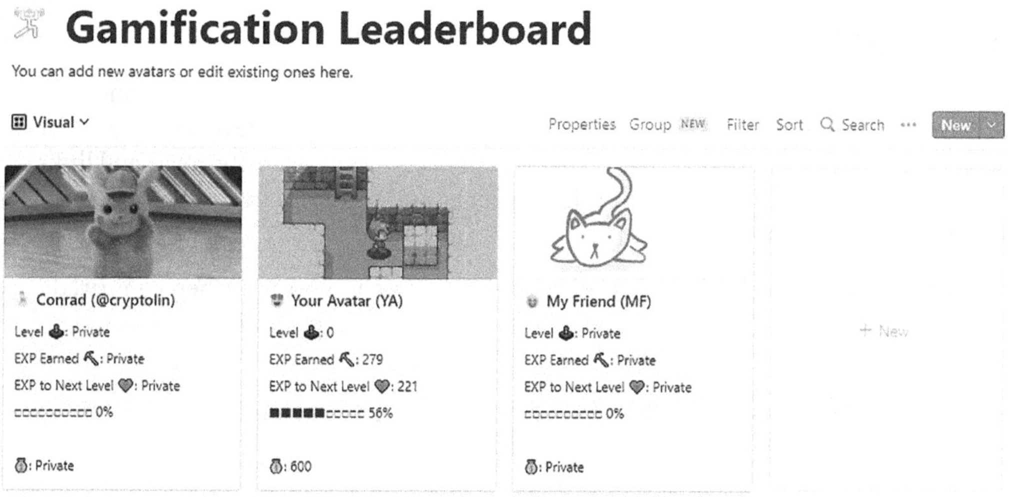

Figure 13.26 – Gamification system by Conrad Lin

Figure 13.26 shows a gallery view of avatars with all the associated information, giving each player a level, showing **EXP Earned** and **EXP to Next Level**, along with a progress bar for visualization. Here are some words from Conrad:

> **#theGamificationProject** *is a huge collaborative project by Conrad Lin and the Co-x3 family that transforms you into your favorite game character, turning tedious tasks into fun and engaging quests that build up your skill tree and includes live leaderboard functionalities to promote friendly competitions between friends, family, and community. Notion +* **#theGamificationProject** *turned my workspace into a highly functional system that motivated me to complete tasks on time. An engaging feedback loop that rewards me for building strong habits. An exciting multiplayer experience I could share with my family.*
>
> *– Conrad Lin*

Using this system is as simple as inputting information, but setting up this workspace can take time and expertise, which is why Conrad shares his work publicly.

For more information, visit the following link: `https://conradlin.com/`.

Bulletproof system

Every system that is mentioned covers all aspects of a user's home and work life and, in the case of **William Nutt**, it is no different. The Bulletproof system leverages the contextual dashboards and expert database concepts once again to create views and links between spaces, organizations, tasks, projects, clients, and all things that relate to being more productive in home and work life.

The Bulletproof system is far less directed or granular in its application when compared to the previous systems covered and is the simplest expression of a basic workspace system creation.

As illustrated in *Figure 13.27*, the Bulletproof system is a combination of linked views, quick links, and pages spread over a home dashboard:

Figure 13.27 – Bulletproof system from William Nutt

Here are a few words from **William Nutt** about Notion:

> *Notion has profoundly influenced my life—personally and professionally.*
> *It's my operating system at work and at home, where I manage virtually*
> *every facet of my life: projects and tasks, clients and relationships, finances*
> *and shopping, media and hobbies, trips and events, goals,*
> *and performance—everything.*
>
> *What began as a nerdy personal interest became the backbone of*
> *my business. On top of publishing free resources at Notion VIP, I consult*
> *users across the globe, manage Notion's certification program, and offer*
> *premium resources. In Notion A-to-Z and my Bulletproof framework,*
> *I apply all my lessons learned and best practices to help other users*
> *accelerate their learning and implementation of Notion, and fall in love*
> *with this miraculously versatile tool, just as I have.*
>
> *– William Nutt*

For more information, visit the following link: `https://www.notion.vip/`.

Every system that is created in Notion can be changed, altered, added to, subtracted from, and evolved into anything any user may need, but it all comes down to knowing how you work and building the right system for you.

Summary

In summary, this final chapter is a window into the various frameworks and systems different Notion ambassadors have created that work for their workflow. Each individual using Notion will find different use cases and different workflows that suit their work process.

The fundamental skills of using the Notion app have been covered alongside other advanced skills and features that this software gives each user. However, just like any other piece of software, working out how it will fit into your life requires application. Find somewhere to start and build from there, making changes as you go, and referring back to this book for solutions.

Index

Other Books You May Enjoy

If you enjoyed this book, you may be interested in these other books by Packt:

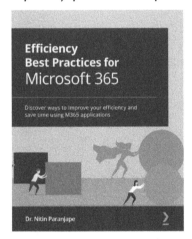

Efficiency Best Practices for Microsoft 365

Dr. Nitin Paranjape

ISBN: 9781801072267

- Understand how different MS 365 tools, such as Office desktop, Teams, Power BI, Lists, and OneDrive, can increase work efficiency
- Identify time-consuming processes and understand how to work through them more efficiently
- Create professional documents quickly with minimal effort
- Work across multiple teams, meetings, and projects without email overload
- Automate mundane, repetitive, and time-consuming manual work
- Manage work, delegation, execution, and project management

Automate It with Zapier

Kelly Goss

ISBN: 9781800208971

- Think creatively to plan your business workflows to overcome specific business problems

- Get to grips with the native features and built-in applications available in Zapier

- Explore different types of third-party business applications that integrate with Zapier

- Configure your workflows optimally to automate business processes and minimize task usage

- Use Zapier's library of pre-built workflows and create advanced workflows from scratch

- Discover the extensive functionality and practical uses of Zapier's built-in apps

Packt is searching for authors like you

If you're interested in becoming an author for Packt, please visit `authors.packtpub.com` and apply today. We have worked with thousands of developers and tech professionals, just like you, to help them share their insight with the global tech community. You can make a general application, apply for a specific hot topic that we are recruiting an author for, or submit your own idea.

Share Your Thoughts

Now you've finished *Enhancing Productivity with Notion*, we'd love to hear your thoughts! Scan the QR code below to go straight to the Amazon review page for this book and share your feedback or leave a review on the site that you purchased it from.

`https://packt.link/r/1-803-23208-0`

Your review is important to us and the tech community and will help us make sure we're delivering excellent quality content.

www.ingramcontent.com/pod-product-compliance
Lightning Source LLC
Chambersburg PA
CBHW062108050326
40690CB00016B/3248